Labor Law

Selected Statutes, Forms, and Agreements 2015–2016

D1299739

Labor Law

Selected Statutes, Forms, and Agreements 2015–2016

Michael C. Harper
Professor of Law and Barreca Labor Relations Scholar
Boston University

Samuel Estreicher
Dwight D. Opperman Professor of Law
New York University

Kati Griffith
Associate Professor of Labor and Employment Law
Cornell University

About Wolters Kluwer Law & Business

Wolters Kluwer Law & Business is a leading global provider of intelligent information and digital solutions for legal and business professionals in key specialty areas, and respected educational resources for professors and law students. Wolters Kluwer Law & Business connects legal and business professionals as well as those in the education market with timely, specialized authoritative content and information-enabled solutions to support success through productivity, accuracy and mobility.

Serving customers worldwide, Wolters Kluwer Law & Business products include those under the Aspen Publishers, CCH, Kluwer Law International, Loislaw, ftwilliam.com and MediRegs family of products.

CCH products have been a trusted resource since 1913, and are highly regarded resources for legal, securities, antitrust and trade regulation, government contracting, banking, pension, payroll, employment and labor, and healthcare reimbursement and compliance professionals.

Aspen Publishers products provide essential information to attorneys, business professionals and law students. Written by preeminent authorities, the product line offers analytical and practical information in a range of specialty practice areas from securities law and intellectual property to mergers and acquisitions and pension/benefits. Aspen's trusted legal education resources provide professors and students with high-quality, up-to-date and effective resources for successful instruction and study in all areas of the law.

Kluwer Law International products provide the global business community with reliable international legal information in English. Legal practitioners, corporate counsel and business executives around the world rely on Kluwer Law journals, looseleafs, books, and electronic products for comprehensive information in many areas of international legal practice.

Loislaw is a comprehensive online legal research product providing legal content to law firm practitioners of various specializations. Loislaw provides attorneys with the ability to quickly and efficiently find the necessary legal information they need, when and where they need it, by facilitating access to primary law as well as state-specific law, records, forms and treatises.

ftwilliam.com offers employee benefits professionals the highest quality plan documents (retirement, welfare and non-qualified) and government forms (5500/PBGC, 1099 and IRS) software at highly competitive prices.

MediRegs products provide integrated health care compliance content and software solutions for professionals in healthcare, higher education and life sciences, including professionals in accounting, law and consulting.

Wolters Kluwer Law & Business, a division of Wolters Kluwer, is headquartered in New York. Wolters Kluwer is a market-leading global information services company focused on professionals.

Contents

SELECTED CROSS-BORDER LABOR LAW INSTRUMENTS

Labor Law

**Selected Statutes, Forms,
and Agreements 2015–2016**

Selected Statutes[*]

Sherman Act — Selected Provisions
26 Stat. 209 (1890), as amended, 15 U.S.C. §§1 et seq.

§1.   (§1) Trusts, etc., in restraint of trade illegal; penalty

Every contract, combination in the form of trust or otherwise, or conspiracy, in restraint of trade or commerce among the several States, or with foreign nations, is declared to be illegal.[*] Every person who shall make any contract or engage in any combination or conspiracy hereby declared to be illegal shall be deemed guilty of a felony, and, on conviction thereof, shall be punished by fine not exceeding $10,000,000 if a corporation, or, if any other person, $350,000, or by imprisonment not exceeding three years, or by both said punishments, in the discretion of the court.

§2.   (§2) Monopolizing trade a felony; penalty

Every person who shall monopolize, or attempt to monopolize, or combine or conspire with any other person or persons, to monopolize any part of the trade or commerce among the several States, or with foreign nations, shall be deemed guilty of a felony, and, on conviction thereof, shall be punished by fine not exceeding $10,000,000 if a corporation, or, if any other person, $350,000, or by imprisonment not exceeding three years, or by both said punishments, in the discretion of the court.

---

* [The section numbers of the statute involved, as originally enacted, are followed (in parentheses) by the corresponding section numbers in the United States Code (2000 ed.) where appropriate. — Eds.]

§4.   (§4) Jurisdiction of courts; duty of United States attorneys; procedure

The several district courts of the United States are invested with jurisdiction to prevent and restrain violations of sections 1 to 7 of this title; and it shall be the duty of the several United States attorneys, in their respective districts, under the direction of the Attorney General, to institute proceedings in equity to prevent and restrain such violations. Such proceedings may be by way of petition setting forth the case and praying that such violation shall be enjoined or otherwise prohibited. When the parties complained of shall have been duly notified of such petition the court shall proceed, as soon as may be, to the hearing and determination of the case; and pending such petition and before final decree, the court may at any time make such temporary restraining order or prohibition as shall be deemed just in the premises.

§8.   (§7) "Person" defined

The word "person", or "persons", wherever used in sections 1 to 7 of this title shall be deemed to include corporations and associations existing under or authorized by the laws of either the United States, the laws of any of the Territories, the laws of any State, or the laws of any foreign country.

Clayton Act — Selected Provisions
38 Stat. 730 (1914), as amended, 15 U.S.C. §§12 et seq.

§1.   (§12) Words defined; short title

(a) "Antitrust laws", as used herein, includes the Act entitled "An Act to protect trade and commerce against unlawful restraints and monopolies", approved July second, eighteen hundred and ninety [Sherman Act, supra]. . . .

(b) This Act may be cited as the "Clayton Act".

§4.   (§15) Suits by persons injured

[A]ny person who shall be injured in his business or property by reason of anything forbidden in the antitrust laws may sue therefor in any district court of the United States in the district in which the defendant resides or is found or has an agent, without regard to the amount in controversy, and shall recover threefold the damages by him sustained, and the cost of the suit, including a reasonable attorney's fee. . . .

§6.   (§17) Antitrust laws not applicable to labor organizations

The labor of a human being is not a commodity or article of commerce. Nothing contained in the antitrust laws shall be construed to forbid the existence and operation of labor, agricultural, or horticultural organizations, instituted for the purposes of mutual help, and not having capital stock or conducted for profit, or to forbid or restrain individual members of such organizations from lawfully carrying out the legitimate objects thereof; nor shall such organizations, or the members thereof, be held or construed to be illegal combinations or conspiracies in restraint of trade, under the antitrust laws.

§16.   (§26) Injunctive relief for private parties; exception; costs

Any person, firm, corporation, or association shall be entitled to sue for and have injunctive relief, in any court of the United States having jurisdiction over the parties, against threatened loss or damage by a violation of the antitrust laws, . . . when and under the same conditions and principles as injunctive relief against threatened conduct that will cause loss or damage is granted by courts of equity, under the rules governing such proceedings, and upon the execution of proper bond against damages for an injunction improvidently granted and a showing that the danger of irreparable loss or damage is immediate, a preliminary injunction may issue. . . . In any action under this section in which the plaintiff substantially prevails, the court shall award the cost of suit, including a reasonable attorney's fee, to such plaintiff.

§20.   (§52) Statutory restriction of injunctive relief

No restraining order or injunction shall be granted by any court of the United States, or a judge or the judges thereof, in any case between an employer and employees, or between employers and employees, or between employees, or between persons employed and persons seeking employment, involving, or growing out of, a dispute concerning terms or conditions of employment, unless necessary to prevent irreparable injury to property, or to a property right, of the party making the application, for which injury there is no adequate remedy at law, and such property or property right must be described with particularity in the application, which must be in writing and sworn to by the applicant or by his agent or attorney.

And no such restraining order or injunction shall prohibit any person or persons, whether singly or in concert, from terminating any relation of employment, or from ceasing to perform any work or labor, or from recommending, advising, or persuading others by peaceful means so to do; or from attending at any place where any such person or persons may lawfully be, for the purpose of peacefully obtaining or communicating information, or from peacefully persuading any person to work or to abstain from working; or from ceasing to patronize or to employ any party to such dispute, or from recommending, advising, or persuading others by peaceful and lawful means so to do; or from paying or giving to, or withholding from, any person engaged in such dispute, any strike benefits or other moneys or things of value; or from peaceably assembling in a lawful manner, and for lawful purposes; or from doing any act or thing which might lawfully be done in the absence of such dispute by any party thereto; nor shall any of the acts specified in this paragraph be considered or held to be violations of any law of the United States.

Railway Labor Act of 1926
44 Stat. 577 (1926), as amended, 45 U.S.C. §§151-188[*]

Subchapter I. GENERAL PROVISIONS

§1.   (§151) Definitions; short title

When used in this chapter and for the purposes of this chapter —

First. The term "carrier" includes any railroad subject to the jurisdiction of the Surface Transportation Board, any express company that would have been, sleeping-car company, carrier by railroad, subject to subtitle IV of Title 49, as of December 31, 1995, and any company which is directly or indirectly owned or controlled by or under common control with any carrier by railroad and which operates any equipment or facilities or performs any service (other than trucking service) in connection with the transportation, receipt, delivery, elevation, transfer in transit, refrigeration or icing, storage, and handling of property transported by railroad, and any receiver, trustee, or other individual or body, judicial or otherwise, when in the possession of the business of any such "carrier": *Provided, however,* That the term "carrier" shall not include any street, interurban, or suburban electric railway, unless such railway is operating as a part of a general steam-railroad system of transportation, but shall not exclude any part of the general steam-railroad system of transportation now or hereafter operated by any other motive power. The Interstate Commerce CommissionSurface Transportation Board is authorized and directed upon request of the Mediation Board or upon complaint of any party interested to determine after hearing whether any line operated by electric power falls within the terms of this proviso. The term "carrier" shall not include any company by reason of its being engaged in the mining of coal, the supplying of coal to a carrier where delivery is not beyond the mine tipple, and the operation of equipment or facilities therefor, or in any of such activities.

Second. The term "Adjustment Board" means the National Railroad Adjustment Board created by this chapter.

Third. The term "Mediation Board" means the National Mediation Board created by this chapter.

Fourth. The term "commerce" means commerce among the several States or between any State, Territory, or the District of Columbia and any foreign nation, or between any Territory or the District of Columbia and any

---

[*] 2012 amendments to the Railway Labor Act are indicated by strike through and underscoring. See FAA Modernization and Reform Act of 2012, Pub. L. 112-95, Title X, §§1001-1004, (Feb. 14, 2012), 126 Stat. 146.

State, or between any Territory and any other Territory, or between any Territory and the District of Columbia, or within any Territory or the District of Columbia, or between points in the same State but through any other State or any Territory or the District of Columbia or any foreign nation.

Fifth. The term "employee" as used herein includes every person in the service of a carrier (subject to its continuing authority to supervise and direct the manner of rendition of his service) who performs any work defined as that of an employee or subordinate official in the orders of the ~~Interstate Commerce Commission~~Surface Transportation Board now in effect, and as the same may be amended or interpreted by orders hereafter entered by the ~~Commission~~ Board pursuant to the authority which is conferred upon it to enter orders amending or interpreting such existing orders: *Provided, however,* That no occupational classification made by order of the ~~Interstate Commerce Commission~~ Surface Transportation Board shall be construed to define the crafts according to which railway employees may be organized by their voluntary action, nor shall the jurisdiction or powers of such employee organizations be regarded as in any way limited or defined by the provisions of this chapter or by the orders of the ~~Commission~~Board.

The term "employee" shall not include any individual while such individual is engaged in the physical operations consisting of the mining of coal, the preparation of coal, the handling (other than movement by rail with standard railroad locomotives) of coal not beyond the mine tipple, or the loading of coal at the tipple.

Sixth. The term "representative" means any person or persons, labor union, organization, or corporation designated either by a carrier or group of carriers or by its or their employees, to act for it or them.

Seventh. The term "district court" includes the United States District Court for the District of Columbia; and the term "court of appeals" includes the United States Court of Appeals for the District of Columbia.

This chapter may be cited as the "Railway Labor Act."

§2.   (§151a) General purposes

The purposes of the chapter are: (1) To avoid any interruption to commerce or to the operation of any carrier engaged therein; (2) to forbid any limitation upon freedom of association among employees or any denial, as a condition of employment or otherwise, of the right of employees to join a labor organization; (3) to provide for the complete independence of carriers and of employees in the matter of self-organization to carry out the purposes of this chapter; (4) to provide for the prompt and orderly settlement of all disputes concerning rates of pay, rules, or working conditions; (5) to provide for the prompt and orderly settlement of all disputes growing out of grievances or out of the interpretation or application of agreements covering rates of pay, rules, or working conditions.

§2. (§152) General duties

First. Duty of carriers and employees to settle disputes

It shall be the duty of all carriers, their officers, agents, and employees to exert every reasonable effort to make and maintain agreements concerning rates of pay, rules, and working conditions, and to settle all disputes, whether arising out of the application of such agreements or otherwise, in order to avoid any interruption to commerce or to the operation of any carrier growing out of any dispute between the carrier and the employees thereof.

Second. Consideration of disputes by representatives

All disputes between a carrier or carriers and its or their employees shall be considered, and, if possible, decided, with all expedition, in conference between representatives designated and authorized so to confer, respectively, by the carrier or carriers and by the employees thereof interested in the dispute.

Third. Designation of representatives

Representatives, for the purposes of this chapter, shall be designated by the respective parties without interference, influence, or coercion by either party over the designation of representatives by the other; and neither party shall in any way interfere with, influence, or coerce the other in its choice of representatives. Representatives of employees for the purposes of this chapter need not be persons in the employ of the carrier, and no carrier shall, by interference, influence, or coercion seek in any manner to prevent the designation by its employees as their representatives of those who or which are not employees of the carrier.

Fourth. Organization and collective bargaining; freedom from interference by carrier; assistance in organizing or maintaining organization by carrier forbidden; deduction of dues from wages forbidden

Employees shall have the right to organize and bargain collectively through representatives of their own choosing. The majority of any craft or class of employees shall have the right to determine who shall be the representative of the craft or class for the purposes of this chapter. No carrier, its officers, or agents shall deny or in any way question the right of its employees to join, organize, or assist in organizing the labor organization of their choice, and it shall be unlawful for any carrier to interfere in any way with the organization of its employees, or to use the funds of the carrier in maintaining or assisting or contributing to any labor organization, labor representative, or other agency of collective bargaining, or in performing any work therefor, or to influence or coerce employees in an effort to induce them to join or remain or not to join or remain members of any labor organization, or to deduct from the wages of employees any dues, fees, assessments, or other contributions payable to labor organizations, or to collect or to assist in the collection of any such dues, fees, assessments, or other contributions: *Provided*, That nothing in this chapter shall be construed to prohibit a carrier from permitting an employee, individually, or local representatives of employees from conferring with management during working hours without loss of time, or to prohibit a carrier from furnishing free transportation to its employees while engaged in the business of a labor organization.

Fifth. Agreements to join or not to join labor organizations forbidden

No carrier, its officers, or agents shall require any person seeking employment to sign any contract or agreement promising to join or not to join a labor organization; and if any such contract has been enforced prior to the effective date of this chapter, then such carrier shall notify the employees by an appropriate order that such contract has been discarded and is no longer binding on them in any way.

Sixth. Conference of representatives; time; place; private agreements

In case of a dispute between a carrier or carriers and its or their employees, arising out of grievances or out of the interpretation or

application of agreements concerning rates of pay, rules, or working conditions, it shall be the duty of the designated representative or representatives of such carrier or carriers and of such employees, within ten days
after the receipt of notice of a desire on the part of either party to confer in
respect to such dispute, to specify a time and place at which such conference shall be held: *Provided,* (1) That the place so specified shall be
situated upon the line of the carrier involved or as otherwise mutually
agreed upon; and (2) that the time so specified shall allow the designated
conferees reasonable opportunity to reach such place of conference, but
shall not exceed twenty days from the receipt of such notice: *And provided
further,* That nothing in this chapter shall be construed to supersede the
provisions of any agreement (as to conferences) then in effect between the
parties.

Seventh. Change in pay, rules, or working conditions contrary to agreement or to section 156 forbidden

No carrier, its officers, or agents shall change the rates of pay, rules, or
working conditions of its employees, as a class, as embodied in agreements
except in the manner prescribed in such agreements or in section 156 of
this title.

Eighth. Notices of manner of settlement of disputes; posting

Every carrier shall notify its employees by printed notices in such form
and posted at such times and places as shall be specified by the Mediation
Board that all disputes between the carrier and its employees will be handled
in accordance with the requirements of this chapter, and in such notices there
shall be printed verbatim, in large type, the third, fourth, and fifth paragraphs
of this section. The provisions of said paragraphs are made a part of the
contract of employment between the carrier and each employee, and shall
be held binding upon the parties, regardless of any other express or implied
agreements between them.

Ninth. Disputes as to identity of representatives; designation by Mediation Board; secret elections

If any dispute shall arise among a carrier's employees as to who are
the representatives of such employees designated and authorized in accordance with the requirements of this chapter, it shall be the duty of the
Mediation Board, upon request of either party to the dispute, to investigate
such dispute and to certify to both parties, in writing, within thirty days

after the receipt of the invocation of its services, the name or names of the individuals or organizations that have been designated and authorized to represent the employees involved in the dispute, and certify the same to the carrier. Upon receipt of such certification the carrier shall treat with the representative so certified as the representative of the craft or class for the purposes of this chapter. In such an investigation, the Mediation Board shall be authorized to take a secret ballot of the employees involved, or to utilize any other appropriate method of ascertaining the names of their duly designated and authorized representatives in such manner as shall insure the choice of representatives by the employees without interference, influence, or coercion exercised by the carrier. In the conduct of any election for the purposes herein indicated the Board shall designate who may participate in the election and establish the rules to govern the election, or may appoint a committee of three neutral persons who after hearing shall within ten days designate the employees who may participate in the election. In any such election for which there are 3 or more options (including the option of not being represented by any labor organization) on the ballot and no such option receives a majority of the valid votes cast, the Mediation Board shall arrange for a second election between the options receiving the largest and the second largest number of votes. The Board shall have access to and have power to make copies of the books and records of the carriers to obtain and utilize such information as may be deemed necessary by it to carry out the purposes and provisions of this paragraph.

Tenth. Violations; prosecution and penalties

The willful failure or refusal of any carrier, its officers or agents, to comply with the terms of the third, fourth, fifth, seventh, or eighth paragraph of this section shall be a misdemeanor, and upon conviction thereof the carrier, officer, or agent offending shall be subject to a fine of not less than $1,000, nor more than $20,000, or imprisonment for not more than six months, or both fine and imprisonment, for each offense, and each day during which such carrier, officer, or agent shall willfully fail or refuse to comply with the terms of the said paragraphs of this section shall constitute a separate offense. It shall be the duty of any United States attorney to whom any duly designated representative of a carrier's employees may apply to institute in the proper court and to prosecute under the direction of the Attorney General of the United States, all necessary proceedings for the enforcement of the provisions of this section, and for the punishment of all violations thereof and the costs and expenses of such prosecution shall be paid out of the appropriation for the expenses of the courts of the United States: *Provided,* That nothing in this chapter shall be construed to require an individual employee to render labor or service without his consent, nor shall anything in this chapter be construed to make the quitting of his labor by an individual employee an illegal act; nor shall any court issue any process to compel the performance by an individual employee of such labor or service, without his consent.

Eleventh. Union security agreements; check-off

Notwithstanding any other provisions of this chapter, or of any other statute or law of the United States, or Territory thereof, or of any State, any carrier or carriers as defined in this chapter and a labor organization or labor organizations duly designated and authorized to represent employees in accordance with the requirements of this chapter shall be permitted —

(a) to make agreements, requiring, as a condition of continued employment, that within sixty days following the beginning of such employment, or the effective date of such agreements, whichever is the later, all employees shall become members of the labor organization representing their craft or class: *Provided,* That no such agreement shall require such condition of employment with respect to employees to whom membership is not available upon the same terms and conditions as are generally applicable to any other member or with respect to employees to whom membership was denied or terminated for any reason other than the failure of the employee to tender the periodic dues, initiation fees, and assessments (not including fines and penalties) uniformly required as a condition of acquiring or retaining membership.

(b) to make agreements providing for the deduction by such carrier or carriers from the wages of its or their employees in a craft or class and payment to the labor organization representing the craft or class of such employees, of any periodic dues, initiation fees, and assessments (not including fines and penalties) uniformly required as a condition of acquiring or retaining membership: *Provided,* That no such agreement shall be effective with respect to any individual employee until he shall have furnished the employer with a written assignment to the labor organization of such membership dues, initiation fees, and assessments, which shall be revocable in writing after the expiration of one year or upon the termination date of the applicable collective agreement, whichever occurs sooner.

(c) The requirement of membership in a labor organization in an agreement made pursuant to subparagraph (a) of this paragraph shall be satisfied, as to both a present or future employee in engine, train, yard, or hostling service, that is, an employee engaged in any of the services or capacities covered in the First division of paragraph (h) of section 153 of this title defining the jurisdictional scope of the First Division of the National Railroad Adjustment

Board, if said employee shall hold or acquire membership in any one of the labor organizations, national in scope, organized in accordance with this chapter and admitting to membership employees of a craft or class in any of said services; and no agreement made pursuant to subparagraph (b) of this paragraph shall provide for deductions from his wages for periodic dues, initiation fees, or assessments payable to any labor organization other than that in which he holds membership: *Provided, however,* That as to an employee in any of said services on a particular carrier at the effective date of any such agreement on a carrier, who is not a member of any one of the labor organizations, national in scope, organized in accordance with this chapter and admitting to membership employees of a craft or class in any of said services, such employee, as a condition of continuing his employment, may be required to become a member of the organization representing the craft in which he is employed on the effective date of the first agreement applicable to him: *Provided, further,* That nothing herein or in any such agreement or agreements shall prevent an employee from changing membership from one organization to another organization admitting to membership employees of a craft or class in any of said services.

(d) Any provisions in paragraphs Fourth and Fifth of this section in conflict herewith are to the extent of such conflict amended.

Twelfth. Showing of interest for representation elections

The Mediation Board, upon receipt of an application requesting that an organization or individual be certified as the representative of any craft or class of employees, shall not direct an election or use any other method to determine who shall be the representative of such craft or class unless the Mediation Board determines that the application is supported by a showing of interest from not less than 50 percent of the employees in the craft or class.

§3.   (§153) National Railroad Adjustment Board

First. Establishment; composition; powers and duties; divisions; hearings and awards; judicial review

There is established a Board, to be known as the "National Railroad Adjustment Board", the members of which shall be selected within thirty days after June 21, 1934, and it is provided—

(a) That the said Adjustment Board shall consist of thirty-four members, seventeen of whom shall be selected by the carriers and seventeen by such labor organizations of the employees, national in scope, as have been or may be organized in accordance with the provisions of sections 151a and 152 of this title.

(b) The carriers, acting each through its board of directors or its receiver or receivers, trustee or trustees, or through an officer or officers designated for that purpose by such board, trustee or trustees, or receiver or receivers, shall prescribe the rules under which its representatives shall be selected and shall select the representatives of the carriers on the Adjustment Board and designate the division on which each such representative shall serve, but no carrier or system of carriers shall have more than one voting representative on any division of the Board.

(c) Except as provided in the second paragraph of subsection (h) of this section, the national labor organizations, as defined in paragraph (a) of this section, acting each through the chief executive or other medium designated by the organization or association thereof, shall prescribe the rules under which the labor members of the Adjustment Board shall be selected and shall select such members and designate the division on which each member shall serve; but no labor organization shall have more than one voting representative on any division of the Board.

(d) In case of a permanent or temporary vacancy on the Adjustment Board, the vacancy shall be filled by selection in the same manner as in the original selection.

(e) If either the carriers or the labor organizations of the employees fail to select and designate representatives to the Adjustment Board, as provided in paragraphs (b) and (c) of this section, respectively, within sixty days after June 21, 1934, in case of any original appointment to office of a member of the Adjustment Board, or in case of a vacancy in any such office within thirty days after such vacancy occurs, the Mediation Board shall thereupon directly make the appointment and shall select an individual associated in interest with the carriers or the group of labor organizations of employees, whichever he is to represent.

(f) In the event a dispute arises as to the right of any national labor organization to participate as per paragraph (c) of this section in the selection and designation of the labor members of the Adjustment Board, the Secretary of Labor shall investigate the claim of such labor organization to participate, and if such claim in the judgment of the Secretary of Labor has merit, the Secretary shall notify the Mediation Board accordingly, and within ten days after receipt of such advice the Mediation Board shall request those national labor organizations duly qualified as per paragraph (c) of this section to participate in the selection and designation of the labor members of the Adjustment Board to select a representative. Such representative, together with a representative likewise designated by the claimant, and a third or neutral party designated by the Mediation Board, constituting a board of three, shall within thirty days after the appointment of the neutral member, investigate the claims of the labor organization desiring participation and decide whether or not it was organized in accordance with sections 151a and 152 of this title and is otherwise properly qualified to participate in the selection of the labor members of the Adjustment Board, and the findings of such boards of three shall be final and binding.

(g) Each member of the Adjustment Board shall be compensated by the party or parties he is to represent. Each third or neutral party selected under the provisions of paragraph (f) of this section shall receive from the Mediation Board such compensation as the Mediation Board may fix, together with his necessary traveling expenses and expenses actually incurred for subsistence, or per diem allowance in lieu thereof, subject to the provisions of law applicable thereto, while serving as such third or neutral party.

(h) The said Adjustment Board shall be composed of four divisions, whose proceedings shall be independent of one another, and the said divisions as well as the number of their members shall be as follows:

First division: To have jurisdiction over disputes involving train- and yard-service employees of carriers; that is, engineers, firemen, hostlers, and outside hostler helpers, conductors, trainmen, and yard-service employees. This division shall consist of eight members, four of whom shall be selected and designated by the carriers and four of whom shall be selected and designated by the labor organizations, national in scope and organized in accordance with sections 151a and 152 of this title and which represent employees in engine, train, yard, or hostling service: *Provided, however,* That each labor organization shall select and designate two members on the First Division and that no labor organization shall have more than one vote in any proceedings of the First Division or in the adoption of any award with respect to any dispute submitted to the First Division: *Provided further,* however, That the carrier members of the First Division shall cast no more than two votes in any proceedings of the division or in the adoption of any award with respect to any dispute submitted to the First Division.

Second division: To have jurisdiction over disputes involving machinists, boilermakers, blacksmiths, sheet-metal workers, electrical workers, carmen, the helpers and apprentices of all the foregoing, coach cleaners, power-house employees, and railroad-shop laborers. This division shall consist of ten members, five of whom shall be selected by the carriers and five by the national labor organizations of the employees.

Third division: To have jurisdiction over disputes involving station, tower, and telegraph employees, train dispatchers, maintenance-of-way men, clerical employees, freight handlers, express, station, and store employees, signal men, sleeping-car conductors, sleeping-car porters, and maids and dining-car employees. This division shall consist of ten members, five of whom shall be selected by the carriers and five by the national labor organizations of employees.

Fourth division: To have jurisdiction over disputes involving employees of carriers directly or indirectly engaged in transportation of passengers or property by water, and all other employees of carriers over which jurisdiction is not given to the first, second, and third divisions. This division shall consist of six members, three of whom shall be selected by the carriers and three by the national labor organizations of the employees.

(i) The disputes between an employee or group of employees and a carrier or carriers growing out of grievances or out of the interpretation or application of agreements concerning rates of pay, rules, or working conditions, including cases pending and unadjusted on June 21, 1934, shall be handled in the usual manner up to and including the chief operating officer of the carrier designated to handle such disputes; but, failing to reach an adjustment in this manner, the disputes may be referred by petition of the parties or by either party to the appropriate division of the Adjustment Board with a full statement of the facts and all supporting data bearing upon the disputes.

(j) Parties may be heard either in person, by counsel, or by other representatives, as they may respectively elect, and the several divisions of the Adjustment Board shall give due notice of all hearings to the employee or employees and the carrier or carriers involved in any disputes submitted to them.

(k) Any division of the Adjustment Board shall have authority to empower two or more of its members to conduct hearings and make findings upon disputes, when properly submitted, at any place designated by the division: *Provided, however,* That except as provided in paragraph (h) of this section, final awards as to any such dispute must be made by the entire division as hereinafter provided.

(*l*) Upon failure of any division to agree upon an award because of a deadlock or inability to secure a majority vote of the division members, as provided in paragraph (n) of this section, then such division shall forthwith agree upon and select a neutral person, to be known as "referee", to sit with the division as a member thereof, and make an award. Should the division fail to agree upon and select a referee within ten days of the date of the deadlock or inability to secure a majority vote, then the division, or any member thereof, or the parties or either party to the dispute may certify that fact to the Mediation Board, which Board shall, within ten days from the date of receiving such certificate, select and name the referee to sit with the division as a member thereof and make an award. The Mediation Board shall be bound by the same provisions in the appointment of these neutral referees as are provided elsewhere in this chapter for the appointment of arbitrators and shall fix and pay the compensation of such referees.

(m) The awards of the several divisions of the Adjustment Board shall be stated in writing. A copy of the awards shall be furnished to the respective parties to the controversy, and the awards shall be final and binding upon both parties to the dispute. In case a dispute arises involving an interpretation of the award, the division of the Board upon request of either party shall interpret the award in the light of the dispute.

(n) A majority vote of all members of the division of the Adjustment Board eligible to vote shall be competent to make an award with respect to any dispute submitted to it.

(o) In case of an award by any division of the Adjustment Board in favor of petitioner, the division of the Board shall make an order, directed to the carrier, to make the award effective and, if the award includes a requirement for the payment of money, to pay to the employee the sum to which he is entitled under the award on or before a day named. In the event any division determines that an award favorable to the petitioner should not be made in any dispute referred to it, the division shall make an order to the petitioner stating such determination.

(p) If a carrier does not comply with an order of a division of the Adjustment Board within the time limit in such order, the petitioner, or any person for whose benefit such order was made, may file in the District Court of the United States for the district in which he resides or in which is located the principal operating office of the carrier, or through which the carrier operates, a petition setting forth briefly the causes for which he claims relief, and the order of the division of the Adjustment Board in the premises. Such suit in the District Court of the United States shall proceed in all respects as other civil suits, except that on the trial of such suit the findings and order of the division of the Adjustment Board shall be conclusive on the parties, and except that the petitioner shall not be liable for costs in the district court nor for costs at any subsequent stage of the proceedings, unless they accrue upon his appeal, and such costs shall be paid out of the appropriation for the expenses of the courts of the United States. If the petitioner shall finally prevail he shall be allowed a reasonable attorney's fee, to be taxed and collected as a part of the costs of the suit. The district courts are empowered, under the rules of the court governing actions at law, to make such order and enter such judgment, by writ of mandamus or otherwise, as may be appropriate to enforce or set aside the order of the division of the Adjustment Board: *Provided, however,* That such order may not be set aside except for failure of the division to comply with the requirements of this chapter, for failure of the order to conform, or confine itself, to matters within the scope of the division's jurisdiction, or for fraud or corruption by a member of the division making the order.

(q) If any employee or group of employees, or any carrier, is aggrieved by the failure of any division of the Adjustment Board to make an award in a dispute referred to it, or is aggrieved by any of the terms of an award or by the failure of the division to include certain terms in such award, then such employee or group of employees or carrier may file in any United States district court in which a petition under paragraph (p) could be filed, a petition for review of the division's order. A copy of the petition shall be forthwith transmitted by the clerk of the court to the Adjustment Board. The Adjustment Board shall file in the court the record of the proceedings on which it based its action. The court shall have jurisdiction to affirm the order of the division or to set it aside, in whole or in part, or it may remand the proceedings to the division for such further action as it may direct. On such review, the findings and order of the division shall be conclusive on the parties, except that the order of the division may be set aside, in whole or in part, or remanded to the division, for failure of the division to comply with the requirements of this chapter, for failure of the order to conform, or confine itself, to matters within the scope of the division's jurisdiction, or for fraud or corruption by a member of the division making the order. The judgment of the court shall be subject to review as provided in sections 1291 and 1254 of Title 28.

(r) All actions at law based upon the provisions of this section shall be begun within two years from the time the cause of action accrues under the award of the division of the Adjustment Board, and not after.

(s) The several divisions of the Adjustment Board shall maintain headquarters in Chicago, Illinois, meet regularly, and continue in session so long as there is pending before the division any matter within its jurisdiction which has been submitted for its consideration and which has not been disposed of.

(t) Whenever practicable, the several divisions or subdivisions of the Adjustment Board shall be supplied with suitable quarters in any Federal building located at its place of meeting.

(u) The Adjustment Board may, subject to the approval of the Mediation Board, employ and fix the compensations of such assistants as it deems necessary in carrying on its proceedings. The compensation of such employees shall be paid by the Mediation Board.

(v) The Adjustment Board shall meet within forty days after June 21, 1934, and adopt such rules as it deems necessary to control proceedings before the respective divisions and not in conflict with the provisions of this section.

Immediately following the meeting of the entire Board and the adoption of such rules, the respective divisions shall meet and organize by the selection of a chairman, a vice chairman, and a secretary. Thereafter each division shall annually designate one of its members to act as chairman and one of its members to act as vice chairman: *Provided, however,* That the chairmanship and vice-chairmanship of any division shall alternate as between the groups, so that both the chairmanship and vice-chairmanship shall be held alternately by a representative of the carriers and a representative of the employees. In case of a vacancy, such vacancy shall be filled for the unexpired term by the selection of a successor from the same group.

(w) Each division of the Adjustment Board shall annually prepare and submit a report of its activities to the Mediation Board, and the substance of such report shall be included in the annual report of the Mediation Board to the Congress of the United States. The reports of each division of the Adjustment Board and the annual report of the Mediation Board shall state in detail all cases heard, all actions taken, the names, salaries, and duties of all agencies, employees, and officers receiving compensation from the United States under the authority of this chapter, and an account of all moneys appropriated by Congress pursuant to the authority conferred by this chapter and disbursed by such agencies, employees, and officers.

(x) Any division of the Adjustment Board shall have authority, in its discretion, to establish regional adjustment boards to act in its place and stead for such limited period as such division may determine to be necessary. Carrier members of such regional boards shall be designated in keeping with rules devised for this purpose by the carrier members of the Adjustment Board and the labor members shall be designated in keeping with rules devised for this purpose by the labor members of the Adjustment Board. Any such regional board shall, during the time for which it is appointed, have the same authority to conduct hearings, make findings upon disputes and adopt the same procedure as the division of the Adjustment Board appointing it, and its decisions shall be enforceable to the same extent and under the same processes. A neutral person, as referee, shall be appointed for service in connection with any such regional adjustment board in the same circumstances and manner as provided in paragraph (l) of this section, with respect to a division of the Adjustment Board.

Second. System, group, or regional boards: establishment by voluntary agreement; special adjustment boards: establishment, composition, designation of representatives by Mediation Board, neutral member, compensation, quorum, finality and enforcement of awards

Nothing in this section shall be construed to prevent any individual carrier, system, or group of carriers and any class or classes of its or their employees, all acting through their representatives, selected in accordance with the provisions of this chapter, from mutually agreeing to the establishment of system, group, or regional boards of adjustment for the purpose of adjusting and deciding disputes of the character specified in this section. In the event that either party to such a system, group, or regional board of adjustment is dissatisfied with such arrangement, it may upon ninety days' notice to the other party elect to come under the jurisdiction of the Adjustment Board.

If written request is made upon any individual carrier by the representative of any craft or class of employees of such carrier for the establishment of a special board of adjustment to resolve disputes otherwise referable to the Adjustment Board, or any dispute which has been pending before the Adjustment Board for twelve months from the date the dispute (claim) is received by the Board, or if any carrier makes such a request upon any such representative, the carrier or the representative upon whom such request is made shall join in an agreement establishing such a board within thirty days from the date such request is made. The cases which may be considered by such board shall be defined in the agreement establishing it. Such board shall consist of one person designated by the carrier and one person designated by the representative of the employees. If such carrier or such representative fails to agree upon the establishment of such a board as provided herein, or to exercise its rights to designate a member of the board, the carrier or representative making the request for the establishment of the special board may request the Mediation Board to designate a member of the special board on behalf of the carrier or representative upon whom such request was made. Upon receipt of a request for such designation the Mediation Board shall promptly make such designation and shall select an individual associated in interest with the carrier or representative he is to represent, who, with the member appointed by the carrier or representative requesting the establishment of the special board, shall constitute the board. Each member of the board shall be compensated by the party he is to represent. The members of the board so designated shall determine all matters not previously agreed upon by the carrier and the representative of the employees with respect to the establishment and jurisdiction of the board. If they are unable to agree such matters shall be determined by a neutral member of the board selected or appointed and compensated in the same manner as is hereinafter provided with respect to situations where the members of the board are unable to agree upon an award. Such neutral member shall cease to be a member of the board when he has determined such matters. If with respect to any dispute or group of disputes the members of the board designated by the carrier and the representative are unable to agree upon an award disposing of the dispute or group of disputes they shall by mutual agreement select a neutral person to be a member of the board for the consideration and disposition of such dispute or group of disputes. In the event the members of the board designated by the parties are unable, within ten days after their failure to agree upon an award, to agree upon the selection of such neutral person, either member of the board may request the Mediation Board to appoint such neutral person and upon receipt of such request the Mediation Board shall promptly make such appointment. The neutral person so selected or appointed shall be compensated and reimbursed for expenses by the Mediation Board. Any two members of the board shall be competent to render an award. Such awards shall be final and binding upon both parties to the dispute and if in favor of the petitioner, shall direct the other party to comply therewith on or before the day named. Compliance with such awards shall be enforceable by proceedings in the United States district courts in the same manner and subject to the same provisions that apply to proceedings for enforcement of compliance with awards of the Adjustment Board.

§4.   (§154) National Mediation Board

First. Board of Mediation abolished; National Mediation Board established; composition; term of office; qualifications; salaries; removal

The Board of Mediation is abolished, effective thirty days from June 21, 1934, and the members, secretary, officers, assistants, employees, and agents thereof, in office upon June 21, 1934, shall continue to function and receive their salaries for a period of thirty days from such date in the same manner as though this chapter had not been passed. There is established, as an independent agency in the executive branch of the Government, a board to be known as the "National Mediation Board", to be composed of three members appointed by the President, by and with the advice and consent of the Senate, not more than two of whom shall be of the same political party. Each member of the Mediation Board in office on January 1, 1965, shall be deemed to have been appointed for a term of office which shall expire on July 1 of the year his term would have otherwise expired. The terms of office of all successors shall expire three years after the expiration of the terms for which their predecessors were appointed; but any member appointed to fill a vacancy occurring prior to the expiration of the term for which his predecessor was appointed shall be appointed only for the unexpired term of his predecessor. Vacancies in the Board shall not impair the powers nor affect the duties of the Board nor of the remaining members of the Board. Two of the members in office shall constitute a quorum for the transaction of the business of the Board. Each member of the Board shall receive necessary traveling and subsistence expenses, or per diem allowance in lieu thereof, subject to the provisions of law applicable thereto, while away from the principal office of the Board on business required by this chapter. No person in the employment of or who is pecuniarily or otherwise interested in any organization of employees or any carrier shall enter upon the duties of or continue to be a member of the Board. Upon the expiration of his term of office a member shall continue to serve until his successor is appointed and shall have qualified.

All cases referred to the Board of Mediation and unsettled on June 21, 1934, shall be handled to conclusion by the Mediation Board.

A member of the Board may be removed by the President for inefficiency, neglect of duty, malfeasance in office, or ineligibility, but for no other cause.

Second. Chairman; principal office; delegation of powers; oaths; seal; report

The Mediation Board shall annually designate a member to act as chairman. The Board shall maintain its principal office in the District of Columbia, but it may meet at any other place whenever it deems it necessary so to do. The Board may designate one or more of its members to exercise the functions of the Board in mediation proceedings. Each member of the Board shall have power to administer oaths and affirmations. The Board shall have a seal which shall be judicially noticed. The Board shall make an annual report to Congress.

Third. Appointment of experts and other employees; salaries of employees; expenditures

The Mediation Board may (1) subject to the provisions of the civil service laws, appoint such experts and assistants to act in a confidential capacity and such other officers and employees as are essential to the effective transaction of the work of the Board; (2) in accordance with chapter 51 and subchapter III of chapter 53 of Title 5, fix the salaries of such experts, assistants, officers, and employees; and (3) make such expenditures (including expenditures for rent and personal services at the seat of government and elsewhere, for law books, periodicals, and books of reference, and for printing and binding, and including expenditures for salaries and compensation, necessary traveling expenses and expenses actually incurred for subsistence, and other necessary expenses of the Mediation Board, Adjustment Board, Regional Adjustment Boards established under paragraph (w) of section 153 of this title, and boards of arbitration, in accordance with the provisions of this section and sections 153 and 157 of this title, respectively), as may be necessary for the execution of the functions vested in the Board, in the Adjustment Board and in the boards of arbitration, and as may be provided for by the Congress from time to time. All expenditures of the Board shall be allowed and paid on the presentation of itemized vouchers therefor approved by the chairman.

Fourth. Delegation of powers and duties

The Mediation Board is authorized by its order to assign, or refer, any portion of its work, business, or functions arising under this chapter or any other Act of Congress, or referred to it by Congress or either branch thereof, to an individual member of the Board or to an employee or employees of the Board to be designated by such order for action thereon, and by its order at any time to amend, modify, supplement, or rescind any such assignment or reference. All such orders shall take effect forthwith and remain in effect until otherwise ordered by the Board. In conformity with and subject to the order or orders of the Mediation Board in the premises, [and] such individual member of the Board or employee designated shall have power and authority to act as to any of said work, business, or functions so assigned or referred to him for action by the Board.

Fifth. Transfer of officers and employees of Board of Mediation; transfer of appropriation

All officers and employees of the Board of Mediation (except the members thereof, whose offices are abolished) whose services in the judgment of the Mediation Board are necessary to the efficient operation of the Board are transferred to the Board, without change in classification or compensation; except that the Board may provide for the adjustment of such classification or compensation to conform to the duties to which such officers and employees may be assigned.

All unexpended appropriations for the operation of the Board of Mediation that are available at the time of the abolition of the Board of Mediation shall be transferred to the Mediation Board and shall be available for its use for salaries and other authorized expenditures.

§5.   (§155) Functions of Mediation Board

First. Disputes within jurisdiction of Mediation Board

The parties, or either party, to a dispute between an employee or group of employees and a carrier may invoke the services of the Mediation Board in any of the following cases:

(a) A dispute concerning changes in rates of pay, rules, or working conditions not adjusted by the parties in conference.

(b) Any other dispute not referable to the National Railroad Adjustment Board and not adjusted in conference between the parties or where conferences are refused.

The Mediation Board may proffer its services in case any labor emergency is found by it to exist at any time.

In either event the said Board shall promptly put itself in communication with the parties to such controversy, and shall use its best efforts, by mediation, to bring them to agreement. If such efforts to bring about an amicable settlement through mediation shall be unsuccessful, the said Board shall at once endeavor as its final required action (except as provided in paragraph third of this section and in section 160 of this title) to induce the parties to submit their controversy to arbitration, in accordance with the provisions of this chapter.

If arbitration at the request of the Board shall be refused by one or both parties, the Board shall at once notify both parties in writing that its mediatory efforts have failed and for thirty days thereafter, unless in the intervening period the parties agree to arbitration, or an emergency board shall be created under section 160 of this title, no change shall be made in the rates of pay, rules, or working conditions or established practices in effect prior to the time the dispute arose.

Second. Interpretation of agreement

In any case in which a controversy arises over the meaning or the application of any agreement reached through mediation under the provisions of this chapter, either party to the said agreement, or both, may apply to the Mediation Board for an interpretation of the meaning or application of such agreement. The said Board shall upon receipt of such request notify the parties to the controversy, and after a hearing of both sides give its interpretation within thirty days.

Third. Duties of Board with respect to arbitration of disputes; arbitrators; acknowledgment of agreement; notice to arbitrators; reconvening of arbitrators; filing contracts with Board; custody of records and documents

The Mediation Board shall have the following duties with respect to the arbitration of disputes under section 157 of this title:

(a) On failure of the arbitrators named by the parties to agree on the remaining arbitrator or arbitrators within the time set by section 157 of this title, it shall be the duty of the Mediation Board to name such remaining arbitrator or arbitrators. It shall be the duty of the Board in naming such arbitrator or arbitrators to appoint only those whom the Board shall deem wholly disinterested in the controversy to be arbitrated and impartial and without bias as between the parties to such arbitration. Should, however, the Board name an arbitrator or arbitrators not so disinterested and impartial, then, upon proper investigation and presentation of the facts, the Board shall promptly remove such arbitrator.

If an arbitrator named by the Mediation Board, in accordance with the provisions of this chapter, shall be removed by such Board as provided by this chapter, or if such an arbitrator refuses or is unable to serve, it shall be the duty of the Mediation Board, promptly, to select another arbitrator, in the same manner as provided in this chapter for an original appointment by the Mediation Board.

(b) Any member of the Mediation Board is authorized to take the acknowledgment of an agreement to arbitrate under this chapter. When so acknowledged, or when acknowledged by the parties before a notary public or the clerk of a district court or a court of appeals of the United States, such agreement to arbitrate shall be delivered to a member of said Board or transmitted to said Board, to be filed in its office.

(c) When an agreement to arbitrate has been filed with the Mediation Board, or with one of its members, as provided by this section, and when the said Board has been furnished the names of the arbitrators chosen by the parties to the controversy it shall be the duty of the Board to cause a notice in writing to be served upon said arbitrators, notifying them of their appointment, requesting them to meet promptly to name the remaining arbitrator or arbitrators necessary to complete the Board of Arbitration, and advising them of the period within which, as provided by the agreement to arbitrate, they are empowered to name such arbitrator or arbitrators.

(d) Either party to an arbitration desiring the reconvening of a board of arbitration to pass upon any controversy arising over the meaning or application of an award may so notify the Mediation Board in writing, stating in such notice the question or questions to be submitted to such reconvened Board. The Mediation Board shall thereupon promptly communicate with the members of the Board of Arbitration, or a subcommittee of such Board appointed for such purpose pursuant to a provision in the agreement to arbitrate, and arrange for the reconvening of said Board of Arbitration or subcommittee, and shall notify the respective parties to the controversy of the time and place at which the Board, or the subcommittee, will meet for hearings upon the matters in controversy to be submitted to it. No evidence other than that contained in the record filed with the original award shall be received or considered by such reconvened Board or subcommittee, except such evidence as may be necessary to illustrate the interpretations suggested by the parties. If any member of the original Board is unable or unwilling to serve on such reconvened Board or subcommittee thereof, another arbitrator shall be named in the same manner and with the same powers and duties as such original arbitrator.

(e) Within sixty days after June 21, 1934, every carrier shall file with the Mediation Board a copy of each contract with its employees in effect on the 1st day of April 1934, covering rates of pay, rules, and working conditions. If no contract with any craft or class of its employees has been entered into, the carrier shall file with the Mediation Board a statement of that fact, including also a statement of the rates of pay, rules, and working conditions applicable in dealing with such craft or class. When any new contract is executed or change is made in an existing contract with any class or craft of its employees covering rates of pay, rules, or working conditions, or in those rates of pay, rules, and working conditions of employees not covered by contract, the carrier shall file the same with the Mediation Board within thirty days after such new contract or change in existing contract has been executed or rates of pay, rules, and working conditions have been made effective.

(f) The Mediation Board shall be the custodian of all papers and documents heretofore filed with or transferred to the Board of Mediation bearing upon the settlement, adjustment, or determination of disputes between carriers and their employees or upon mediation or arbitration proceedings held under or pursuant to the provisions of any Act of Congress in respect thereto; and the President is authorized to designate a custodian of the records and property of the Board of Mediation until the transfer and delivery of such records to the Mediation Board and to require the transfer and delivery to the Mediation Board of any and all such papers and documents filed with it or in its possession.

§6.   (§156) Procedure in changing rates of pay, rules, and working conditions

Carriers and representatives of the employees shall give at least thirty days' written notice of an intended change in agreements affecting rates of pay, rules, or working conditions, and the time and place for the beginning of conference between the representatives of the parties interested in such intended changes shall be agreed upon within ten days after the receipt of said notice, and said time shall be within the thirty days provided in the notice. In every case where such notice of intended change has been given, or conferences are being held with reference thereto, or the services of the Mediation Board have been requested by either party, or said Board has proffered its services, rates of pay, rules, or working conditions shall not be altered by the carrier until the controversy has been finally acted upon, as required by section 155 of this title, by the Mediation Board, unless a period of ten days has elapsed after termination of conferences without request for or proffer of the services of the Mediation Board.

§7.   (§157) Arbitration

First. Submission of controversy to arbitration

Whenever a controversy shall arise between a carrier or carriers and its or their employees which is not settled either in conference between representatives of the parties or by the appropriate adjustment board or through mediation, in the manner provided in sections 151 to 156 of this title, such controversy may, by agreement of the parties to such controversy, be submitted to the arbitration of a board of three (or, if the parties to the controversy so stipulate, of six) persons: *Provided, however,* That the failure or refusal of either party to submit a controversy to arbitration shall not be construed as a violation of any legal obligation imposed upon such party by the terms of this chapter or otherwise.

Second. Manner of selecting board of arbitration

Such board of arbitration shall be chosen in the following manner:

(a) In the case of a board of three the carrier or carriers and the representatives of the employees, parties respectively to the agreement to arbitrate, shall each name one arbitrator; the two arbitrators thus chosen shall select a third arbitrator. If the arbitrators chosen by the parties shall fail to name the third arbitrator within five days after their first meeting, such third arbitrator shall be named by the Mediation Board.

(b) In the case of a board of six the carrier or carriers and the representatives of the employees, parties respectively to the agreement to arbitrate, shall each name two arbitrators; the four arbitrators thus chosen shall, by a majority vote, select the remaining two arbitrators. If the arbitrators chosen by the parties shall fail to name the two arbitrators within fifteen days after their first meeting, the said two arbitrators, or as many of them as have not been named, shall be named by the Mediation Board.

Third. Board of arbitration; organization; compensation; procedure

(a) Notice of selection or failure to select arbitrators. When the arbitrators selected by the respective parties have agreed upon the remaining arbitrator or arbitrators, they shall notify the Mediation Board; and, in the event of their failure to agree upon any or upon all of the necessary arbitrators within the period fixed by this chapter, they shall, at the expiration of such period, notify the Mediation Board of the arbitrators selected, if any, or of their failure to make or to complete such selection.

(b) Organization of board; procedure. The board of arbitration shall organize and select its own chairman and make all necessary rules for conducting its hearings: *Provided, however,* That the board of arbitration shall be bound to give the parties to the controversy a full and fair hearing, which shall

include an opportunity to present evidence in support of their claims, and an opportunity to present their case in person, by counsel, or by other representative as they may respectively elect.

(c) Duty to reconvene; questions considered. Upon notice from the Mediation Board that the parties, or either party, to an arbitration desire the reconvening of the board of arbitration (or a subcommittee of such board of arbitration appointed for such purpose pursuant to the agreement to arbitrate) to pass upon any controversy over the meaning or application of their award, the board, or its subcommittee, shall at once reconvene. No question other than, or in addition to, the questions relating to the meaning or application of the award, submitted by the party or parties in writing, shall be considered by the reconvened board of arbitration or its subcommittee.

Such rulings shall be acknowledged by such board or subcommittee thereof in the same manner, and filed in the same district court clerk's office, as the original award and become a part thereof.

(d) Competency of arbitrators. No arbitrator, except those chosen by the Mediation Board, shall be incompetent to act as an arbitrator because of his interest in the controversy to be arbitrated, or because of his connection with or partiality to either of the parties to the arbitration.

(e) Compensation and expenses. Each member of any board of arbitration created under the provisions of this chapter named by either party to the arbitration shall be compensated by the party naming him. Each arbitrator selected by the arbitrators or named by the Mediation Board shall receive from the Mediation Board such compensation as the Mediation Board may fix, together with his necessary traveling expenses and expenses actually incurred for subsistence, while serving as an arbitrator.

(f) Award; disposition of original and copies. The board of arbitration shall furnish a certified copy of its award to the respective parties to the controversy, and shall transmit the original, together with the papers and proceedings and a transcript of the evidence taken at the hearings, certified under the hands of at least a majority of the arbitrators, to the clerk of the district court of the United States for the district wherein the controversy arose or the arbitration is entered into, to be filed in said clerk's office as hereinafter provided. The said board shall also furnish a certified copy of its award, and the papers and proceedings, including testimony relating thereto, to the Mediation Board to be filed in its office; and in addition a certified copy of its award shall be filed in the office of the Interstate Commerce Commission: *Provided, however,* That such award shall not be construed to diminish or

extinguish any of the powers or duties of the Interstate Commerce Commission, under subtitle IV of Title 49.[*]

(g) Compensation of assistants to board of arbitration; expenses; quarters. A board of arbitration may, subject to the approval of the Mediation Board, employ and fix the compensation of such assistants as it deems necessary in carrying on the arbitration proceedings. The compensation of such employees, together with their necessary traveling expenses and expenses actually incurred for subsistence, while so employed, and the necessary expenses of boards of arbitration, shall be paid by the Mediation Board.

Whenever practicable, the board shall be supplied with suitable quarters in any Federal building located at its place of meeting or at any place where the board may conduct its proceedings or deliberations.

(h) Testimony before board; oaths; attendance of witnesses; production of documents; subpoenas; fees. All testimony before said board shall be given under oath or affirmation, and any member of the board shall have the power to administer oaths or affirmations. The board of arbitration, or any member thereof, shall have the power to require the attendance of witnesses and the production of such books, papers, contracts, agreements, and documents as may be deemed by the board of arbitration material to a just determination of the matters submitted to its arbitration, and may for that purpose request the clerk of the district court of the United States for the district wherein said arbitration is being conducted to issue the necessary subpoenas, and upon such request the said clerk or his duly authorized deputy shall be, and he is, authorized, and it shall be his duty, to issue such subpoenas.

Any witness appearing before a board of arbitration shall receive the same fees and mileage as witnesses in courts of the United States, to be paid by the party securing the subpoena.

§8.   (§158) Agreement to arbitrate; form and contents; signatures and acknowledgment; revocation

The agreement to arbitrate —
(a) Shall be in writing;
(b) Shall stipulate that the arbitration is ~~held~~ had under the provisions of this chapter;

---

[*] The Interstate Commerce Commission was abolished, and its functions transferred to the Surface Transportation Board, effective Jan. 1, 1996. See Pub. L. 104-88, especially §205 (Dec. 29, 1995), 109 Stat. 803.

(c) Shall state whether the board of arbitration is to consist of three or of six members;

(d) Shall be signed by the duly accredited representatives of the carrier or carriers and the employees, parties respectively to the agreement to arbitrate, and shall be acknowledged by said parties before a notary public, the clerk of a district court or court of appeals of the United States, or before a member of the Mediation Board, and, when so acknowledged, shall be filed in the office of the Mediation Board;

(e) Shall state specifically the questions to be submitted to the said board for decision; and that, in its award or awards, the said board shall confine itself strictly to decisions as to the questions so specifically submitted to it;

(f) Shall provide that the questions, or any one or more of them, submitted by the parties to the board of arbitration may be withdrawn from arbitration on notice to that effect signed by the duly accredited representatives of all the parties and served on the board of arbitration;

(g) Shall stipulate that the signatures of a majority of said board of arbitration affixed to their award shall be competent to constitute a valid and binding award;

(h) Shall fix a period from the date of the appointment of the arbitrator or arbitrators necessary to complete the board (as provided for in the agreement) within which the said board shall commence its hearings;

(i) Shall fix a period from the beginning of the hearings within which the said board shall make and file its award: *Provided,* That the parties may agree at any time upon an extension of this period;

(j) Shall provide for the date from which the award shall become effective and shall fix the period during which the award shall continue in force;

(k) Shall provide that the award of the board of arbitration and the evidence of the proceedings before the board relating thereto, when certified under the hands of at least a majority of the arbitrators, shall be filed in the clerk's office of the district court of the United States for the district wherein the controversy arose or the arbitration was entered into, which district shall be designated in the agreement; and, when so filed, such award and proceedings shall constitute the full and complete record of the arbitration;

(*l*) Shall provide that the award, when so filed, shall be final and conclusive upon the parties as to the facts determined by said award and as to the merits of the controversy decided;

(m) Shall provide that any difference arising as to the meaning, or the application of the provisions, of an award made by a board of arbitration shall be referred back for a ruling to the same board, or, by agreement, to a subcommittee of such board; and that such ruling, when acknowledged in the same manner, and filed in the same district court clerk's office, as the original award, shall be a part of and shall have the same force and effect as such original award; and

(n) Shall provide that the respective parties to the award will each faithfully execute the same.

The said agreement to arbitrate, when properly signed and acknowledged as herein provided, shall not be revoked by a party to such agreement: *Provided, however,* That such agreement to arbitrate may at any time be revoked and canceled by the written agreement of both parties, signed by their duly accredited representatives, and (if no board of arbitration has yet been constituted under the agreement) delivered to the Mediation Board or any member thereof; or, if the board of arbitration has been constituted as provided by this chapter, delivered to such board of arbitration.

§9. (§159) Award and judgment thereon; effect of chapter on individual employee

First. Filing of award

The award of a board of arbitration, having been acknowledged as herein provided, shall be filed in the clerk's office of the district court designated in the agreement to arbitrate.

Second. Conclusiveness of award; judgment

An award acknowledged and filed as herein provided shall be conclusive on the parties as to the merits and facts of the controversy submitted to arbitration, and unless, within ten days after the filing of the award, a petition to impeach the award, on the grounds hereinafter set forth, shall be filed in the clerk's office of the court in which the award has been filed, the court shall enter judgment on the award, which judgment shall be final and conclusive on the parties.

Third. Impeachment of award; grounds

Such petition for the impeachment or contesting of any award so filed shall be entertained by the court only on one or more of the following grounds:

(a) That the award plainly does not conform to the substantive requirements laid down by this chapter for such awards, or that the proceedings were not substantially in conformity with this chapter;

(b) That the award does not conform, nor confine itself, to the stipulations of the agreement to arbitrate; or

(c) That a member of the board of arbitration rendering the award was guilty of fraud or corruption; or that a party to the arbitration practiced fraud or corruption which fraud or corruption affected the result of the arbitration: *Provided, however,* That no court shall entertain any such petition on the ground that an award is invalid for uncertainty; in such case the proper remedy shall be a submission of such award to a reconvened board, or subcommittee thereof, for interpretation, as provided by this chapter: *Provided further,* That an award contested as herein provided shall be construed liberally by the court, with a view to favoring its validity, and that no award shall be set aside for trivial irregularity or clerical error, going only to form and not to substance.

Fourth. Effect of partial invalidity of award

If the court shall determine that a part of the award is invalid on some ground or grounds designated in this section as a ground of invalidity, but shall determine that a part of the award is valid, the court shall set aside the entire award: *Provided, however,* That, if the parties shall agree thereto, and if such valid and invalid parts are separable, the court shall set aside the invalid part, and order judgment to stand as to the valid part.

Fifth. Appeal; record

At the expiration of 10 days from the decision of the district court upon the petition filed as aforesaid, final judgment shall be entered in accordance with said decision, unless during said 10 days either party shall appeal therefrom to the court of appeals. In such case only such portion of the record shall be transmitted to the appellate court as is necessary to the proper understanding and consideration of the questions of law presented by said petition and to be decided.

Sixth. Finality of decision of court of appeals

The determination of said court of appeals upon said questions shall be final, and, being certified by the clerk thereof to said district court, judgment pursuant thereto shall thereupon be entered by said district court.

Seventh. Judgment where petitioner's contentions are sustained

If the petitioner's contentions are finally sustained, judgment shall be entered setting aside the award in whole or, if the parties so agree, in part; but in such case the parties may agree upon a judgment to be entered disposing of the subject matter of the controversy, which judgment when entered shall have the same force and effect as judgment entered upon an award.

Eighth. Duty of employee to render service without consent; right to quit

Nothing in this chapter shall be construed to require an individual employee to render labor or service without his consent, nor shall anything in this chapter be construed to make the quitting of his labor or service by an individual employee an illegal act; nor shall any court issue any process to compel the performance by an individual employee of such labor or service, without his consent.

§9A. (§159a) Special procedure for commuter service

(a) Applicability of provisions.[*] Except as provided in section 590(h) of this title, the provisions of this section shall apply to any dispute subject to this chapter between a publicly funded and publicly operated carrier providing rail commuter service (including the Amtrak Commuter Services Corporation) and its employees.

(b) Request for establishment of emergency board. If a dispute between the parties described in subsection (a) of this section is not adjusted under the foregoing provisions of this chapter and the President does not, under section 160 of this title, create an emergency board to investigate and report on such dispute, then any party to the dispute or the Governor of any State through which the service that is the subject of the dispute is operated may request the President to establish such an emergency board.

(c) Establishment of emergency board. (1) Upon the request of a party or a Governor under subsection (b) of this section, the President shall create an

---

[*] This section was added by Pub. L. 97-35, Title XI, §1157, 95 Stat. 681 (1981).

emergency board to investigate and report on the dispute in accordance with section 160 of this title. For purposes of this subsection, the period during which no change, except by agreement, shall be made by the parties in the conditions out of which the dispute arose shall be 120 days from the day of the creation of such emergency board.

(2) If the President, in his discretion, creates a board to investigate and report on a dispute between the parties described in subsection (a) of this section, the provisions of this section shall apply to the same extent as if such board had been created pursuant to paragraph (1) of this subsection.

(d) Public hearing by National Mediation Board upon failure of emergency board to effectuate settlement of dispute. Within 60 days after the creation of an emergency board under this section, if there has been no settlement between the parties, the National Mediation Board shall conduct a public hearing on the dispute at which each party shall appear and provide testimony setting forth the reasons it has not accepted the recommendations of the emergency board for settlement of the dispute.

(e) Establishment of second emergency board. If no settlement in the dispute is reached at the end of the 120-day period beginning on the date of the creation of the emergency board, any party to the dispute or the Governor of any State through which the service that is the subject of the dispute is operated may request the President to establish another emergency board, in which case the President shall establish such emergency board.

(f) Submission of final offers to second emergency board by parties. Within 30 days after creation of a board under subsection (e) of this section, the parties to the dispute shall submit to the board final offers for settlement of the dispute.

(g) Report of second emergency board. Within 30 days after the submission of final offers under subsection (f) of this section, the emergency board shall submit a report to the President setting forth its selection of the most reasonable offer.

(h) Maintenance of status quo during dispute period. From the time a request to establish a board is made under subsection (e) of this section until 60 days after such board makes its report under subsection (g) of this section, no change, except by agreement, shall be made by the parties in the conditions out of which the dispute arose.

(i) Work stoppages by employees subsequent to carrier offer selected; eligibility of employees for benefits. If the emergency board selects the final offer submitted by the carrier and, after the expiration of the 60-day period described in subsection (h) of this section, the employees of such carrier

engage in any work stoppage arising out of the dispute, such employees shall not be eligible during the period of such work stoppage for benefits under the Railroad Unemployment Insurance Act [45 U.S.C. §351 et seq.].

(j) Work stoppages by employees subsequent to employees offer selected; eligibility of employer for benefits. If the emergency board selects the final offer submitted by the employees and, after the expiration of the 60-day period described in subsection (h) of this section, the carrier refuses to accept the final offer submitted by the employees and the employees of such carrier engage in any work stoppage arising out of the dispute, the carrier shall not participate in any benefits of any agreement between carriers which is designed to provide benefits to such carriers during a work stoppage.

§10. (§160) Emergency Board

If a dispute between a carrier and its employees be not adjusted under the foregoing provisions of this chapter and should, in the judgment of the Mediation Board, threaten substantially to interrupt interstate commerce to a degree such as to deprive any section of the country of essential transportation service, the Mediation Board shall notify the President, who may thereupon, in his discretion, create a board to investigate and report respecting such dispute. Such board shall be composed of such number of persons as to the President may seem desirable: *Provided, however,* That no member appointed shall be pecuniarily or otherwise interested in any organization of employees or any carrier. The compensation of the members of any such board shall be fixed by the President. Such board shall be created separately in each instance and it shall investigate promptly the facts as to the dispute and make a report thereon to the President within thirty days from the date of its creation.

There is authorized to be appropriated such sums as may be necessary for the expenses of such board, including the compensation and the necessary traveling expenses and expenses actually incurred for subsistence, of the members of the board. All expenditures of the board shall be allowed and paid on the presentation of itemized vouchers therefor approved by the chairman.

After the creation of such board and for thirty days after such board has made its report to the President, no change, except by agreement, shall be made by the parties to the controversy in the conditions out of which the dispute arose.

§160a Rules and regulations

(a) In general. The Mediation Board shall have the authority from time to time to make, amend, and rescind in the manner prescribed by section 553 of Title 5 and after opportunity for a public hearing, such rules and regulations as may be necessary to carry out the provisions of this chapter.

(b) Application. The requirements of subsection (a) shall not apply to any rule or proposed rule to which the third sentence of section 553(b) of Title 5 applies.

§11.   (§161) Effect of partial invalidity of chapter

If any provision of this chapter, or the application thereof to any person or circumstance, is held invalid, the remainder of the chapter, and the application of such provision to other persons or circumstances, shall not be affected thereby.~~section, subsection, sentence, clause, or phrase of this chapter is for any reason held to be unconstitutional, such decision shall not affect the validity of the remaining portions of this chapter. All Acts or parts of Acts inconsistent with the provisions of this chapter are repealed.~~

§12.   (§162) Authorization of appropriations

There is authorized to be appropriated such sums as may be necessary for expenditure by the Mediation Board in carrying out the provisions of this chapter.

§14.   (§163) Repeal of prior legislation; exception

Chapters 6 and 7 of this title, providing for mediation, conciliation, and arbitration, and all Acts and parts of Acts in conflict with the provisions of this chapter are repealed, except that the members, secretary, officers, employees, and agents of the Railroad Labor Board, in office on May 20, 1926, shall receive their salaries for a period of 30 days from such date, in the same manner as though this chapter had not been passed.

(§165) Evaluation and audit of Mediation Board

(a) Evaluation and audit of Mediation Board. (1) *In general.* In order to promote economy, efficiency, and effectiveness in the administration of the

programs, operations, and activities of the Mediation Board, the Comptroller General of the United States shall evaluate and audit the programs and expenditures of the Mediation Board. Such an evaluation and audit shall be conducted not less frequently than every 2 years, but may be conducted as determined necessary by the Comptroller General or the appropriate congressional committees.

(2) Responsibility of Comptroller General. In carrying out the evaluation and audit required under paragraph (1), the Comptroller General shall evaluate and audit the programs, operations, and activities of the Mediation Board, including, at a minimum—

(A) information management and security, including privacy protection of personally identifiable information;

(B) resource management;

(C) workforce development;

(D) procurement and contracting planning, practices, and policies;

(E) the extent to which the Mediation Board follows leading practices in selected management areas; and

(F) the processes the mediation board follows to address challenges in—

(i) initial investigations of applications requesting that an organization or individual be certified as the representative of any craft or class of employees;

(ii) determining and certifying representatives of employees; and

(iii) ensuring that the process occurs without interference, influence, or coercion.

(b) Immediate review of certification procedures. Not later than 180 days after February 14, 2012, the Comptroller General shall review the processes applied by the Mediation Board to certify or decertify representation of employees by a labor organization and make recommendations to the Board and appropriate congressional committees regarding actions that may be taken by the Board or Congress to ensure that the processes are fair and reasonable for all parties. Such review shall be conducted separately from any evaluation and audit under subsection (a) and shall include, at a minimum—

(1) an evaluation of the existing processes and changes to such processes that have occurred since the establishment of the Mediation Board and whether those changes are consistent with congressional intent; and

(2) a description of the extent to which such processes are consistent with similar processes applied to other Federal or State agencies with

jurisdiction over labor relations, and an evaluation of any justifications for any discrepancies between the processes of the Mediation Board and such similar Federal or State processes.

(c) Appropriate congressional committee defined. In this section, the term "appropriate congressional committees" means the Committee on Transportation and Infrastructure of the House of Representatives, the Committee on Commerce, Science, and Transportation of the Senate, and the Committee on Health, Education, Labor, and Pensions of the Senate.

SUBCHAPTER II. CARRIERS BY AIR

§201.   (§181) Application of subchapter I to carriers by air

All of the provisions of subchapter I of this chapter except section 153 of this title are extended to and shall cover every common carrier by air engaged in interstate or foreign commerce, and every carrier by air transporting mail for or under contract with the United States Government, and every air pilot or other person who performs any work as an employee or subordinate official of such carrier or carriers, subject to its or their continuing authority to supervise and direct the manner of rendition of his service.[*]

§202.   (§182) Duties, penalties, benefits, and privileges
of subchapter I applicable

The duties, requirements, penalties, benefits, and privileges prescribed and established by the provisions of subchapter I of this chapter except section 153 of this title shall apply to said carriers by air and their employees in the same manner and to the same extent as though such carriers and their employees were specifically included within the definition of "carrier" and "employee", respectively, in section 151 of this title.

§203.   (§183) Disputes within jurisdiction of Mediation Board

The parties or either party to a dispute between an employee or a group of employees and a carrier or carriers by air may invoke the services of the

---

[*] Added April 10, 1936, c.166, 49 Stat. 1189 et seq.

National Mediation Board and the jurisdiction of said Mediation Board is extended to any of the following cases:

(a) A dispute concerning changes in rates of pay, rules, or working conditions not adjusted by the parties in conference.

(b) Any other dispute not referable to an adjustment board, as hereinafter provided, and not adjusted in conference between the parties, or where conferences are refused.

The National Mediation Board may proffer its services in case any labor emergency is found by it to exist at any time.

The services of the Mediation Board may be invoked in a case under this subchapter in the same manner and to the same extent as are the disputes covered by section 155 of this title.

§204. (§184) System, group, or regional boards of adjustment

The disputes between an employee or group of employees and a carrier or carriers by air growing out of grievances, or out of the interpretation or application of agreements concerning rates of pay, rules, or working conditions, including cases pending and unadjusted on April 10, 1936 before the National Labor Relations Board, shall be handled in the usual manner up to and including the chief operating officer of the carrier designated to handle such disputes; but, failing to reach an adjustment in this manner, the disputes may be referred by petition of the parties or by either party to an appropriate adjustment board, as hereinafter provided, with a full statement of the facts and supporting data bearing upon the disputes.

It shall be the duty of every carrier and of its employees, acting through their representatives, selected in accordance with the provisions of this subchapter, to establish a board of adjustment of jurisdiction not exceeding the jurisdiction which may be lawfully exercised by system, group, or regional boards of adjustment, under the authority of section 153 of this title.

Such boards of adjustment may be established by agreement between employees and carriers either on any individual carrier, or system, or group of carriers by air and any class or classes of its or their employees; or pending the establishment of a permanent National Board of Adjustment as hereinafter provided. Nothing in this chapter shall prevent said carriers by air, or any class or classes of their employees, both acting through their representatives selected in accordance with provisions of this subchapter, from mutually agreeing to the establishment of a National Board of Adjustment of temporary duration and of similarly limited jurisdiction.

§205.   (§185) National Air Transport Adjustment Board

When, in the judgment of the National Mediation Board, it shall be necessary to have a permanent national board of adjustment in order to provide for the prompt and orderly settlement of disputes between said carriers by air, or any of them, and its or their employees, growing out of grievances or out of the interpretation or application of agreements between said carriers by air or any of them, and any class or classes of its or their employees, covering rates of pay, rules, or working conditions, the National Mediation Board is empowered and directed, by its order duly made, published, and served, to direct the said carriers by air and such labor organizations of their employees, national in scope, as have been or may be recognized in accordance with the provisions of this chapter, to select and designate four representatives who shall constitute a board which shall be known as the "National Air Transport Adjustment Board." Two members of said National Air Transport Adjustment Board shall be selected by said carriers by air and two members by the said labor organizations of the employees, within thirty days after the date of the order of the National Mediation Board, in the manner and by the procedure prescribed by section 153 of this title for the selection and designation of members of the National Railroad Adjustment Board. The National Air Transport Adjustment Board shall meet within forty days after the date of the order of the National Mediation Board directing the selection and designation of its members and shall organize and adopt rules for conducting its proceedings, in the manner prescribed in section 153 of this title. Vacancies in membership or office shall be filled, members shall be appointed in case of failure of the carriers or of labor organizations of the employees to select and designate representatives, members of the National Air Transport Adjustment Board shall be compensated, hearings shall be held, findings and awards made, stated, served, and enforced, and the number and compensation of any necessary assistants shall be determined and the compensation of such employees shall be paid, all in the same manner and to the same extent as provided with reference to the National Railroad Adjustment Board by section 153 of this title. The powers and duties prescribed and established by the provisions of section 153 of this title with reference to the National Railroad Adjustment Board and the several divisions thereof are conferred upon and shall be exercised and performed in like manner and to the same extent by the said National Air Transport Adjustment Board, not exceeding, however, the jurisdiction conferred upon said National Air Transport Adjustment Board by the provisions of this subchapter. From and after the organization of the National Air Transport Adjustment Board, if any system, group, or regional board of adjustment established by any carrier or carriers by air and any class or classes of its or their employees is not satisfactory to either party thereto, the said party, upon ninety days' notice to the other party, may elect to come under the jurisdiction of the National Air Transport Adjustment Board.

[This section (May 20, 1926, ch 347, Title II, §206, as added Apr. 10, 1936, 49 Stat. 1191) was omitted as executed. The section related to the transfer of certain cases from the NLRB to the NMB. — EDS.]

§207. (§187) Separability ~~of provisions~~

If any provision of this subchapter or application thereof to any person or circumstance is held invalid, the remainder of such sections and the application of such provision to other persons or circumstances shall not be affected thereby.

§208. (§188) Authorization of appropriations

There is authorized to be appropriated such sums as may be necessary for expenditure by the Mediation Board in carrying out the provisions of this chapter.

Norris-LaGuardia Act of 1932
47 Stat. 70 (1932), as amended, 29 U.S.C. §§101-115

§1.   (§101) Issuance of restraining orders and injunctions; limitation; public policy

No court of the United States, as defined in this chapter, shall have jurisdiction to issue any restraining order or temporary or permanent injunction in a case involving or growing out of a labor dispute, except in a strict conformity with the provisions of this chapter; nor shall any such restraining order or temporary or permanent injunction be issued contrary to the public policy declared in this chapter.

§2.   (§102) Public policy in labor matters declared

In the interpretation of this chapter and in determining the jurisdiction and authority of the courts of the United States, as such jurisdiction and authority are defined and limited in this chapter, the public policy of the United States is declared as follows:

Whereas under prevailing economic conditions, developed with the aid of governmental authority for owners of property to organize in the corporate and other forms of ownership association, the individual unorganized worker is commonly helpless to exercise actual liberty of contract and to protect his freedom of labor, and thereby to obtain acceptable terms and conditions of employment, wherefore, though he should be free to decline to associate with his fellows, it is necessary that he have full freedom of association, self-organization, and designation of representatives of his own choosing, to negotiate the terms and conditions of his employment, and that he shall be free from the interference, restraint, or coercion of employers of labor, or their agents, in the designation of such representatives or in self-organization or in other concerted activities for the purpose of collective bargaining or other mutual aid or protection; therefore, the following definitions of and limitations upon the jurisdiction and authority of the courts of the United States are enacted.

§3. (§103) Nonenforceability of undertakings in conflict with public policy; "yellow dog" contracts

Any undertaking or promise, such as is described in this section, or any other undertaking or promise in conflict with the public policy declared in section 102 of this title, is declared to be contrary to the public policy of the United States, shall not be enforceable in any court of the United States and shall not afford any basis for the granting of legal or equitable relief by any such court, including specifically the following:

Every undertaking or promise hereafter made, whether written or oral, express or implied, constituting or contained in any contract or agreement of hiring or employment between any individual, firm, company, association, or corporation, and any employee or prospective employee of the same, whereby

(a) Either party to such contract or agreement undertakes or promises not to join, become, or remain a member of any labor organization or of any employer organization; or

(b) Either party to such contract or agreement undertakes or promises that he will withdraw from an employment relation in the event that he joins, becomes, or remains a member of any labor organization or of any employer organization.

§4. (§104) Enumeration of specific acts not subject to restraining orders or injunctions

No court of the United States shall have jurisdiction to issue any restraining order or temporary or permanent injunction in any case involving or growing out of any labor dispute to prohibit any person or persons participating or interested in such dispute (as these terms are herein defined) from doing, whether singly or in concert, any of the following acts:

(a) Ceasing or refusing to perform any work or to remain in any relation of employment;

(b) Becoming or remaining a member of any labor organization or of any employer organization, regardless of any such undertaking or promise as is described in section 103 of this title;

(c) Paying or giving to, or withholding from, any person participating or interested in such labor dispute, any strike or unemployment benefits or insurance, or other moneys or things of value;

(d) By all lawful means aiding any person participating or interested in any labor dispute who is being proceeded against in, or is prosecuting, any action or suit in any court of the United States or of any State;

(e) Giving publicity to the existence of, or the facts involved in, any labor dispute, whether by advertising, speaking, patrolling, or by any other method not involving fraud or violence;

(f) Assembling peaceably to act or to organize to act in promotion of their interests in a labor dispute;

(g) Advising or notifying any person of an intention to do any of the acts heretofore specified;

(h) Agreeing with other persons to do or not to do any of the acts heretofore specified; and

(i) Advising, urging, or otherwise causing or inducing without fraud or violence the acts heretofore specified, regardless of any such undertaking or promise as is described in section 103 of this title.

§5. (§105) Doing in concert of certain acts as constituting unlawful combination or conspiracy subjecting person to injunctive remedies

No court of the United States shall have jurisdiction to issue a restraining order or temporary or permanent injunction upon the ground that any of the persons participating or interested in a labor dispute constitute or are engaged in an unlawful combination or conspiracy because of the doing in concert of the acts enumerated in section 104 of this title.

§6. (§106) Responsibility of officers and members of associations or their organizations for unlawful acts of individual officers, members, and agents

No officer or member of any association or organization, and no association or organization participating or interested in a labor dispute, shall be held responsible or liable in any court of the United States for the unlawful acts of individual officers, members, or agents, except upon clear proof of actual participation in, or actual authorization of, such acts, or of ratification of such acts after actual knowledge thereof.

§7. (§107) Issuance of injunctions in labor disputes; hearing; findings of court; notice to affected persons; temporary restraining order; undertakings

No court of the United States shall have jurisdiction to issue a temporary or permanent injunction in any case involving or growing out of a labor dispute, as defined in this chapter, except after hearing the testimony of witnesses in open court (with opportunity for cross-examination) in support of the allegations of a complaint made under oath, and testimony in opposition thereto, if offered, and except after findings of fact by the court, to the effect—

(a) That unlawful acts have been threatened and will be committed unless restrained or have been committed and will be continued unless restrained, but no injunction or temporary restraining order shall be issued on account of any threat or unlawful act excepting against the person or persons, association, or organization making the threat or committing the unlawful act or actually authorizing or ratifying the same after actual knowledge thereof;

(b) That substantial and irreparable injury to complainant's property will follow;

(c) That as to each item of relief granted greater injury will be inflicted upon complainant by the denial of relief than will be inflicted upon defendants by the granting of relief;

(d) That complainant has no adequate remedy at law; and

(e) That the public officers charged with the duty to protect complainant's property are unable or unwilling to furnish adequate protection.

Such hearing shall be held after due and personal notice thereof has been given, in such manner as the court shall direct, to all known persons against whom relief is sought, and also to the chief of those public officials of the county and city within which the unlawful acts have been threatened or committed charged with the duty to protect complainant's property: *Provided, however,* That if a complainant shall also allege that, unless a temporary restraining order shall be issued without notice, a substantial and irreparable injury to complainant's property will be unavoidable, such a temporary restraining order may be issued upon testimony under oath, sufficient, if sustained, to justify the court in issuing a temporary injunction upon a hearing after notice. Such a temporary restraining order shall be effective for no longer than five days and shall become void at the expiration of said five days. No temporary restraining order or temporary injunction shall be issued except on condition that complainant shall first file an undertaking with adequate security in an amount to be fixed by the court sufficient to recompense those enjoined for any loss, expense, or damage caused by the improvident or erroneous issuance of such order or injunction, including all reasonable costs (together with a reasonable attorney's fee) and expense of defense against the order or against the granting of any injunctive relief sought in the same proceeding and subsequently denied by the court.

The undertaking mentioned in this section shall be understood to signify an agreement entered into by the complainant and the surety upon which a decree may be rendered in the same suit or proceeding against said complainant and surety, upon a hearing to assess damages of which hearing complainant and surety shall have reasonable notice, the said complainant and surety submitting themselves to the jurisdiction of the court for that purpose. But nothing in this section contained shall deprive any party having a claim or cause of action under or upon such undertaking from electing to pursue his ordinary remedy by suit at law or in equity.

§8.   (§108) Noncompliance with obligations involved in labor disputes or failure to settle by negotiation or arbitration as preventing injunctive relief

No restraining order or injunctive relief shall be granted to any complainant who has failed to comply with any obligation imposed by law which is involved in the labor dispute in question, or who has failed to make every reasonable effort to settle such dispute either by negotiation or with the aid of any available governmental machinery of mediation or voluntary arbitration.

§9.   (§109) Granting of restraining order or injunction as dependent on previous findings of fact; limitation on prohibitions included in restraining orders and injunctions

No restraining order or temporary or permanent injunction shall be granted in a case involving or growing out of a labor dispute, except on the basis of findings of fact made and filed by the court in the record of the case prior to the issuance of such restraining order or injunction; and every restraining order or injunction granted in a case involving or growing out of a labor dispute shall include only a prohibition of such specific act or acts as may be expressly complained of in the bill of complaint or petition filed in such case and as shall be expressly included in said findings of fact made and filed by the court as provided in this chapter.

§10. (§110) Review by Court of Appeals of issuance or denial of temporary injunctions; record

Whenever any court of the United States shall issue or deny any temporary injunction in a case involving or growing out of a labor dispute, the court shall, upon the request of any party to the proceedings and on his filing the usual bond for costs, forthwith certify as in ordinary cases the record of the case to the court of appeals for its review. Upon the filing of such record in the court of appeals, the appeal shall be heard and the temporary injunctive order affirmed, modified, or set aside expeditiously.

§§11, 12. (§§111, 112) [Repealed June 25, 1948, c.645, §21, 62 Stat. 862, eff. Sept. 1, 1948.]

§13. (§113) Definitions of terms and words used in chapter

When used in this chapter, and for the purposes of this chapter —

(a) A case shall be held to involve or to grow out of a labor dispute when the case involves persons who are engaged in the same industry, trade, craft, or occupation; or have direct or indirect interests therein; or who are employees of the same employer; or who are members of the same or an affiliated organization of employers or employees; whether such dispute is (1) between one or more employers or associations of employers and one or more employees or associations of employees; (2) between one or more employers or associations of employers and one or more employers or associations of employers; or (3) between one or more employees or associations of employees and one or more employees or associations of employees; or when the case involves any conflicting or competing interests in a "labor dispute" (as defined in this section) of "persons participating or interested" therein (as defined in this section).

(b) A person or association shall be held to be a person participating or interested in a labor dispute if relief is sought against him or it, and if he or it is engaged in the same industry, trade, craft, or occupation in which such dispute occurs, or has a direct or indirect interest therein, or is a member, officer, or agent of any association composed in whole or in part of employers or employees engaged in such industry, trade, craft, or occupation.

(c) The term "labor dispute" includes any controversy concerning terms or conditions of employment, or concerning the association or representation of persons in negotiating, fixing, maintaining, changing, or seeking to arrange terms or conditions of employment, regardless of whether or not the disputants stand in the proximate relation of employer and employee.

(d) The term "court of the United States" means any court of the United States whose jurisdiction has been or may be conferred or defined or limited by Act of Congress, including the courts of the District of Columbia.

§14. (§114) Separability of provisions

If any provision of this chapter or the application thereof to any person or circumstance is held unconstitutional or otherwise invalid, the remaining provisions of this chapter and the application of such provisions to other persons or circumstances shall not be affected thereby.

§15. (§115) Repeal of conflicting acts

All acts and parts of acts in conflict with the provisions of this chapter are repealed.

National Labor Relations Act of 1935[*]
49 Stat. 449 (1935), as amended, 29 U.S.C. §§151-169

FINDINGS AND POLICIES

§1. (§151) The denial by **some** employers of the right of employees to organize and the refusal by **some** employers to accept the procedure of collective bargaining lead to strikes and other forms of industrial strife or unrest, which have the intent or the necessary effect of burdening or obstructing commerce by (a) impairing the efficiency, safety, or operation of the instrumentalities of commerce; (b) occurring in the current of commerce; (c) materially affecting, restraining, or controlling the flow of raw materials or manufactured or processed goods from or into the channels of commerce, or the prices of such materials or goods in commerce; or (d) causing diminution of employment and wages in such volume as substantially to impair or disrupt the market for goods flowing from or into the channels of commerce.[*]

The inequality of bargaining power between employees who do not possess full freedom of association or actual liberty of contract, and employers who are organized in the corporate or other forms of ownership association substantially burdens and affects the flow of commerce, and tends to aggravate recurrent business depressions, by depressing wage rates and the purchasing power of wage earners in industry and by preventing the stabilization of competitive wage rates and working conditions within and between industries.

Experience has proved that protection by law of the right of employees to organize and bargain collectively safeguards commerce from injury, impairment, or interruption, and promotes the flow of commerce by removing certain recognized sources of industrial strife and unrest, by encouraging practices fundamental to the friendly adjustment of industrial disputes arising out of differences as to wages, hours, or other working conditions, and by restoring equality of bargaining power between employers and employees.

Experience has further demonstrated that certain practices by some labor organizations, their officers, and members have the intent or the

---

* [Internal section references are to the NLRA of 1935 (Wagner Act), as amended, and not to the United States Code; references within parentheticals are to the Code. The text of the original Wagner Act is printed in regular roman type; the Taft-Hartley amendments of 1947 are in boldface type; the Landrum-Griffin amendments of 1959 are in italics; and the 1974 amendments are underscored. Deleted matter is in brackets; bracketed matter in regular roman type was deleted in 1947; and bracketed matter in boldface type was deleted in 1959. Other amendments and deletions are specifically noted. — EDS.]

necessary effect of burdening or obstructing commerce by preventing the free flow of goods in such commerce through strikes and other forms of industrial unrest or through concerted activities which impair the interest of the public in the free flow of such commerce. The elimination of such practices is a necessary condition to the assurance of the rights herein guaranteed.

It is hereby declared to be the policy of the United States to eliminate the causes of certain substantial obstructions to the free flow of commerce and to mitigate and eliminate these obstructions when they have occurred by encouraging the practice and procedure of collective bargaining and by protecting the exercise by workers of full freedom of association, self-organization, and designation of representatives of their own choosing, for the purpose of negotiating the terms and conditions of their employment or other mutual aid or protection.

DEFINITIONS

§2. (§152) When used in this Act —

(1) The term "person" includes one or more individuals, labor organizations, partnerships, associations, corporations, legal representatives, trustees, trustees in cases under Title 11,[*] or receivers.

(2) The term "employer" includes any person acting [in the interest of] **as an agent** of an employer, directly or indirectly, but shall not include the United States **or any wholly owned Government corporation, or any Federal Reserve Bank**, or any State or political subdivision thereof, [**or any corporation or association operating a hospital, if no part of the net earnings inures to the benefit of any private shareholder or individual,**[**]] or any person subject to the Railway Labor Act, as amended from time to time, or any labor organization (other than when acting as an employer), or anyone acting in the capacity of officer or agent of such labor organization.

(3) The term "employee" shall include any employee, and shall not be limited to the employees of a particular employer, unless the Act explicitly states otherwise, and shall include any individual whose work has ceased as a consequence of, or in connection with, any current labor dispute or because of any unfair labor practice, and who has not obtained any other regular and substantially equivalent employment, but shall not include any individual

---

[*] Bankruptcy. Provision as amended by Pub. L. 95-598, Nov. 6, 1978.
[**] The bracketed matter was deleted by Pub. L. 93-360, July 26, 1974.

employed as an agricultural laborer, or in the domestic service of any family or person at his home, or any individual employed by his parent or spouse, **or any individual having the status of an independent contractor, or any individual employed as a supervisor, or any individual employed by an employer subject to the Railway Labor Act, as amended from time to time, or by any other person who is not an employer as herein defined**.

(4) The term "representatives" includes any individual or labor organization.

(5) The term "labor organization" means any organization of any kind, or any agency or employee representation committee or plan, in which employees participate and which exists for the purpose, in whole or in part, of dealing with employers concerning grievances, labor disputes, wages, rates of pay, hours of employment, or conditions of work.

(6) The term "commerce" means trade, traffic, commerce, transportation, or communication among the several States, or between the District of Columbia or any Territory of the United States and any State or other Territory, or between any foreign country and any State, Territory, or the District of Columbia, or within the District of Columbia or any Territory, or between points in the same State but through any other State or any Territory or the District of Columbia or any foreign country.

(7) The term "affecting commerce" means in commerce, or burdening or obstructing commerce or the free flow of commerce, or having led or tending to lead to a labor dispute burdening or obstructing commerce or the free flow of commerce.

(8) The term "unfair labor practice" means any unfair labor practice listed in section 8.

(9) The term "labor dispute" includes any controversy concerning terms, tenure or conditions of employment, or concerning the association or representation of persons in negotiating, fixing, maintaining, changing, or seeking to arrange terms or conditions of employment, regardless of whether the disputants stand in the proximate relation of employer and employee.

(10) The term "National Labor Relations Board" means the National Labor Relations Board provided for in section 3 of this Act.

(11) The term "supervisor" means any individual having authority, in the interest of the employer, to hire, transfer, suspend, lay off, recall, promote, discharge, assign, reward, or discipline other employees, or responsibly to direct them, or to adjust their grievances, or effectively to recommend such action, if in connection with the foregoing the exercise of such authority is not of a merely routine or clerical nature, but requires the use of independent judgment.

(12) The term "professional employee" means —

(a) any employee engaged in work (i) predominantly intellectual and varied in character as opposed to routine mental, manual, mechanical, or physical work; (ii) involving the consistent exercise of discretion and judgment in its performance; (iii) of such a character that the output produced or the result accomplished cannot be standardized in relation to a given period of time; (iv) requiring knowledge of an advanced type in a field of science or learning customarily acquired by a prolonged course of specialized intellectual instruction and study in an institution of higher learning or a hospital, as distinguished from a general academic education or from an apprenticeship or from training in the performance of routine mental, manual, or physical processes; or

(b) any employee, who (i) has completed the courses of specialized intellectual instruction and study described in clause (iv) of paragraph (a), and (ii) is performing related work under the supervision of a professional person to qualify himself to become a professional employee as defined in paragraph (a).

(13) In determining whether any person is acting as an "agent" of another person so as to make such other person responsible for his acts, the question of whether the specific acts performed were actually authorized or subsequently ratified shall not be controlling.

(14) The term "health care institution" shall include any hospital, convalescent hospital, health maintenance organization, health clinic, nursing home, extended care facility, or other institution devoted to the care of sick, infirm, or aged person (sic).

NATIONAL LABOR RELATIONS BOARD

§3. (§153) (a) The National Labor Relations Board (hereinafter called the "Board") created by this Act prior to its amendment by the Labor Management Relations Act, 1947, is hereby continued as an agency of the United States, except that the Board shall consist of five instead of three members, appointed by the President by and with the advice and consent of the Senate.* Of the two additional members so provided for, one shall be appointed for a term of five years and the

---

* [Because §§3 and 4 were amended so extensively in 1947, the 1935 version of those sections is not reproduced below; only the 1947 and 1959 amendments are set forth. — EDS.]

other for a term of two years. Their successors, and the successors of the other members, shall be appointed for terms of five years each, excepting that any individual chosen to fill a vacancy shall be appointed only for the unexpired term of the member whom he shall succeed. The President shall designate one member to serve as Chairman of the Board. Any member of the Board may be removed by the President, upon notice and hearing, for neglect of duty or malfeasance in office, but for no other cause.

(b) The Board is authorized to delegate to any group of three or more members any or all of the powers which it may itself exercise. *The Board is also authorized to delegate to its regional directors its powers under section 9 to determine the unit appropriate for the purpose of collective bargaining, to investigate and provide for hearings, and determine whether a question of representation exists, and to direct an election or take a secret ballot under subsection (c) or (e) of section 9 and certify the results thereof, except that upon the filing of a request therefor with the Board by any interested person, the Board may review any action of a regional director delegated to him under this paragraph, but such a review shall not, unless specifically ordered by the Board, operate as a stay of any action taken by the regional director.* A vacancy in the Board shall not impair the right of the remaining members to exercise all of the powers of the Board, and three members of the Board shall, at all times, constitute a quorum of the Board, except that two members shall constitute a quorum of any group designated pursuant to the first sentence hereof. The Board shall have an official seal which shall be judicially noticed.

(c) The Board shall at the close of each fiscal year make a report in writing to Congress and to the President summarizing significant case activities and operations for that fiscal year.[*]

(d) There shall be a General Counsel of the Board who shall be appointed by the President, by and with the advice and consent of the Senate, for a term of four years. The General Counsel of the Board shall exercise general supervision over all attorneys employed by the Board (other than administrative law judges[**] and legal assistants to Board members) and over the officers and employees in the regional offices. He shall have final authority, on behalf of the Board, in respect of the investigation of charges and issuance of complaints under section 10, and

---

[*] As amended by Pub. L. 93-608, Jan. 2, 1975, and Pub. L. 97-375, Dec. 21, 1982.

[**] "Administrative law judge" was substituted for "trial examiner" throughout the Act pursuant to §3105 of Title 5 and §3 of Pub. L. 95-251, Mar. 27, 1978, 92 Stat. 184.

in respect of the prosecution of such complaints before the Board, and shall have such other duties as the Board may prescribe or as may be provided by law. *In case of a vacancy in the office of the General Counsel the President is authorized to designate the officer or employee who shall act as General Counsel during such vacancy, but no person or persons so designated shall so act (1) for more than forty days when the Congress is in session unless a nomination to fill such vacancy shall have been submitted to the Senate, or (2) after the adjournment sine die of the session of the Senate in which such nomination was submitted.*

§4. (§154) **(a)** Each member of the Board and the General Counsel of the Board [shall receive a salary of $12,000 a year,*] shall be eligible for reappointment, and shall not engage in any other business, vocation, or employment. The Board shall appoint an executive secretary, and such attorneys, examiners, and regional directors, and such other employees as it may from time to time find necessary for the proper performance of its duties. The Board may not employ any attorneys for the purpose of reviewing transcripts of hearings or preparing drafts of opinions except that any attorney employed for assignment as a legal assistant to any Board member may for such Board member review such transcripts and prepare such drafts. No administrative law judge's report shall be reviewed, either before or after its publication, by any person other than a member of the Board or his legal assistant, and no administrative law judge shall advise or consult with the Board with respect to exceptions taken to his findings, rulings, or recommendations. The Board may establish or utilize such regional, local, or other agencies, and utilize such voluntary and uncompensated services, as may from time to time be needed. Attorneys appointed under this section may, at the direction of the Board, appear for and represent the Board in any case in court. Nothing in this Act shall be construed to authorize the Board to appoint individuals for the purpose of conciliation or mediation, or for economic analysis.

(b) All of the expenses of the Board, including all necessary traveling and subsistence expenses outside the District of Columbia incurred by the members or employees of the Board under its orders, shall be allowed and paid on the presentation of itemized vouchers therefor approved by the Board or by any individual it designates for that purpose.

---

*Deleted pursuant to §§5311 et seq. of Title V, Government Organization and Employees.

§5. (§155) The principal office of the Board shall be in the District of Columbia, but it may meet and exercise any or all of its powers at any other place. The Board may, by one or more of its members or by such agents or agencies as it may designate, prosecute any inquiry necessary to its functions in any part of the United States. A member who participates in such an inquiry shall not be disqualified from subsequently participating in a decision of the Board in the same case.

§6. (§156) The Board shall have authority from time to time to make, amend, and rescind, **in the manner prescribed by the Administrative Procedure Act,**[*] such rules and regulations as may be necessary to carry out the provisions of this Act. [Such rules and regulations shall be effective upon publication in the manner which the Board shall prescribe.]

RIGHTS OF EMPLOYEES

§7. (§157) <u>Employees</u> shall have the right to self-organization, to form, join, or assist labor organizations, to bargain collectively through representatives of their own choosing, and to engage in other concerted activities for the purpose of collective bargaining or other mutual aid or protection, **and shall also have the right to refrain from any or all of such activities except to the extent that such right may be affected by an agreement requiring membership in a labor organization as a condition of employment as authorized in section 8(a)(3).**

UNFAIR LABOR PRACTICES

§8. (§158) (a) It shall be an unfair labor practice for an employer —
    (1) to interfere with, restrain, or coerce employees in the exercise of the rights guaranteed in section 7;
    (2) to dominate or interfere with the formation or administration of any labor organization or contribute financial or other support to it: *Provided,* That subject to rules and regulations made and published by the Board pursuant to section 6, an employer shall not be prohibited from permitting employees to confer with him during working hours without loss of time or pay;

---

* [5 U.S.C. §§551 et seq. — EDS.]

(3) by discrimination in regard to hire or tenure of employment or any term or condition of employment to encourage or discourage membership in any labor organization: *Provided,* That nothing in this Act, or in any other statute of the United States, shall preclude an employer from making an agreement with a labor organization (not established, maintained, or assisted by any action defined in **section 8(a) of** this Act as an unfair labor practice) to require as a condition of employment membership therein **on or after the thirtieth day following the beginning of such employment or the effective date of such agreement, whichever is the later, (i)** if such labor organization is the representative of the employees as provided in section 9(a), in the appropriate collective-bargaining unit covered by such agreement when made, **[and has at the time the agreement was made or within the preceding twelve months received from the Board a notice of compliance with sections 9(f), (g), (h)], and (ii) unless following an election held as provided in section 9(e) within one year preceding the effective date of such agreement, the Board shall have certified that at least a majority of the employees eligible to vote in such election have voted to rescind the authority of such labor organization to make such an agreement:** * *Provided further,* **That no employer shall justify any discrimination against an employee for nonmembership in a labor organization (A) if he has reasonable grounds for believing that such membership was not available to the employee on the same terms and conditions generally applicable to other members, or (B) if he has reasonable grounds for believing that membership was denied or terminated for reasons other than the failure of the employee to tender the periodic dues and the initiation fees uniformly required as a condition of acquiring or retaining membership;**

(4) to discharge or otherwise discriminate against an employee because he has filed charges or given testimony under this Act;

(5) to refuse to bargain collectively with the representatives of his employees, subject to the provisions of section 9(a).

(b) It shall be an unfair labor practice for a labor organization or its agents —

(1) to restrain or coerce (A) employees in the exercise of the rights guaranteed in section 7: *Provided,* That this paragraph shall not impair the right of a labor organization to prescribe its own rules with respect to the acquisition or retention of membership therein;

---

*Clause (ii) was added in 1951 by 65 Stat. 601.

or (B) an employer in the selection of his representatives for the purposes of collective bargaining or the adjustment of grievances;

(2) to cause or attempt to cause an employer to discriminate against an employee in violation of subsection (a)(3) or to discriminate against an employee with respect to whom membership in such organization has been denied or terminated on some ground other than his failure to tender the periodic dues and the initiation fees uniformly required as a condition of acquiring or retaining membership;

(3) to refuse to bargain collectively with an employer, provided it is the representative of his employees subject to the provisions of section 9(a);

(4)(*i*) to engage in, or to induce or encourage [the employees of any employer] *any individual employed by any person engaged in commerce or in an industry affecting commerce* to engage in, a strike or a [concerted] refusal in the course of [their] *his* employment to use, manufacture, process, transport, or otherwise handle or work on any goods, articles, materials, or commodities or to perform any services[,]*; or (ii) to threaten, coerce, or restrain any person engaged in commerce or in an industry affecting commerce,* where *in either case* an object thereof is —

(A) forcing or requiring any employer or self-employed person to join any labor or employer organization or [any employer or other person to cease using, selling, handling, transporting, or otherwise dealing in the products of any other producer, processor, or manufacturer, or to cease doing business with any other person] *to enter into any agreement which is prohibited by section (e);*

(B) *forcing or requiring any person to cease using, selling, handling, transporting, or otherwise dealing in the products of any other producer, processor, or manufacturer, or to cease doing business with any other person, or* forcing or requiring any other employer to recognize or bargain with a labor organization as the representative of his employees unless such labor organization has been certified as the representative of such employees under the provisions of section 9[;]*: Provided, That nothing contained in this clause (B) shall be construed to make unlawful, where not otherwise unlawful, any primary strike or primary picketing;*

(C) forcing or requiring any employer to recognize or bargain with a particular labor organization as the representative of his employees if another labor organization has been certified as the representative of such employees under the provisions of section 9;

(D) forcing or requiring any employer to assign particular work to employees in a particular labor organization or in a particular trade, craft, or class rather than to employees in another labor organization or in another trade, craft, or class, unless such employer is failing to conform to an order or certification of the Board determining the bargaining representative for employees performing such work:

Provided, That nothing contained in subsection (b) shall be construed to make unlawful a refusal by any person to enter upon the premises of any employer (other than his own employer), if the employees of such employer are engaged in a strike ratified or approved by a representative of such employees whom such employer is required to recognize under this Act[;]*: Provided further, That for the purposes of this paragraph (4) only, nothing contained in such paragraph shall be construed to prohibit publicity, other than picketing, for the purpose of truthfully advising the public, including consumers and members of a labor organization, that a product or products are produced by an employer with whom the labor organization has a primary dispute and are distributed by another employer, as long as such publicity does not have an effect of inducing any individual employed by any person other than the primary employer in the course of his employment to refuse to pick up, deliver, or transport any goods, or not to perform any services, at the establishment of the employer engaged in such distribution;*

(5) to require of employees covered by an agreement authorized under subsection (a)(3) of this section the payment, as a condition precedent to becoming a member of such organization, of a fee in an amount which the Board finds excessive or discriminatory under all the circumstances. In making such a finding, the Board shall consider, among other relevant factors, the practices and customs of labor organizations in the particular industry, and the wages currently paid to the employees affected; [and]

(6) to cause or attempt to cause an employer to pay or deliver or agree to pay or deliver any money or other thing of value, in the nature of an exaction, for services which are not performed or not to be performed[.]; *and*

(7) to picket or cause to be picketed, or threaten to picket or cause to be picketed, any employer where an object thereof is forcing or requiring

an employer to recognize or bargain with a labor organization as the representative of his employees, or forcing or requiring the employees of an employer to accept or select such labor organization as their collective bargaining representative, unless such labor organization is currently certified as the representative of such employees:

(A) where the employer has lawfully recognized in accordance with this Act any other labor organization and a question concerning representation may not appropriately be raised under section 9(c) of this Act,

(B) where within the preceding twelve months a valid election under section 9(c) of this Act has been conducted, or

(C) where such picketing has been conducted without a petition under section 9(c) of this Act being filed within a reasonable period of time not to exceed thirty days from the commencement of such picketing: Provided, That when such a petition has been filed the Board shall forthwith, without regard to the provisions of section 9(c)(1) of this Act or the absence of a showing of a substantial interest on the part of the labor organization, direct an election in such unit as the Board finds to be appropriate and shall certify the results thereof: Provided further, That nothing in this subparagraph (C) shall be construed to prohibit any picketing or other publicity for the purpose of truthfully advising the public (including consumers) that an employer does not employ members of, or have a contract with, a labor organization, unless an effect of such picketing is to induce any individual employed by any other person in the course of his employment, not to pick up, deliver or transport any goods or not to perform any services.

Nothing in this paragraph (7) shall be construed to permit any act which would otherwise be an unfair labor practice under this section 8(b).

(c) The expressing of any views, argument, or opinion, or the dissemination thereof, whether in written, printed, graphic, or visual form, shall not constitute or be evidence of an unfair labor practice under any of the provisions of this Act, if such expression contains no threat of reprisal or force or promise of benefit.

(d) For the purposes of this section, to bargain collectively is the performance of the mutual obligation of the employer and the representative of the employees to meet at reasonable times and confer in good faith with respect to wages, hours, and other terms and conditions of employment, or the negotiation of an agreement, or any question arising thereunder, and the execution of a written contract incorporating any agreement reached if requested by either party, but such obligation does not compel either party to agree to a proposal or require the making of a concession: *Provided,* That where there is in effect a collective-bargaining contract covering employees in an industry affecting commerce, the duty to bargain collectively shall also mean that no party to such contract shall terminate or modify such contract, unless the party desiring such termination or modification —

(1) serves a written notice upon the other party to the contract of the proposed termination or modification sixty days prior to the expiration date thereof, or in the event such contract contains no expiration date, sixty days prior to the time it is proposed to make such termination or modification;

(2) offers to meet and confer with the other party for the purpose of negotiating a new contract or a contract containing the proposed modifications;

(3) notifies the Federal Mediation and Conciliation Service within thirty days after such notice of the existence of a dispute, and simultaneously therewith notifies any State or Territorial agency established to mediate and conciliate disputes within the State or Territory where the dispute occurred, provided no agreement has been reached by that time; and

(4) continues in full force and effect, without resorting to strike or lock-out, all the terms and conditions of the existing contract for a period of sixty days after such notice is given or until the expiration date of such contract, whichever occurs later:

The duties imposed upon employers, employees, and labor organizations by paragraphs (2), (3), and (4) shall become inapplicable upon an intervening certification of the Board, under which the labor organization or individual, which is a party to the contract, has been superseded as or ceased to be the representative of the employees subject to the provisions of section 9(a), and the duties so imposed shall not be construed as requiring either party to discuss or agree to any modification of the terms and conditions contained in a contract for a fixed period, if such modification is to become effective before such terms and conditions can be reopened under the provisions of the contract. Any employee who engages in a strike within the [sixty-day] any notice period specified in this subsection, or who engages in any strike within the appropriate period specified in subsection (g) of this section, shall lose his status as an employee of the employer engaged in the particular labor dispute, for the purposes of sections 8, 9, and 10 of this Act, but such loss of status for such employee shall terminate if and when he is

reemployed by such employer. Whenever the collective bargaining involves employees of a health care institution, the provisions of this subsection shall be modified as follows:

(A) The notice of paragraph (1) of this subsection shall be ninety days; the notice of paragraph (3) of this subsection shall be sixty days; and the contract period of paragraph (4) of this subsection shall be ninety days.

(B) Where the bargaining is for an initial agreement following certification or recognition, at least thirty days' notice of the existence of a dispute shall be given by the labor organization to the agencies set forth in paragraph (3) of this subsection.

(C) After notice is given to the Federal Mediation and Conciliation Service under either clause (A) or (B) of this sentence, the Service shall promptly communicate with the parties and use its best efforts, by mediation and conciliation, to bring them to agreement. The parties shall participate fully and promptly in such meetings as may be undertaken by the Service for the purpose of aiding in a settlement of the dispute.

(e) It shall be an unfair labor practice for any labor organization and any employer to enter into any contract or agreement, express or implied, whereby such employer ceases or refrains or agrees to cease or refrain from handling, using, selling, transporting or otherwise dealing in any of the products of any other employer, or to cease doing business with any other person, and any contract or agreement entered into heretofore or hereafter containing such an agreement shall be to such extent unenforcible (sic) *and void: Provided, That nothing in this subsection (e) shall apply to an agreement between a labor organization and an employer in the construction industry relating to the contracting or subcontracting of work to be done at the site of the construction, alteration, painting, or repair of a building, structure, or other work: Provided further, That for the purposes of this subsection (e) and subsection (b)(4)(B) of this section the terms "any employer", "any person engaged in commerce or an industry affecting commerce", and "any person" when used in relation to the terms "any other producer, processor, or manufacturer", "any other employer", or "any other person" shall not include persons in the relation of a jobber, manufacturer, contractor, or subcontractor working on the goods or premises of the jobber or manufacturer or performing parts of an integrated process of production in the apparel and clothing industry: Provided further, That nothing in this Act shall prohibit the enforcement of any agreement which is within the foregoing exception.*

(f) It shall not be an unfair labor practice under subsections (a) and (b) of this section for an employer engaged primarily in the building and construction industry to make an agreement covering employees engaged (or who,

*upon their employment, will be engaged) in the building and construction industry with a labor organization of which building and construction employees are members (not established, maintained, or assisted by any action defined in subsection (a) of this section as an unfair labor practice) because (1) the majority status of such labor organization has not been established under the provisions of section 9 of this Act prior to the making of such agreement, or (2) such agreement requires as a condition of employment, membership in such labor organization after the seventh day following the beginning of such employment or the effective date of the agreement, whichever is later, or (3) such agreement requires the employer to notify such labor organization of opportunities for employment with such employer, or gives such labor organization an opportunity to refer qualified applicants for such employment, or (4) such agreement specifies minimum training or experience qualifications for employment or provides for priority in opportunities for employment based upon length of service with such employer, in the industry or in the particular geographical area: Provided, That nothing in this subsection shall set aside the final proviso to section 8(a)(3) of this Act: Provided further, That any agreement which would be invalid, but for clause (1) of this subsection, shall not be a bar to a petition filed pursuant to section 9(c) or 9(e).**

(g) A labor organization before engaging in any strike, picketing, or other concerted refusal to work at any health care institution shall, not less than ten days prior to such action, notify the institution in writing and the Federal Mediation and Conciliation Service of that intention, except that in the case of bargaining for an initial agreement following certification or recognition the notice required by this subsection shall not be given until the expiration of the period specified in clause (B) of the last sentence of section (8)(d) of this Act. The notice shall state the date and time that such action will commence. The notice, once given, may be extended by the written agreement of both parties.

---

* Section 8(f) was inserted in the Act by §705(a) of Pub. L. 86-257, Sept. 14, 1959. Section 705(b) of that law provides:

Nothing contained in the amendment made by subsection (a) shall be construed as authorizing the execution or application of agreements requiring membership in a labor organization as a condition of employment in any State or Territory in which such execution or application is prohibited by State or Territorial Law.

REPRESENTATIVES AND ELECTIONS

§9. (§159) (a) Representatives designated or selected for the purposes of collective bargaining by the majority of the employees in a unit appropriate for such purposes, shall be the exclusive representatives of all the employees in such unit for the purposes of collective bargaining in respect to rates of pay, wages, hours of employment, or other conditions of employment: ***Provided,*** That any individual employee or a group of employees shall have the right at any time to present grievances to their employer **and to have such grievances adjusted, without the intervention of the bargaining representative, as long as the adjustment is not inconsistent with the terms of a collective-bargaining contract or agreement then in effect:** *Provided further,* **That the bargaining representative has been given opportunity to be present at such adjustment.**

(b) The Board shall decide in each case whether, in order to assure to employees the fullest freedom in exercising the rights guaranteed by this Act, the unit appropriate for the purposes of collective bargaining shall be the employer unit, craft unit, plant unit, or subdivision thereof: ***Provided,*** **That the Board shall not (1) decide that any unit is appropriate for such purposes if such unit includes both professional employees and employees who are not professional employees unless a majority of such professional employees vote for inclusion in such unit; or (2) decide that any craft unit is inappropriate for such purposes on the ground that a different unit has been established by a prior Board determination, unless a majority of the employees in the proposed craft unit vote against separate representation or (3) decide that any unit is appropriate for such purposes if it includes, together with other employees, any individual employed as a guard to enforce against employees and other persons rules to protect property of the employer or to protect the safety of persons on the employer's premises; but no labor organization shall be certified as the representative of employees in a bargaining unit of guards if such organization admits to membership, or is affiliated directly or indirectly with an organization which admits to membership, employees other than guards.**

[(c) Whenever a question affecting commerce arises concerning the representation of employees, the Board may investigate such controversy and certify to the parties, in writing, the name or names of the representatives that have been designated or selected. In any such investigation, the Board shall provide for an appropriate hearing upon due notice, either in conjunction with a proceeding under section 10 or otherwise, and may take a secret ballot of employees, or utilize any other suitable method to ascertain such representatives.]

(c)(1) Whenever a petition shall have been filed, in accordance with such regulations as may be prescribed by the Board —

(A) by an employee or group of employees or any individual or labor organization acting in their behalf alleging that a substantial number of employees (i) wish to be represented for collective bargaining and that their employer declines to recognize their representative as the representative defined in section 9(a), or (ii) assert that the individual or labor organization, which has been certified or is being currently recognized by their employer as the bargaining representative, is no longer a representative as defined in section 9(a); or

(B) by an employer, alleging that one or more individuals or labor organizations have presented to him a claim to be recognized as the representative defined in section 9(a);

the Board shall investigate such petition and if it has reasonable cause to believe that a question of representation affecting commerce exists shall provide for an appropriate hearing upon due notice. Such hearing may be conducted by an officer or employee of the regional office, who shall not make any recommendations with respect thereto. If the Board finds upon the record of such hearing that such a question of representation exists, it shall direct an election by secret ballot and shall certify the results thereof.

(2) In determining whether or not a question of representation affecting commerce exists, the same regulations and rules of decision shall apply irrespective of the identity of the persons filing the petition or the kind of relief sought and in no case shall the Board deny a labor organization a place on the ballot by reason of an order with respect to such labor organization or its predecessor not issued in conformity with section 10(c).

(3) No election shall be directed in any bargaining unit or any subdivision within which in the preceding twelve-month period, a valid election shall have been held. Employees [on strike] *engaged in an economic strike* who are not entitled to reinstatement shall [not] be eligible to vote *under such regulations as the Board shall find are consistent with the purposes and provisions of this Act in any election conducted within twelve months after the commencement of the strike.* In any election where none of the choices on the ballot receives a majority, a run-off shall be conducted, the ballot providing for a selection between the two choices receiving the largest and second largest number of valid votes cast in the election.

(4) Nothing in this section shall be construed to prohibit the waiving of hearings by stipulation for the purpose of a consent

election in conformity with regulations and rules of decision of the Board.

(5) In determining whether a unit is appropriate for the purposes specified in subsection (b) of this section the extent to which the employees have organized shall not be controlling.

(d) Whenever an order of the Board made pursuant to section 10(c) is based in whole or in part upon facts certified following an investigation pursuant to subsection (c) of this section and there is a petition for the enforcement or review of such order, such certification and the record of such investigation shall be included in the transcript of the entire record required to be filed under section 10(e) or 10(f), and thereupon the decree of the court enforcing, modifying, or setting aside in whole or in part the order of the Board shall be made and entered upon the pleadings, testimony, and proceedings set forth in such transcript.

(e)(1) Upon the filing with the Board, by 30 per centum or more of the employees in a bargaining unit covered by an agreement between their employer and a labor organization made pursuant to section 8(a)(3), of a petition alleging they desire that such authority be rescinded, the Board shall take a secret ballot of the employees in such unit and shall certify the results thereof to such labor organization and to the employer.

(2) No election shall be conducted pursuant to this subsection in any bargaining unit or any subdivision within which, in the preceding twelve-month period, a valid election shall have been held.[*]

[Subsections (f), (g), and (h) were deleted by the Labor-Management Reporting and Disclosure Act of 1959. — Eds.]

---

[*] [As enacted in 1947, Section 9(e) had three subsections. In 1951, the first subsection was deleted, and the two remaining subsections were renumbered (1) and (2). 65 Stat. 601. The deleted subsection required, as a prerequisite to the inclusion of a union security clause in a labor agreement, authorization by a majority of unit employees in a Board-conducted election. — Eds.]

PREVENTION OF UNFAIR LABOR PRACTICES

§10. (§160) (a) The Board is empowered, as hereinafter provided, to prevent any person from engaging in any unfair labor practice (listed in section 8) affecting commerce. This power shall not be affected by any other means of adjustment or prevention that has been or may be established by agreement, law, or otherwise: **Provided, That the Board is empowered by agreement with any agency of any State or Territory to cede to such agency jurisdiction over any cases in any industry (other than mining, manufacturing, communications, and transportation except where predominantly local in character) even though such cases may involve labor disputes affecting commerce, unless the provision of the State or Territorial statute applicable to the determination of such cases by such agency is inconsistent with the corresponding provision of this Act or has received a construction inconsistent therewith.**

(b) Whenever it is charged that any person has engaged in or is engaging in any such unfair labor practice, the Board, or any agent or agency designated by the Board for such purposes, shall have power to issue and cause to be served upon such person a complaint stating the charges in that respect, and containing a notice of hearing before the Board or a member thereof, or before a designated agent or agency, at a place therein fixed, not less than five days after the serving of said complaint: **Provided, That no complaint shall issue based upon any unfair labor practice occurring more than six months prior to the filing of the charge with the Board and the service of a copy thereof upon the person against whom such charge is made, unless the person aggrieved thereby was prevented from filing such charge by reason of service in the armed forces, in which event the six-month period shall be computed from the day of his discharge.** Any such complaint may be amended by the member, agent, or agency conducting the hearing or the Board in its discretion at any time prior to the issuance of an order based thereon. The person so complained of shall have the right to file an answer to the original or amended complaint and to appear in person or otherwise and give testimony at the place and time fixed in the complaint. In the discretion of the member, agent, or agency conducting the hearing or the Board, any other person may be allowed to intervene in the said proceeding and to present testimony. [In any such proceeding the rules of evidence prevailing in courts of law or equity shall not be controlling.] **Any such proceeding shall, so far as practicable, be conducted in accordance with the rules of evidence applicable in the district courts of the United**

States under the rules of civil procedure for the district courts of the United States, adopted by the Supreme Court of the United States pursuant to section 2072 of Title 28.

(c) The testimony taken by such member, agent, or agency or the Board shall be reduced to writing and filed with the Board. Thereafter, in its discretion, the Board upon notice may take further testimony or hear argument. If upon [all] **the preponderance of** the testimony taken the Board shall be of the opinion that any person named in the complaint has engaged in or is engaging in any such unfair labor practice, then the Board shall state its findings of fact and shall issue and cause to be served on such person an order requiring such person to cease and desist from such unfair labor practice, and to take such affirmative action including reinstatement of employees with or without back pay, as will effectuate the policies of this Act: *Provided,* **That where an order directs reinstatement of an employee, back pay may be required of the employer or labor organization, as the case may be, responsible for the discrimination suffered by him:** *And provided further,* **That in determining whether a complaint shall issue alleging a violation of section 8(a)(1) or section 8(a)(2), and in deciding such cases, the same regulations and rules of decision shall apply irrespective of whether or not the labor organization affected is affiliated with a labor organization national or international in scope.** Such order may further require such person to make reports from time to time showing the extent to which it has complied with the order. If upon [all] **the preponderance of** the testimony taken the Board shall not be of the opinion that the person named in the complaint has engaged in or is engaging in any such unfair labor practice, then the Board shall state its findings of fact and shall issue an order dismissing the said complaint. **No order of the Board shall require the reinstatement of any individual as an employee who has been suspended or discharged, or the payment to him of any back pay, if such individual was suspended or discharged for cause. In case the evidence is presented before a member of the Board, or before an administrative law judge or judges thereof, such member, or such judge or judges as the case may be, shall issue and cause to be served on the parties to the proceeding a proposed report, together with a recommended order, which shall be filed with the Board, and if no exceptions are filed within twenty days after service thereof upon such parties, or within such further period as the Board may authorize, such recommended order shall become the order of the Board and become effective as therein prescribed.**

(d) Until **[a transcript of]** the record in a case shall have been filed in a court, as hereinafter provided, the Board may at any time upon reasonable notice and in such manner as it shall deem proper, modify or set aside, in whole or in part, any finding or order made or issued by it.

(e) The Board shall have power to petition any [circuit] court of appeals of the United States [(including the **United States** Court of Appeals [of] **for** the District of Columbia)], or if all the [circuit] courts of appeals to which application may be made are in vacation, any district court of the United States [(including the **District** Court of the **United States for the** District of Columbia)], within any circuit or district, respectively, wherein the unfair labor practice in question occurred or wherein such person resides or transacts business, for the enforcement of such order and for appropriate temporary relief or restraining order, and shall [certify and] file in the court the record in the proceedings, *as provided in section 2112 of Title 28.* Upon [such filing] *the filing of such petition*, the court shall cause notice thereof to be served upon such person, and thereupon shall have jurisdiction of the proceeding and of the question determined therein, and shall have power to grant such temporary relief or restraining order as it deems just and proper, and to make and enter [upon the pleadings, testimony, and proceedings set forth in such transcript] a decree enforcing, modifying and enforcing as so modified, or setting aside in whole or in part the order of the Board. No objection that has not been urged before the Board, its member, agent, or agency, shall be considered by the court, unless the failure or neglect to urge such objection shall be excused because of extraordinary circumstances. The findings of the Board [as to the facts,] **with respect to questions of fact** if supported by **substantial** evidence[,] **on the record considered as a whole** shall be conclusive. If either party shall apply to the court for leave to adduce additional evidence and shall show to the satisfaction of the court that such additional evidence is material and that there were reasonable grounds for the failure to adduce such evidence in the hearing before the Board, its member, agent, or agency, the court may order such additional evidence to be taken before the Board, its member, agent, or agency, and to be made a part of the [transcript] *record*. The Board may modify its findings as to the facts, or make new findings by reason of additional evidence so taken and filed, and it shall file such modified or new findings, which **findings with respect to questions of fact** if supported by **substantial** evidence **on the record considered as a whole** shall be conclusive, and shall file its recommendations, if any, for the modification or setting aside of its original order. *Upon the filing of the record with it* the jurisdiction of the court shall be exclusive and its judgment and decree shall be final, except that the same shall be subject to review by the appropriate United States court of appeals if application was made to the district court as hereinabove provided, and by the Supreme Court of the United States upon writ of certiorari or certification as provided in section 1254 of Title 28.*

(f)* Any person aggrieved by a final order of the Board granting or denying in whole or in part the relief sought may obtain a review of such order in any United States court of appeals in the circuit wherein the unfair labor practice in question was alleged to have been engaged in or wherein such person resides or transacts business, or in the **United States** Court of Appeals [of] **for** the District of Columbia, by filing in such a court a written petition praying that the order of the Board be modified or set aside. A copy of such petition shall be forthwith [served upon the Board] *transmitted by the clerk of the court to the Board,* and thereupon the aggrieved party shall file in the court [a transcript of] the [entire] record in the proceeding, certified by the Board [including the pleading and testimony upon which the order complained of was entered and the findings and order of the Board], *as provided in section 2112 of Title 28.* Upon [such filing] *the filing of such petition,* the court shall proceed in the same manner as in the case of an application by the Board under subsection (e) of this section, and shall have the same jurisdiction to grant to the Board such temporary relief or restraining order as it deems just and proper, and in like manner to make and enter a decree enforcing, modifying, and enforcing as so modified, or setting aside in whole or in part the order of the Board; [and] the findings of the Board [as to the facts] **with respect to questions of fact** if supported by **substantial** evidence[,] **on the record considered as a whole** shall in like manner be conclusive.

(g) The commencement of proceedings under subsection (e) or (f) of this section shall not, unless specifically ordered by the court, operate as a stay of the Board's order.

(h) When granting appropriate temporary relief or a restraining order, or making and entering a decree enforcing, modifying, and enforcing as so modified or setting aside in whole or in part an order of the Board, as provided in this section, the jurisdiction of courts sitting in equity shall not be limited by the Act entitled "An Act to amend the judicial Code and to define and limit the jurisdiction of courts sitting in equity, and for

---

* Sections 10(e) and 10(f) are rendered as amended by Pub. L. 85-791, §§13(b) and (c), Aug. 28, 1958, as well as by the 1947 and 1959 amendments.

other purposes", approved March 23, 1932 (U.S.C., Supp. VII, title 29, secs. 101-115).*

(i) [Repealed.]

(j) The Board shall have power, upon issuance of a complaint as provided in subsection (b) of this section charging that any person has engaged in or is engaging in an unfair labor practice, to petition any United States district court,** within any district wherein the unfair labor practice in question is alleged to have occurred or wherein such person resides or transacts business, for appropriate temporary relief or restraining order. Upon the filing of any such petition the court shall cause notice thereof to be served upon such person, and thereupon shall have jurisdiction to grant to the Board such temporary relief or restraining order as it deems just and proper.

(k) Whenever it is charged that any person has engaged in an unfair labor practice within the meaning of paragraph (4)(D) of section 8(b) of this Act, the Board is empowered and directed to hear and determine the dispute out of which such unfair labor practice shall have arisen, unless, within ten days after notice that such charge has been filed, the parties to such dispute submit to the Board satisfactory evidence that they have adjusted, or agreed upon methods for the voluntary adjustment of, the dispute. Upon compliance by the parties to the dispute with the decision of the Board or upon such voluntary adjustment of the dispute, such charge shall be dismissed.

(*l*) Whenever it is charged that any person has engaged in an unfair labor practice within the meaning of paragraph (4)(A), (B), or (C) of section 8(b) *or section 8(e) or section 8(b)(7),* **the preliminary investigation of such charge shall be made forthwith and given priority over all other cases except cases of like character in the office where it is filed or to which it is referred. If, after such investigation, the officer or regional attorney to whom the matter may be referred has reasonable cause to believe such charge is true and that a complaint should issue, he shall, on behalf of the Board, petition any United States district court within any district where the unfair labor practice in question has occurred, is alleged to have occurred, or wherein such person resides or transacts business, for appropriate injunctive relief pending the final adjudication of the Board with respect to such matter. Upon the filing of any such petition the district court shall have jurisdiction to grant such injunctive relief or temporary restraining order as it deems just and proper,**

---

* [The Norris-LaGuardia Act of 1932. — Eds.]

** Section 10(j) and subsequent sections as rendered reflect the enactment of 28 U.S.C. §132(a) and 28 U.S.C. §88, June 25, 1948, concerning the United States District Courts.

notwithstanding any other provision of law: *Provided further,* **That no temporary restraining order shall be issued without notice unless a petition alleges that substantial and irreparable injury to the charging party will be unavoidable and such temporary restraining order shall be effective for no longer than five days and will become void at the expiration of such period[.]**: *Provided further, That such officer or regional attorney shall not apply for any restraining order under section 8(b)(7) if a charge against the employer under section 8(a)(2) has been filed and after the preliminary investigation, he has reasonable cause to believe that such charge is true and that a complaint should issue.* **Upon filing of any such petition the courts shall cause notice thereof to be served upon any person involved in the charge and such person, including the charging party, shall be given an opportunity to appear by counsel and present any relevant testimony:** *Provided further,* **That for the purposes of this subsection district courts shall be deemed to have jurisdiction of a labor organization (1) in the district in which such organization maintains its principal office, or (2) in any district in which its duly authorized officers or agents are engaged in promoting or protecting the interests of employee members. The service of legal process upon such officer or agent shall constitute service upon the labor organization and make such organization a party to the suit. In situations where such relief is appropriate the procedure specified herein shall apply to charges with respect to section 8(b)(4)(D).**

(m) Whenever it is charged that any person has engaged in an unfair labor practice within the meaning of subsection (a)(3) or (b)(2) of section 8, such charge shall be given priority over all other cases except cases of like character in the office where it is filed or to which it is referred and cases given priority under subsection (l) of this section.

INVESTIGATORY POWERS

§11. (§161) For the purpose of all hearings and investigations, which, in the opinion of the Board, are necessary and proper for the exercise of the powers vested in it by sections 9 and 10 —

(1) The Board, or its duly authorized agents or agencies, shall at all reasonable times have access to, for the purpose of examination, and the right to copy any evidence of any person being investigated or proceeded against that relates to any matter under investigation or in question. The Board, or any member thereof, shall upon application of any party to such proceedings, forthwith issue to such party subpenas requiring the attendance and testimony of witnesses or the production of any evidence

in such proceeding or investigation requested in such application. **Within five days after the service of a subpena on any person requiring the production of any evidence in his possession or under his control, such person may petition the Board to revoke, and the Board shall revoke, such subpena if in its opinion the evidence whose production is required does not relate to any matter under investigation, or any matter in question in such proceedings, or if in its opinion such subpena does not describe with sufficient particularity the evidence whose production is required.** Any member of the Board, or any agent or agency designated by the Board for such purposes, may administer oaths and affirmations, examine witnesses, and receive evidence. Such attendance of witnesses and the production of such evidence may be required from any place in the United States or any Territory or possession thereof, at any designated place of hearing.

(2) In case of contumacy or refusal to obey a subpena issued to any person, any district court of the United States or the United States courts of any Territory or possession, within the jurisdiction of which the inquiry is carried on or within the jurisdiction of which said person guilty of contumacy or refusal to obey is found or resides or transacts business, upon application by the Board shall have jurisdiction to issue to such person an order requiring such person to appear before the Board, its member, agent, or agency, there to produce evidence if so ordered, or there to give testimony touching the matter under investigation or in question; and any failure to obey such order of the court may be punished by said court as a contempt thereof.

[(3) No person shall be excused from attending and testifying or from producing books, records, correspondence, documents, or other evidence in obedience to the subpena of the Board, on the ground that the testimony or evidence required of him may tend to incriminate him or subject him to a penalty or forfeiture; but no individual shall be prosecuted or subjected to any penalty or forfeiture for or on account of any transaction, matter, or thing concerning which he is compelled, after having claimed his privilege against self-incrimination, to testify or produce evidence, except that such individual so testifying shall not be exempt from prosecution and punishment for perjury committed in so testifying.[*]]

---

[*] [Section 11(3) was repealed in 1970, by 84 Stat. 930. Similar provisions were substituted; see 18 U.S.C. §§6001, 6002, 6004 (1970). — EDS.]

(4) Complaints, orders, and other process and papers of the Board, its member, agent, or agency, may be served either personally or by registered mail or by telegraph or by leaving a copy thereof at the principal office or place of business of the person required to be served. The verified return by the individual so serving the same setting forth the manner of such service shall be proof of the same, and the return post office receipt or telegraph receipt therefor when registered or certified and mailed or when telegraphed as aforesaid shall be proof of service of the same. Witnesses summoned before the Board, its member, agent, or agency, shall be paid the same fees and mileage that are paid witnesses in the courts of the United States, and witnesses whose depositions are taken and the persons taking the same shall severally be entitled to the same fees as are paid for like services in the courts of the United States.

(5) All process of any court to which application may be made under this Act may be served in the judicial district wherein the defendant or other person required to be served resides or may be found.

(6) The several departments and agencies of the Government, when directed by the President, shall furnish the Board, upon its request, all records, papers, and information in their possession relating to any matter before the Board.

§12. (§162) Any person who shall willfully resist, prevent, impede, or interfere with any member of the Board or any of its agents or agencies in the performance of duties pursuant to this Act shall be punished by a fine of not more than $5,000 or by imprisonment for not more than one year, or both.

LIMITATIONS

§13. (§163) Nothing in this Act, **except as specifically provided for herein,** shall be construed so as either to interfere with or impede or diminish in any way the right to strike, **or to affect the limitations or qualifications on that right.**

§14. (§164) **(a) Nothing herein shall prohibit any individual employed as a supervisor from becoming or remaining a member of a labor organization, but no employer subject to this Act shall be compelled to deem individuals defined herein as supervisors as employees for the purpose of any law, either national or local, relating to collective bargaining.**

(b) Nothing in this Act shall be construed as authorizing the execution or application of agreements requiring membership in a labor organization as a condition of employment in any State or Territory in which such execution or application is prohibited by State or Territorial Law.

(c)(1) The Board, in its discretion, may, by rule of decision or by published rules adopted pursuant to subchapter II of chapter 5 of Title 5, decline to assert jurisdiction over any labor dispute involving any class or category of employers, where, in the opinion of the Board, the effect of such labor dispute on commerce is not sufficiently substantial to warrant the exercise of its jurisdiction: Provided, That the Board shall not decline to assert jurisdiction over any labor dispute over which it would assert jurisdiction under the standards prevailing upon August 1, 1959.*

(2) Nothing in this Act shall be deemed to prevent or bar any agency or the courts of any State or Territory (including the Commonwealth of Puerto Rico, Guam, and the Virgin Islands), from assuming and asserting jurisdiction over labor disputes over which the Board declines, pursuant to paragraph (1) of this subsection, to assert jurisdiction.

§15. (§165) [Reference to repealed provisions of Bankruptcy Act of 1898. — Eds.]

§16. (§166) If any provision of this Act, or the application of such provision to any person or circumstances, shall be held invalid, the remainder of this Act, or the application of such provision to persons or circumstances other than those as to which it is held invalid, shall not be affected thereby.

§17. (§167) This Act may be cited as the "National Labor Relations Act".

§18. (§168) [Reference to repealed sections 9(f), (g), and (h). — Eds.]

§19. (§169) Any employee who is a member of and adheres to established and traditional tenets or teachings of a bona fide religion, body, or sect which has historically held conscientious objections to joining or financially supporting labor organizations shall not be required to join or financially support any labor organization as a condition of employment; except that

---

* [The Administrative Procedure Act. Provision as amended by §7(b) of Pub. L. 89-544, Sept. 6, 1966. — Eds.]

such employee may be required in a contract between such employees' employer and a labor organization in lieu of periodic dues and initiation fees, to pay sums equal to such dues and initiation fees to a nonreligious, nonlabor organization charitable fund exempt from taxation under section 501(c)(3) of Title 26,[*] chosen by such employee from a list of at least three such funds, designated in such contract or if the contract fails to designate such funds, then to any such fund chosen by the employee. If such employee who holds conscientious objections pursuant to this section requests the labor organization to use the grievance-arbitration procedure on the employee's behalf, the labor organization is authorized to charge the employee for the reasonable cost of using such procedure.[**]

---

[*] [The Internal Revenue Code. — Eds.]
[**] This section was added by Pub. L. 93-360, July 26, 1974, 88 Stat. 397, and amended by Pub. L. 96-593, Dec. 24, 1980, 94 Stat. 3452.

Labor Management Relations Act of 1947[*]
61 Stat. 136 (1947), as amended, 29 U.S.C. §§141-197.

Short Title and Declaration of Policy

§1. (§141) (a) This Act may be cited as the "Labor Management Relations Act, 1947."[*]

(b) Industrial strife which interferes with the normal flow of commerce and with the full production of articles and commodities for commerce, can be avoided or substantially minimized if employers, employees, and labor organizations each recognize under law one another's legitimate rights in their relations with each other, and above all recognize under law that neither party has any right in its relations with any other to engage in acts or practices which jeopardize the public health, safety, or interest.

It is the purpose and policy of this Act, in order to promote the full flow of commerce, to prescribe the legitimate rights of both employees and employers in their relations affecting commerce, to provide orderly and peaceful procedures for preventing the interference by either with the legitimate rights of the other, to protect the rights of individual employees in their relations with labor organizations whose activities affect commerce, to define and proscribe practices on the part of labor and management which affect commerce and are inimical to the general welfare, and to protect the rights of the public in connection with labor disputes affecting commerce.

TITLE I. AMENDMENT OF NATIONAL LABOR RELATIONS ACT

§101. [The text of the National Labor Relations Act as amended is set forth supra.]

---

[*] [Unless otherwise indicated, internal section references are to the NLRA or LMRA, and not to the United States Code; references within parentheticals are to the Code. Provisions added by the LMRDA (1959) are in italics; provisions added by the Health Care Institutions Act (1974) are capitalized. Material deleted by the amendments is enclosed in brackets. Other amendments and deletions are specifically noted. — EDS.]

TITLE II. CONCILIATION OF LABOR DISPUTES; NATIONAL EMERGENCIES

§201. (§171) It is the policy of the United States that —

(a) sound and stable industrial peace and the advancement of the general welfare, health, and safety of the Nation and of the best interests of employers and employees can most satisfactorily be secured by the settlement of issues between employers and employees through the processes of conference and collective bargaining between employers and the representatives of their employees;

(b) the settlement of issues between employers and employees through collective bargaining may be advanced by making available full and adequate government facilities for conciliation, mediation, and voluntary arbitration to aid and encourage employers and the representatives of their employees to reach and maintain agreements concerning rates of pay, hours, and working conditions, and to make all reasonable efforts to settle their differences by mutual agreement reached through conferences and collective bargaining or by such methods as may be provided for in any applicable agreement for the settlement of disputes; and

(c) certain controversies which arise between parties to collective-bargaining agreements may be avoided or minimized by making available full and adequate governmental facilities for furnishing assistance to employers and the representatives of their employees in formulating for inclusion within such agreements provision for adequate notice of any proposed changes in the terms of such agreements, for the final adjustment of grievances or questions regarding the application or interpretation of such agreements, and other provisions designed to prevent the subsequent arising of such controversies.

§202. (§172) (a) There is hereby created an independent agency to be known as the Federal Mediation and Conciliation Service (herein referred to as the "Service", except that for sixty days after June 23, 1947, such term shall refer to the Conciliation Service of the Department of Labor). The Service shall be under the direction of a Federal Mediation and Conciliation Director (hereinafter referred to as the "Director"), who shall be appointed by the President by and with the advice and consent of the Senate. The Director shall not engage in any other business, vocation, or employment.

(b) The Director is authorized, subject to the civil service laws, to appoint such clerical and other personnel as may be necessary for the execution of the functions of the Service, and shall fix their compensation in accordance with chapter 51 and subchapter III of chapter 53 of Title 5,[*] and may, without regard to the provisions of the civil service laws, appoint such conciliators and mediators as may be necessary to carry out the functions of the Service. The Director is authorized to make such expenditures for supplies, facilities, and services as he deems necessary. Such expenditures shall be allowed and paid upon presentation of itemized vouchers therefor approved by the Director or by any employee designated by him for that purpose.

(c) The principal office of the Service shall be in the District of Columbia, but the Director may establish regional offices convenient to localities in which labor controversies are likely to arise. The Director may by order, subject to revocation at any time, delegate any authority and discretion conferred upon him by this Act to any regional director, or other officer or employee of the Service. The Director may establish suitable procedures for cooperation with State and local mediation agencies. The Director shall make an annual report in writing to Congress at the end of the fiscal year.

(d) All mediation and conciliation functions of the Secretary of Labor or the United States Conciliation Service under section 51 of this title, and all functions of the United States Conciliation Service under any other law are transferred to the Federal Mediation and Conciliation Service, together with the personnel and records of the United States Conciliation Service. Such transfer shall take effect upon the sixtieth day after June 23, 1947. Such transfer shall not affect any proceedings pending before the United States Conciliation Service or any certification, order, rule, or regulation theretofore made by it or by the Secretary of Labor. The Director and the Service shall not be subject in any way to the jurisdiction or authority of the Secretary of Labor or any official or division of the Department of Labor.

Functions of the Service

§203. (§173) (a) It shall be the duty of the Service, in order to prevent or minimize interruptions of the free flow of commerce growing out of labor disputes, to assist parties to labor disputes in industries affecting commerce to settle such disputes through conciliation and mediation.

(b) The Service may proffer its services in any labor dispute in any industry affecting commerce, either upon its own motion or upon the request of one or more of the parties to the dispute, whenever in its judgment such dispute threatens to cause a substantial interruption of

---

[*] As amended following enactment of Pub. L. 89-554, Sept. 6, 1966, 80 Stat. 631.

commerce. The Director and the Service are directed to avoid attempting to mediate disputes which would have only a minor effect on interstate commerce if State or other conciliation services are available to the parties. Whenever the Service does proffer its services in any dispute, it shall be the duty of the Service promptly to put itself in communication with the parties and to use its best efforts, by mediation and conciliation, to bring them to agreement.

(c) If the Director is not able to bring the parties to agreement by conciliation within a reasonable time, he shall seek to induce the parties voluntarily to seek other means of settling the dispute without resort to strike, lock-out, or other coercion, including submission to the employees in the bargaining unit of the employer's last offer of settlement for approval or rejection in a secret ballot. The failure or refusal of either party to agree to any procedure suggested by the Director shall not be deemed a violation of any duty or obligation imposed by this Act.

(d) Final adjustment by a method agreed upon by the parties is declared to be the desirable method for settlement of grievance disputes arising over the application or interpretation of an existing collective-bargaining agreement. The Service is directed to make its conciliation and mediation services available in the settlement of such grievance disputes only as a last resort and in exceptional cases.

(e) The Service is authorized and directed to encourage and support the establishment and operation of joint labor management activities conducted by plant, area, and industrywide committees designed to improve labor management relationships, job security and organizational effectiveness, in accordance with the provisions of section 205A.[*]

(f) The Service may make its services available to Federal agencies to aid in the resolution of disputes under the provisions of subchapter IV of chapter 5 of Title 5. Functions performed by the Service may include assisting parties to disputes related to administrative programs, training persons in skills and procedures employed in alternative means of dispute resolution, and furnishing officers and employees of the Service to act as neutrals. Only officers and employees who are qualified in accordance with section 573 of Title 5 may be assigned to act as neutrals. The Service shall consult with the agency designated by, or the interagency committee designated or established by, the President under section 573 of Title 5 in

---

[*] Subsection (e) was added in 1978 by Pub. L. 95-524, §6(c)(1), 92 Stat. 2020.

maintaining rosters of neutrals and arbitrators, and to adopt such procedures and rules as are necessary to carry out the services authorized in this subsection.[*]

§204. (§174) (a) In order to prevent or minimize interruptions of the free flow of commerce growing out of labor disputes, employers and employees and their representatives, in any industry affecting commerce, shall —

(1) exert every reasonable effort to make and maintain agreements concerning rates of pay, hours, and working conditions, including provision for adequate notice of any proposed change in the terms of such agreements;

(2) whenever a dispute arises over the terms or application of a collective-bargaining agreement and a conference is requested by a party or prospective party thereto, arrange promptly for such a conference to be held and endeavor in such conference to settle such dispute expeditiously; and

(3) in case such dispute is not settled by conference, participate fully and promptly in such meetings as may be undertaken by the Service under this Act for the purpose of aiding in a settlement of the dispute.

§205. (§175) (a) There is created a National Labor-Management Panel which shall be composed of twelve members appointed by the President, six of whom shall be selected from among persons outstanding in the field of management and six of whom shall be selected from among persons outstanding in the field of labor. Each member shall hold office for a term of three years, except that any member appointed to fill a vacancy occurring prior to the expiration of the term for which his predecessor was appointed shall be appointed for the remainder of such term, and the terms of office of the members first taking office shall expire, as designated by the President at the time of appointment, four at the end of the first year, four at the end of the second year, and four at the end of the third year after the date of appointment. Members of the panel, when serving on business of the panel, shall be paid compensation at the rate of $25 per day, and shall also be entitled to receive an allowance for actual and necessary travel and subsistence expenses while so serving away from their places of residence.

(b) It shall be the duty of the panel, at the request of the Director, to advise in the avoidance of industrial controversies and the manner in which

---

[*] As added by §7 of Pub. L. 101-552, Nov. 15, 1990; see also Pub. L. 104-320, §9, Oct. 19, 1996.

mediation and voluntary adjustment shall be administered, particularly with reference to controversies affecting the general welfare of the country.

§205A. (§175a)[*] (a)(1) The Service is authorized and directed to provide assistance in the establishment and operation of plant, area and industrywide labor management committees which —

(A) have been organized jointly by employers and labor organizations representing employees in that plant, area, or industry; and

(B) are established for the purpose of improving labor management relationships, job security, organizational effectiveness, enhancing economic development or involving workers in decisions affecting their jobs including improving communication with respect to subjects of mutual interest and concern.

(2) The Service is authorized and directed to enter into contracts and to make grants, where necessary or appropriate, to fulfill its responsibilities under this section.

(b)(1) No grant may be made, no contract may be entered into and no other assistance may be provided under the provisions of this section to a plant labor management committee unless the employees in that plant are represented by a labor organization and there is in effect at that plant a collective bargaining agreement.

(2) No grant may be made, no contract may be entered into and no other assistance may be provided under the provisions of this section to an area or industrywide labor management committee unless its participants include any labor organizations certified or recognized as the representative of the employees of an employer participating in such committee. Nothing in this clause shall prohibit participation in an area or industrywide committee by an employer whose employees are not represented by a labor organization.

(3) No grant may be made under the provisions of this section to any labor management committee which the Service finds to have as one of its purposes the discouragement of the exercise of rights contained in section 157 of this title, or the interference with collective bargaining in any plant, or industry.

(c) The Service shall carry out the provisions of this section through an office established for that purpose.

(d) There are authorized to be appropriated to carry out the provisions of this section $10,000,000 for the fiscal year 1979, and such sums as may be necessary thereafter.

---

* This section was added in 1978 by Pub. L. 95-524, §6(c)(2), 92 Stat. 2020.

National Emergencies

§206. (§176) Whenever in the opinion of the President of the United States, a threatened or actual strike or lock-out affecting an entire industry or a substantial part thereof engaged in trade, commerce, transportation, transmission, or communication among the several States or with foreign nations, or engaged in the production of goods for commerce, will, if permitted to occur or to continue, imperil the national health or safety, he may appoint a board of inquiry to inquire into the issues involved in the dispute and to make a written report to him within such time as he shall prescribe. Such report shall include a statement of the facts with respect to the dispute, including each party's statement of its position but shall not contain any recommendations. The President shall file a copy of such report with the Service and shall make its contents available to the public.

§207. (§177) (a) A board of inquiry shall be composed of a chairman and such other members as the President shall determine, and shall have power to sit and act in any place within the United States and to conduct such hearings either in public or in private, as it may deem necessary or proper, to ascertain the facts with respect to the causes and circumstances of the dispute.

(b) Members of a board of inquiry shall receive compensation at the rate of $50 for each day actually spent by them in the work of the board, together with necessary travel and subsistence expenses.

(c) For the purpose of any hearing or inquiry conducted by any board appointed under this title, the provisions of sections 49 and 50 of Title 15 (relating to the attendance of witnesses and the production of books, papers, and documents) are made applicable to the powers and duties of such board.

§208. (§178) (a) Upon receiving a report from a board of inquiry the President may direct the Attorney General to petition any district court of the United States having jurisdiction of the parties to enjoin such strike or lock-out or the continuing thereof, and if the court finds that such threatened or actual strike or lock-out —

(i) affects an entire industry or a substantial part thereof engaged in trade, commerce, transportation, transmission, or communication among the several States or with foreign nations, or engaged in the production of goods for commerce; and

(ii) if permitted to occur or to continue, will imperil the national health or safety, it shall have jurisdiction to enjoin any such strike or lockout, or the continuing thereof, and to make such other orders as may be appropriate.

(b) In any case, the provisions of chapter 6 of this title[*] shall not be applicable.

(c) The order or orders of the court shall be subject to review by the appropriate United States court of appeals and by the Supreme Court upon writ of certiorari or certification as provided in section 1254 of Title 28.

§209. (§179) (a) Whenever a district court has issued an order under section 208 enjoining acts or practices which imperil or threaten to imperil the national health or safety, it shall be the duty of the parties to the labor dispute giving rise to such order to make every effort to adjust and settle their differences, with the assistance of the Service created by this Act. Neither party shall be under any duty to accept, in whole or in part, any proposal of settlement made by the Service.

(b) Upon the issuance of such order, the President shall reconvene the board of inquiry which has previously reported with respect to the dispute. At the end of a sixty-day period (unless the dispute has been settled by that time), the board of inquiry shall report to the President the current position of the parties and the efforts which have been made for settlement, and shall include a statement by each party of its position and a statement of the employer's last offer of settlement. The President shall make such report available to the public. The National Labor Relations Board, within the succeeding fifteen days, shall take a secret ballot of the employees of each employer involved in the dispute on the question of whether they wish to accept the final offer of settlement made by their employer as stated by him and shall certify the results thereof to the Attorney General within five days thereafter.

§210. (§180) Upon the certification of the results of such ballot or upon a settlement being reached, whichever happens sooner, the Attorney General shall move the court to discharge the injunction, which motion shall then be granted and the injunction discharged. When such motion is granted, the President shall submit to the Congress a full and comprehensive report of the proceedings, including the findings of the board of inquiry and the ballot taken by the National Labor Relations Board, together with such recommendations as he may see fit to make for consideration and appropriate action.

* [The Norris-LaGuardia Act. — EDS.]

Compilation of Collective Bargaining Agreements, etc.

§211. (§181) (a) For the guidance and information of interested representatives of employers, employees, and the general public, the Bureau of Labor Statistics of the Department of Labor shall maintain a file of copies of all available collective bargaining agreements and other available agreements and actions thereunder settling or adjusting labor disputes. Such file shall be open to inspection under appropriate conditions prescribed by the Secretary of Labor, except that no specific information submitted in confidence shall be disclosed.

(b) The Bureau of Labor Statistics in the Department of Labor is authorized to furnish upon request of the Service, or employers, employees, or their representatives, all available data and factual information which may aid in the settlement of any labor dispute, except that no specific information submitted in confidence shall be disclosed.

Exemption of Railway Labor Act

§212. (§182) The provisions of this subchapter shall not be applicable with respect to any matter which is subject to the provisions of the Railway Labor Act, as amended from time to time.

Conciliation of Labor Disputes in the Health Care Industry[*]

§213. (§183) (a) If, in the opinion of the Director of the Federal Mediation and Conciliation Service, a threatened or actual strike or lockout affecting a health care institution will, if permitted to occur or to continue, substantially interrupt the delivery of health care in the locality concerned, the Director may further assist in the resolution of the impasse by establishing within 30 days after the notice to the Federal Mediation and Conciliation Service under clause (A) of the last sentence of section 8(d) (which is required by clause (3) of such section 8(d)), or within 10 days after the notice under clause (B), an impartial Board of Inquiry to investigate the issues involved in the dispute and to make a written report thereon to the parties within fifteen (15) days after the establishment of such a Board.[*] The written report shall contain the findings of fact together with the Board's recommendations for settling the dispute, with the objective of achieving a prompt, peaceful and just settlement of the dispute. Each such Board shall be composed of such number of individuals as the Director may deem desirable. No member

---

[*] Added by Act of July 26, 1974, Pub. L. 93-360, §2, 88 Stat. 396.

appointed under this section shall have any interest or involvement in the health care institutions or the employee organizations involved in the dispute.

(b)(1) Members of any board established under this section who are otherwise employed by the Federal Government shall serve without compensation but shall be reimbursed for travel, subsistence, and other necessary expenses incurred by them in carrying out its duties under this section.

(2) Members of any board established under this section who are not subject to paragraph (1) shall receive compensation at a rate prescribed by the Director but not to exceed the daily rate prescribed for GS-18 of the General Schedule under section 5332 of Title 5, including travel for each day they are engaged in the performance of their duties under this section and shall be entitled to reimbursement for travel, subsistence, and other necessary expenses incurred by them in carrying out their duties under this section.

(c) After the establishment of a board under subsection (a) of this section and for 15 days after any such board has issued its report, no change in the status quo in effect prior to the expiration of the contract in the case of negotiations for a contract renewal, or in effect prior to the time of the impasse in the case of an initial bargaining negotiation, except by agreement, shall be made by the parties to the controversy.

(d) There are authorized to be appropriated such sums as may be necessary to carry out the provisions of this section.

TITLE III. SUITS BY AND AGAINST LABOR ORGANIZATIONS

§301. (§185) (a) Suits for violation of contracts between an employer and a labor organization representing employees in an industry affecting commerce as defined in this Act, or between any such labor organizations, may be brought in any district court of the United States having jurisdiction of the parties, without respect to the amount in controversy or without regard to the citizenship of the parties.

(b) Any labor organization which represents employees in an industry affecting commerce as defined in this Act and any employer whose activities affect commerce as defined in this Act shall be bound by the acts of its agents. Any such labor organization may sue or be sued as an entity and in behalf of the employees whom it represents in the courts of the United States. Any money judgment against a labor organization in a district court of the United States shall be enforceable only against the organization as an entity and against its assets, and shall not be enforceable against any individual member or his assets.

(c) For the purposes of actions and proceedings by or against labor organizations in the district courts of the United States, district courts shall be deemed to have jurisdiction of a labor organization (1) in the district in which such organization maintains its principal office, or (2) in any district in which its duly authorized officers or agents are engaged in representing or acting for employee members.

(d) The service of summons, subpena, or other legal process of any court of the United States upon an officer or agent of a labor organization, in his capacity as such, shall constitute service upon the labor organization.

(e) For the purposes of this section, in determining whether any person is acting as an "agent" of another person so as to make such other person responsible for his acts, the question of whether the specific acts performed were actually authorized or subsequently ratified shall not be controlling.

Restrictions on Payments to Employee Representatives

§302. (§186) (a) It shall be unlawful for any employer *or association of employers or any person who acts as a labor relations expert, adviser, or consultant to an employer or who acts in the interest of an employer* to pay, *lend,* or deliver, or [to] agree to pay, *lend,* or deliver, any money or other thing of value —

(1) to any representative of any of his employees who are employed in an industry affecting commerce[.]*; or*

(2) to any labor organization, or any officer or employee thereof, which represents, seeks to represent, or would admit to membership, any of the employees of such employer who are employed in an industry affecting commerce; or

(3) to any employee or group or committee of employees of such employer employed in an industry affecting commerce in excess of their normal compensation for the purpose of causing such employee or group or committee directly or indirectly to influence any other employees in the exercise of the right to organize and bargain collectively through representatives of their own choosing; or

(4) to any officer or employee of a labor organization engaged in an industry affecting commerce with intent to influence him in respect to any of his actions, decisions, or duties as a representative of employees or as such officer or employee of such labor organization.

(b)(1) It shall be unlawful for any [representative of any employees who are employed in an industry affecting commerce] *person* to *request, demand,* receive, or accept, or [to] agree to receive or accept [from the employer of such employees], *any payment, loan, or delivery of* any money or other thing of value[.] *prohibited by subsection (a) of this section.*

   (2) It shall be unlawful for any labor organization, or for any person acting as an officer, agent, representative, or employee of such labor organization, to demand or accept from the operator of any motor vehicle (as defined in section 13102 of Title 49) employed in the transportation of property in commerce, or the employer of any such operator, any money or other thing of value payable to such organization or to an officer, agent, representative or employee thereof as a fee or charge for the unloading, or in connection with the unloading, of the cargo of such vehicle: Provided, That nothing in this paragraph shall be construed to make unlawful any payment by an employer to any of his employees as compensation for their services as employees.

(c) The provisions of this section shall not be applicable (1) [with] *in* respect to any money or other thing of value payable by an employer *to any of his employees whose established duties include acting openly for such employer in matters of labor relations or personnel administration or* to any representative *of his employees, or to any officer or employee of a labor organization,* who is *also* an employee or former employee of such employer, as compensation for, or by reason of, his service[s] as an employee of such employer; (2) with respect to the payment or delivery of any money or other thing of value in satisfaction of a judgment of any court or a decision or award of an arbitrator or impartial chairman or in compromise, adjustment, settlement, or release of any claim, complaint, grievance, or dispute in the absence of fraud or duress; (3) with respect to the sale or purchase of an article or commodity at the prevailing market price in the regular course of business; (4) with respect to money deducted from the wages of employees in payment of membership dues in a labor organization: *Provided,* That the employer has received from each employee, on whose account such deductions are made, a written assignment which shall not be irrevocable for a period of more than one year, or beyond the termination date of the applicable collective agreement, whichever occurs sooner; [or] (5) with respect to money or other thing of value paid to a trust fund established by such representative, for the sole and exclusive benefit of the employees of such employer, and their families and dependents (or of such employees, families, and dependents jointly with the employees of other employers making similar payments, and their families and dependents): *Provided,* That (A) such payments are held in trust for the purpose of paying, either from principal or income or both, for the benefit of employees, their families and dependents, for medical or hospital care, pensions on retirement or death of employees, compensation for injuries or illness resulting from occupational activity or insurance to provide any of the foregoing, or unemployment benefits or life insurance, disability and sickness insurance, or accident insurance; (B) the detailed basis on which such payments are to be made is specified in a written agreement with the employer, and employees and employers are equally represented in the administration of such fund, together with such neutral persons as the representatives of the employers and the representatives of [the] employees may agree upon and in the event the employer and employee groups deadlock on the administration of such fund and there are no neutral persons empowered to break such deadlock, such agreement provides that the two groups shall agree on an impartial umpire to decide such dispute, or in event of their failure to agree within a reasonable length of time, an impartial umpire to decide such dispute shall, on petition of either group, be appointed by the district court of the United States for the district where the trust fund has its principal office, and shall also contain provisions for an annual audit of the trust fund, a statement of the results of which shall be available for inspection by interested persons at the principal office of the trust fund and at such other places as may be designated in such written agreement; and (C) such payments as are intended to be used for the purpose of providing pensions or annuities for employees are made to a separate trust which provides that the funds held therein cannot be used for any purpose other than paying such pensions or annuities[.]*; or (6) with respect to money or other thing of value paid by any employer to a trust fund established by such representative for the purpose of pooled vacation, holiday, severance or similar benefits, or defraying costs of apprenticeship or other training programs: Provided, That the requirements of clause (B) of the proviso to clause (5) of this subsection shall apply to such trust funds;* (7) with respect to money or other thing of value paid by any employer to a pooled or individual trust fund established by such representative for the purpose of (A) scholarships for the benefit of employees, their families, and dependents for study at educational institutions, (B) child care centers for preschool and school age dependents of employees or (C) financial assistance for employee housing: *Provided,* That no labor organization or employer shall be required to bargain on the establishment of any such trust fund, and refusal to do so shall not constitute an unfair labor practice: *Provided further,* That the requirements of clause (B) of the proviso to clause (5) of this subsection shall apply to such trust funds; (8) with respect to money or any other thing of value paid by any employer to a trust fund established by such representative for the purpose of defraying the costs of legal services for employees, their families, and dependents for counsel or plan of their choice: *Provided,* That the requirements of clause (B) of the proviso to clause (5) of this subsection shall apply to such trust funds: *Provided further,* That no such legal services shall be furnished: (A) to initiate any proceeding directed (i) against any such employer or its officers or agents except in workman's compensation cases, or (ii) against such labor organization, or its parent or subordinate bodies, or their officers or agents, or (iii) against any other employer or labor organization, or their officers or agents, in any matter arising under the National Labor Relations Act, as amended, or this Act; and (B) in any proceeding where a labor organization would be prohibited from defraying the costs of legal services by the provisions of the Labor-Management Reporting and Disclosure Act of 1959; or (9) with respect to money or other things of value paid by an employer to a plant, area or industrywide labor management committee established for one or more of the purposes set forth in section 5(b) of the Labor Management Cooperation Act of 1978.[*]

(d)(1) Any person who participates in a transaction involving a payment, loan, or delivery of money or other thing of value to a labor organization in payment of membership dues or to a joint labor-management trust fund as defined by clause (B) of the proviso to clause (5) of subsection (c) of this section or to a plant, area, or industry-wide labor-management committee that is received and used by such labor organization, trust fund, or committee, which transaction does not satisfy all the applicable requirements of subsections (c)(4) through (c)(9) of this section, and willfully and with intent to benefit himself or to benefit other persons he knows are not permitted to receive a payment, loan, money, or other thing of value under subsections (c)(4) through (c)(9) violates this subsection, shall, upon conviction thereof, be guilty of a felony and be subject to a fine of not more than $15,000, or imprisoned for not more than five years, or both; but if the value of the amount of money or thing of value involved in any violation of the provisions of this section does not exceed $1,000, such person shall be guilty of a misdemeanor and be subject to a fine of not more than $10,000, or imprisoned for not more than one year, or both.

---

[*] Clause (7) of §302(c) was added by Pub. L. 91-96, Oct. 14, 1969, 83 Stat. 133; Clause (8) by Pub. L. 93-95, Aug. 15, 1973, 87 Stat. 314; and Clause (9) by Pub. L. 95-524, Oct. 27, 1978, 92 Stat. 2021.

(2) Except for violations involving transactions covered by subsection (d)(1) of this section, any person who willfully violates this section shall, upon conviction thereof, be guilty of a felony and be subject to a fine of not more than $15,000, or imprisoned for not more than five years, or both; but if the value of the amount of money or thing of value involved in any violation of the provisions of this section does not exceed $1,000, such person shall be guilty of a misdemeanor and be subject to a fine of not more than $10,000, or imprisoned for not more than one year, or both.[*]

(e) The district courts of the United States and the United States courts of the Territories and possessions shall have jurisdiction, for cause shown, and subject to the provisions of section 381 of Title 28 (relating to notice to opposite party) to restrain violations of this section, without regard to the provisions of section 17 of Title 15 and section 52 of this title, and the provisions of chapter 6 of this title.[**]

(f) This section shall not apply to any contract in force on June 23, 1947, until the expiration of such contract, or until July 1, 1948, whichever first occurs.

(g) Compliance with the restrictions contained in subsection (c)(5)(B) of this section upon contributions to trust funds, otherwise lawful, shall not be applicable to contributions to such trust funds established by collective agreement prior to January 1, 1946, nor shall subsection (c)(5)(A) of this section be construed as prohibiting contributions to such trust funds if prior to January 1, 1947, such funds contained provisions for pooled vacation benefits.

Unlawful Activities or Conduct

§303. (§187) (a) It shall be unlawful, for the purpose[s] of this section only, in an industry or activity affecting commerce, for any labor organization to engage in *any activity or conduct defined as an unfair labor practice in section 8(b)(4) of the National Labor Relations Act, as amended.* [, or to induce or encourage the employees of any employer to engage in, a strike or a concerted refusal in the course of their employment to use, manufacture, process, transport, or otherwise handle or work on any goods, articles, materials, or commodities or to perform any services, where an object thereof is —

---

[*] Section 302(d) was amended by Pub. L. 98-473, Oct. 12, 1984, 98 Stat. 2131.
[**] [The Norris-LaGuardia Act. — Eds.]

(1) forcing or requiring any employer or self-employed person to join any labor or employer organization or any employer or other person to cease using, selling, handling, transporting, or otherwise dealing in the products of any other producer, processor, or manufacturer, or to cease doing business with any other person;

(2) forcing or requiring any other employer to recognize or bargain with a labor organization as the representative of his employees unless such labor organization has been certified as the representative of such employees under the provisions of section 9 of the National Labor Relations Act;

(3) forcing or requiring any employer to recognize or bargain with a particular labor organization as the representative of his employees if another labor organization has been certified as the representative of such employees under the provisions of section 9 of the National Labor Relations Act;

(4) forcing or requiring any employer to assign particular work to employees in a particular labor organization or in a particular trade, craft, or class rather than to employees in another labor organization or in another trade, craft, or class unless such employer is failing to conform to an order or certification of the National Labor Relations Board determining the bargaining representative for employees performing such work. Nothing contained in this subsection shall be construed to make unlawful a refusal by any person to enter upon the premises of any employer (other than his own employer), if the employees of such employer are engaged in a strike ratified or approved by a representative of such employees whom such employer is required to recognize under the National Labor Relations Act.]

(b) Whoever shall be injured in his business or property by reason or (sic) any violation of subsection (a) may sue therefor in any district court of the United States subject to the limitations and provisions of section 301 hereof without respect to the amount in controversy, or in any other court having jurisdiction of the parties, and shall recover the damages by him sustained and the cost of the suit.

Restriction on Political Contributions

[Section 304 of the LMRA was repealed and reenacted in other statutes, first in 1948 and then in the 1976 Federal Election Campaign Act. — EDS.]

Strikes by Government Employees [Repealed][*]

[§305. (§188) It shall be unlawful for any individual employed by the United States or any agency thereof including wholly owned Government corporations to participate in any strike.[*] Any individual employed by the United States or by any such agency who strikes shall be discharged immediately from his employment, and shall forfeit his civil-service status, if any, and shall not be eligible for reemployment for three years by the United States or any such agency.]

TITLE IV. CREATION OF JOINT COMMITTEE TO STUDY AND REPORT ON BASIC PROBLEMS AFFECTING FRIENDLY LABOR RELATIONS AND PRODUCTIVITY

[Text omitted.]

TITLE V. DEFINITIONS

§501. (§142) When used in this Act —

(1) The term "industry affecting commerce" means any industry or activity in commerce or in which a labor dispute would burden or obstruct commerce or tend to burden or obstruct commerce or the free flow of commerce.

(2) The term "strike" includes any strike or other concerted stoppage of work by employees (including a stoppage by reason of the expiration of a collective-bargaining agreement) and any concerted slowdown or other concerted interruption of operations by employees.

(3) The terms "commerce", "labor disputes", "employer", "employee", "labor organization", "representative", "person", and "supervisor" shall have the same meaning as when used in the National Labor Relations Act as amended by this Act.

---

* [Section 305 was repealed by Act of Aug. 9, 1955, c.690, §4(3), 69 Stat. 625. Congress instead enacted 5 U.S.C. §§118p-118r (now 5 U.S.C. §§3333, 7311; 18 U.S.C. §1918). Those provisions make strikes by federal employees a felony. The Civil Service Reform Act of 1978 also makes strikes and other work stoppages by federal employees unfair labor practices (5 U.S.C. §§7116(b)(7)(A) and (B)), and provides for decertification of unions that strike (5 U.S.C. §7120(f)). — EDS.]

Saving Provisions

§502. (§143) Nothing in this Act shall be construed to require an individual employee to render labor or service without his consent, nor shall anything in this Act be construed to make the quitting of his labor by an individual employee an illegal act; nor shall any court issue any process to compel the performance by an individual employee of such labor or service, without his consent; nor shall the quitting of labor by an employee or employees in good faith because of abnormally dangerous conditions for work at the place of employment of such employee or employees be deemed a strike under this Act.

Separability

§503. (§144) If any provision of this Act, or the application of such provision to any person or circumstance, shall be held invalid, the remainder of this Act, or the application of such provision to persons or circumstances other than those as to which it is held invalid, shall not be affected thereby.

Labor-Management Reporting and Disclosure Act of 1959
73 Stat. 519 (1959), as amended, 29 U.S.C. §§401-531

§2.   (§401) Congressional declaration of findings, purposes, and policy

(a) *Standards for labor-management relations.* The Congress finds that, in the public interest, it continues to be the responsibility of the Federal Government to protect employees' rights to organize, choose their own representatives, bargain collectively, and otherwise engage in concerted activities for their mutual aid or protection; that the relations between employers and labor organizations and the millions of workers they represent have a substantial impact on the commerce of the Nation; and that in order to accomplish the objective of a free flow of commerce it is essential that labor organizations, employers, and their officials adhere to the highest standards of responsibility and ethical conduct in administering the affairs of their organizations, particularly as they affect labor-management relations.

(b) *Protection of rights of employees and the public.* The Congress further finds, from recent investigations in the labor and management fields, that there have been a number of instances of breach of trust, corruption, disregard of the rights of individual employees, and other failures to observe high standards of responsibility and ethical conduct which require further and supplementary legislation that will afford necessary protection of the rights and interests of employees and the public generally as they relate to the activities of labor organizations, employers, labor relations consultants, and their officers and representatives.

(c) *Necessity to eliminate or prevent improper practices.* The Congress, therefore, further finds and declares that the enactment of this chapter is necessary to eliminate or prevent improper practices on the part of labor organizations, employers, labor relations consultants, and their officers and representatives which distort and defeat the policies of the Labor Management Relations Act, 1947, as amended [29 U.S.C. §141 et seq.], and the Railway Labor Act, as amended [45 U.S.C. §151 et seq.], and have the tendency or necessary effect of burdening or obstructing commerce by (1) impairing the efficiency, safety, or operation of the instrumentalities of commerce; (2) occurring in the current of commerce; (3) materially affecting, restraining, or controlling the flow of raw materials or manufactured or processed goods into or from the channels of commerce, or the prices of such materials or goods in commerce; or (4) causing diminution of employment and wages in such volume as substantially to impair or disrupt the market for goods flowing into or from the channels of commerce.

§3.   (§402) Definitions

For the purposes of this chapter—

(a) "Commerce" means trade, traffic, commerce, transportation, transmission, or communication among the several States or between any State and any place outside thereof.

(b) "State" includes any State of the United States, the District of Columbia, Puerto Rico, the Virgin Islands, American Samoa, Guam, Wake Island, the Canal Zone, and Outer Continental Shelf lands defined in the Outer Continental Shelf Lands Act [43 U.S.C. §1331 et seq.].

(c) "Industry affecting commerce" means any activity, business, or industry in commerce or in which a labor dispute would hinder or obstruct commerce or the free flow of commerce and includes any activity or industry "affecting commerce" within the meaning of the Labor Management Relations Act, 1947, as amended [29 U.S.C. §141 et seq.], or the Railway Labor Act, as amended [45 U.S.C. §151 et seq.].

(d) "Person" includes one or more individuals, labor organizations, partnerships, associations, corporations, legal representatives, mutual companies, joint-stock companies, trusts, unincorporated organizations, trustees, trustees in cases under title 11, or receivers.

(e) "Employer" means any employer or any group or association of employers engaged in an industry affecting commerce (1) which is, with respect to employees engaged in an industry affecting commerce, an employer within the meaning of any law of the United States relating to the employment of any employees or (2) which may deal with any labor organization concerning grievances, labor disputes, wages, rates of pay, hours of employment, or conditions of work, and includes any person acting directly or indirectly as an employer or as an agent of an employer in relation to an employee but does not include the United States or any corporation wholly owned by the Government of the United States or any State or political subdivision thereof.

(f) "Employee" means any individual employed by an employer, and includes any individual whose work has ceased as a consequence of, or in connection with, any current labor dispute or because of any unfair labor practice or because of exclusion or expulsion from a labor organization in any manner or for any reason inconsistent with the requirements of this chapter.

(g) "Labor dispute" includes any controversy concerning terms, tenure, or conditions of employment, or concerning the association or representation of persons in negotiating, fixing, maintaining, changing, or seeking to arrange terms or conditions of employment, regardless of whether the disputants stand in the proximate relation of employer and employee.

(h) "Trusteeship" means any receivership, trusteeship, or other method of supervision or control whereby a labor organization suspends the autonomy otherwise available to a subordinate body under its constitution or bylaws.

(i) "Labor organization" means a labor organization engaged in an industry affecting commerce and includes any organization of any kind, any agency, or employee representation committee, group, association, or plan so engaged in which employees participate and which exists for the purpose, in whole or in part, of dealing with employers concerning grievances, labor disputes, wages, rates of pay, hours, or other terms or conditions of employment, and any conference, general committee, joint or system board, or joint council so engaged which is subordinate to a national or international labor organization, other than a State or local central body.

(j) A labor organization shall be deemed to be engaged in an industry affecting commerce if it —

(1) is the certified representative of employees under the provisions of the National Labor Relations Act, as amended [29 U.S.C. §151 et seq.], or the Railway Labor Act, as amended [45 U.S.C. §151 et seq.]; or

(2) although not certified, is a national or international labor organization or a local labor organization recognized or acting as the representative of employees of an employer or employers engaged in an industry affecting commerce; or

(3) has chartered a local labor organization or subsidiary body which is representing or actively seeking to represent employees of employers within the meaning of paragraph (1) or (2); or

(4) has been chartered by a labor organization representing or actively seeking to represent employees within the meaning of paragraph (1) or (2) as the local or subordinate body through which such employees may enjoy membership or become affiliated with such labor organization; or

(5) is a conference, general committee, joint or system board, or joint council, subordinate to a national or international labor organization, which includes a labor organization engaged in an industry

affecting commerce within the meaning of any of the preceding paragraphs of this subsection, other than a State or local central body.

(k) "Secret ballot" means the expression by ballot, voting machine, or otherwise, but in no event by proxy, of a choice with respect to any election or vote taken upon any matter, which is cast in such a manner that the person expressing such choice cannot be identified with the choice expressed.

(*l*) "Trust in which a labor organization is interested" means a trust or other fund or organization (1) which was created or established by a labor organization, or one or more of the trustees or one or more members of the governing body of which is selected or appointed by a labor organization, and (2) a primary purpose of which is to provide benefits for the members of such labor organization or their beneficiaries.

(m) "Labor relations consultant" means any person who, for compensation, advises or represents an employer, employer organization, or labor organization concerning employee organizing, concerted activities, or collective bargaining activities.

(n) "Officer" means any constitutional officer, any person authorized to perform the functions of president, vice president, secretary, treasurer, or other executive functions of a labor organization, and any member of its executive board or similar governing body.

(*o*) "Member" or "member in good standing", when used in reference to a labor organization, includes any person who has fulfilled the requirements for membership in such organization, and who neither has voluntarily withdrawn from membership nor has been expelled or suspended from membership after appropriate proceedings consistent with lawful provisions of the constitution and bylaws of such organization.

(p) "Secretary" means the Secretary of Labor.

(q) "Officer, agent, shop steward, or other representative," when used with respect to a labor organization, includes elected officials and key administrative personnel, whether elected or appointed (such as business agents, heads of departments or major units, and organizers who exercise substantial independent authority), but does not include salaried nonsupervisory professional staff, stenographic, and service personnel.

(r) "District court of the United States" means a United States district court and a United States court of any place subject to the jurisdiction of the United States.

Title I. Bill of Rights of Members of Labor Organization

§101.   (§411) Bill of rights; constitution and bylaws of labor organizations

(a)(1) Equal rights. Every member of a labor organization shall have equal rights and privileges within such organization to nominate candidates, to vote in elections or referendums of the labor organization, to attend membership meetings, and to participate in the deliberations and voting upon the business of such meetings, subject to reasonable rules and regulations in such organization's constitution and bylaws.

(2) Freedom of speech and assembly. Every member of any labor organization shall have the right to meet and assemble freely with other members; and to express any views, arguments, or opinions; and to express at meetings of the labor organization his views, upon candidates in an election of the labor organization or upon any business properly before the meeting, subject to the organization's established and reasonable rules pertaining to the conduct of meetings: *Provided,* That nothing herein shall be construed to impair the right of a labor organization to adopt and enforce reasonable rules as to the responsibility of every member toward the organization as an institution and to his refraining from conduct that would interfere with its performance of its legal or contractual obligations.

(3) Dues, initiation fees, and assessments. Except in the case of a federation of national or international labor organizations, the rates of dues and initiation fees payable by members of any labor organization in effect on September 14, 1959 shall not be increased, and no general or special assessment shall be levied upon such members, except —

(A) in the case of a local labor organization, (i) by majority vote by secret ballot of the members in good standing voting at a general or special membership meeting, after reasonable notice of the intention to vote upon such question, or (ii) by majority vote of the members in good standing voting in a membership referendum conducted by secret ballot; or

(B) in the case of a labor organization, other than a local labor organization or a federation of national or international labor organizations, (i) by majority vote of the delegates voting at a regular convention, or at a special convention of such labor organization held upon not less than thirty days' written notice to the principal office of each local or constituent labor organization entitled to such notice, or (ii) by majority vote of the members in good standing of such labor organization voting in a membership referendum conducted by secret ballot, or (iii) by majority vote of the members of the executive board or similar governing body of such labor organization, pursuant to express authority contained in the constitution and bylaws of such labor organization: *Provided,* That any such action on the part of the executive board or similar governing body shall be effective only until the next regular convention of such labor organization.

(4) Protection of the right to sue. No labor organization shall limit the right of any member thereof to institute an action in any court, or in a proceeding before any administrative agency, irrespective of whether or not the labor organization or its officers are named as defendants or respondents in such action or proceeding, or the right of any member of a labor organization to appear as a witness in any judicial, administrative, or legislative proceeding, or to petition any legislature or to communicate with any legislator: *Provided,* That such member may be required to exhaust reasonable hearing procedures (but not to exceed a four-month lapse of time) within such organization, before instituting legal or administrative proceedings against such organizations or any officer thereof: *And provided further,* That no interested employer or employer association shall directly or indirectly finance, encourage, or participate in, except as a party, any such action, proceeding, appearance, or petition.

(5) Safeguards against improper disciplinary action. No member of any labor organization may be fined, suspended, expelled, or otherwise disciplined except for nonpayment of dues by such organization or by any officer thereof unless such member has been (A) served with written specific charges; (B) given a reasonable time to prepare his defense; (C) afforded a full and fair hearing.

(b) Invalidity of constitution and bylaws. Any provision of the constitution and bylaws of any labor organization which is inconsistent with the provisions of this section shall be of no force or effect.

§102. (§412) Civil action for infringement of rights; jurisdiction

Any person whose rights secured by the provisions of this subchapter have been infringed by any violation of this subchapter may bring a civil action in a district court of the United States for such relief (including injunctions) as may be appropriate. Any such action against a labor organization shall be brought in the district court of the United States for the district where the alleged violation occurred, or where the principal office of such labor organization is located.

§103. (§413) Retention of existing rights of members

Nothing contained in this subchapter shall limit the rights and remedies of any member of a labor organization under any State or Federal law or before any court or other tribunal, or under the constitution and bylaws of any labor organization.

§104. (§414) Right to copies of collective bargaining agreements

It shall be the duty of the secretary or corresponding principal officer of each labor organization, in the case of a local labor organization, to forward a copy of each collective bargaining agreement made by such labor organization with any employer to any employee who requests such a copy and whose rights as such employee are directly affected by such agreement, and in the case of a labor organization other than a local labor organization, to forward a copy of any such agreement to each constituent unit which has members directly affected by such agreement; and such officer shall maintain at the principal office of the labor organization of which he is an officer copies of any such agreement made or received by such labor organization, which copies shall be available for inspection by any member or by any employee whose rights are affected by such agreement. The provisions of section 440 of this title shall be applicable in the enforcement of this section.

§105. (§415) Information to members of provisions of chapter

Every labor organization shall inform its members concerning the provisions of this chapter.

TITLE II. REPORTING BY LABOR ORGANIZATIONS, OFFICERS AND
EMPLOYEES OF LABOR ORGANIZATIONS, AND EMPLOYERS

§201.   (§431) Report of labor organizations

(a) Adoption and filing of constitution and bylaws; contents of report.
Every labor organization shall adopt a constitution and bylaws and shall file a
copy thereof with the Secretary, together with a report, signed by its president
and secretary or corresponding principal officers, containing the following
information —

(1) the name of the labor organization, its mailing address, and any
other address at which it maintains its principal office or at which it keeps
the records referred to in this subchapter;

(2) the name and title of each of its officers;

(3) the initiation fee or fees required from a new or transferred
member and fees for work permits required by the reporting labor
organization;

(4) the regular dues or fees or other periodic payments required to
remain a member of the reporting labor organization; and

(5) detailed statements, or references to specific provisions of documents filed under this subsection which contain such statements, showing the provision made and procedures followed with respect to each of
the following: (A) qualifications for or restrictions on membership,
(B) levying of assessments, (C) participation in insurance or other benefit
plans, (D) authorization for disbursement of funds of the labor
organization, (E) audit of financial transactions of the labor organization,
(F) the calling of regular and special meetings, (G) the selection of
officers and stewards and of any representatives to other bodies composed of labor organizations' representatives, with a specific statement
of the manner in which each officer was elected, appointed, or otherwise
selected, (H) discipline or removal of officers or agents for breaches of
their trust, (1) imposition of fines, suspensions, and expulsions of members, including the grounds for such action and any provision made
for notice, hearing, judgment on the evidence, and appeal procedures,
(J) authorization for bargaining demands, (K) ratification of contract
terms, (L) authorization for strikes, and (M) issuance of work permits.
Any change in the information required by this subsection shall be
reported to the Secretary at the time the reporting labor organization
files with the Secretary the annual financial report required by subsection
(b) of this section.

(b) Annual financial report; filing; contents. Every labor organization
shall file annually with the Secretary a financial report signed by its

president and treasurer or corresponding principal officers containing the following information in such detail as may be necessary accurately to disclose its financial condition and operations for its preceding fiscal year—

(1) assets and liabilities at the beginning and end of the fiscal year;

(2) receipts of any kind and the sources thereof;

(3) salary, allowances, and other direct or indirect disbursements (including reimbursed expenses) to each officer and also to each employee who, during such fiscal year, received more than $10,000 in the aggregate from such labor organization and any other labor organization affiliated with it or with which it is affiliated, or which is affiliated with the same national or international labor organization;

(4) direct and indirect loans made to any officer, employee, or member, which aggregated more than $250 during the fiscal year, together with a statement of the purpose, security, if any, and arrangements for repayment;

(5) direct and indirect loans to any business enterprise, together with a statement of the purpose, security, if any, and arrangements for repayment; and

(6) other disbursements made by it including the purposes thereof, all in such categories as the Secretary may prescribe.

(c) Availability of information to members; examination of books, records, and accounts. Every labor organization required to submit a report under this subchapter shall make available the information required to be contained in such report to all of its members, and every such labor organization and its officers shall be under a duty enforceable at the suit of any member of such organization in any State court of competent jurisdiction or in the district court of the United States for the district in which such labor organization maintains its principal office, to permit such member for just cause to examine any books, records, and accounts necessary to verify such report. The court in such action may, in its discretion, in addition to any judgment awarded to the plaintiff or plaintiffs, allow a reasonable attorney's fee to be paid by the defendant, and costs of the action.

§202.   (§432) Report of officers and employees of labor organizations

(a) Filing; contents of report. Every officer of a labor organization and every employee of a labor organization (other than an employee performing

exclusively clerical or custodial services) shall file with the Secretary a signed report listing and describing for his preceding fiscal year —

(1) any stock, bond, security, or other interest, legal or equitable, which he or his spouse or minor child directly or indirectly held in, and any income or any other benefit with monetary value (including reimbursed expenses) which he or his spouse or minor child derived directly or indirectly from, an employer whose employees such labor organization represents or is actively seeking to represent, except payments and other benefits received as a bona fide employee of such employer;

(2) any transaction in which he or his spouse or minor child engaged, directly or indirectly, involving any stock, bond, security, or loan to or from, or other legal or equitable interest in the business of an employer whose employees such labor organization represents or is actively seeking to represent;

(3) any stock, bond, security, or other interest, legal or equitable, which he or his spouse or minor child directly or indirectly held in, and any income or any other benefit with monetary value (including reimbursed expenses) which he or his spouse or minor child directly or indirectly derived from, any business a substantial part of which consists of buying from, selling or leasing to, or otherwise dealing with, the business of an employer whose employees such labor organization represents or is actively seeking to represent;

(4) any stock, bond, security, or other interest, legal or equitable, which he or his spouse or minor child directly or indirectly held in, and any income or any other benefit with monetary value (including reimbursed expenses) which he or his spouse or minor child directly or indirectly derived from, a business any part of which consists of buying from, or selling or leasing directly or indirectly to, or otherwise dealing with such labor organization;

(5) any direct or indirect business transaction or arrangement between him or his spouse or minor child and any employer whose employees his organization represents or is actively seeking to represent, except work performed and payments and benefits received as a bona fide employee of such employer and except purchases and sales of goods or services in the regular course of business at prices generally available to any employee of such employer; and

(6) any payment of money or other thing of value (including reimbursed expenses) which he or his spouse or minor child received directly or indirectly from any employer or any person who acts as a labor

relations consultant to an employer, except payments of the kinds referred to in section 186(c) of this title.

(b) Report of certain bona fide investments. The provisions of paragraphs (1), (2), (3), (4), and (5) of subsection (a) of this section shall not be construed to require any such officer or employee to report his bona fide investments in securities traded on a securities exchange registered as a national securities exchange under the Securities Exchange Act of 1934 [15 U.S.C. §78a et seq.], in shares in an investment company registered under the Investment Company Act of 1940 [15 U.S.C. §§80a-1 et seq.], or in securities of a public utility holding company registered under the Public Utility Holding Company Act of 1935 [15 U.S.C. §§79 et seq.], or to report any income derived therefrom.

(c) Exemption from filing requirement. Nothing contained in this section shall be construed to require any officer or employee of a labor organization to file a report under subsection (a) of this section unless he or his spouse or minor child holds or has held an interest, has received income or any other benefit with monetary value or a loan, or has engaged in a transaction described therein.

§203.   (§433) Report of employers

(a) Filing and contents of report of payments, loans, promises, agreements, or arrangements. Every employer who in any fiscal year made —

(1) any payment or loan, direct or indirect, of money or other thing of value (including reimbursed expenses), or any promise or agreement therefor, to any labor organization or officer, agent, shop steward, or other representative of a labor organization, or employee of any labor organization, except (A) payments or loans made by any national or State bank, credit union, insurance company, savings and loan association or other credit institution and (B) payments of the kind referred to in section 186(c) of this title;

(2) any payment (including reimbursed expenses) to any of his employees, or any group or committee of such employees, for the purpose of causing such employee or group or committee of employees to persuade other employees to exercise or not to exercise, or as the manner of exercising, the right to organize and bargain collectively through representatives of their own choosing unless such payments were contemporaneously or previously disclosed to such other employees;

(3) any expenditure, during the fiscal year, where an object thereof, directly or indirectly, is to interfere with, restrain, or coerce employees in the exercise of the right to organize and bargain collectively through representatives of their own choosing, or is to obtain information concerning the activities of employees or a labor organization in connection with a labor dispute involving such employer, except for use solely in conjunction with an administrative or arbitral proceeding or a criminal or civil judicial proceeding;

(4) any agreement or arrangement with a labor relations consultant or other independent contractor or organization pursuant to which such person undertakes activities where an object thereof, directly or indirectly, is to persuade employees to exercise or not to exercise, or persuade employees as to the manner of exercising, the right to organize and bargain collectively through representatives of their own choosing, or undertakes to supply such employer with information concerning the activities of employees or a labor organization in connection with a labor dispute involving such employer, except information for use solely in conjunction with an administrative or arbitral proceeding or a criminal or civil judicial proceeding; or

(5) any payment (including reimbursed expenses) pursuant to an agreement or arrangement described in subdivision (4);

shall file with the Secretary a report, in a form prescribed by him, signed by its president and treasurer or corresponding principal officers showing in detail the date and amount of each such payment, loan, promise, agreement, or arrangement and the name, address, and position, if any, in any firm or labor organization of the person to whom it was made and a full explanation of the circumstances of all such payments, including the terms of any agreement or understanding pursuant to which they were made.

(b) Persuasive activities relating to the fight to organize and bargain collectively; supplying information of activities in connection with labor disputes; filing and contents of report of agreement or arrangement. Every person who pursuant to any agreement or arrangement with an employer undertakes activities where an object thereof is, directly or indirectly —

(1) to persuade employees to exercise or not to exercise, or persuade employees as to the manner of exercising, the right to organize and bargain collectively through representatives of their own choosing; or

(2) to supply an employer with information concerning the activities of employees or a labor organization in connection with a labor dispute involving such employer, except information for use solely in

conjunction with an administrative or arbitral proceeding or a criminal or civil judicial proceeding;

shall file within thirty days after entering into such agreement or arrangement a report with the Secretary, signed by its president and treasurer or corresponding principal officers, containing the name under which such person is engaged in doing business and the address of its principal office, and a detailed statement of the terms and conditions of such agreement or arrangement. Every such person shall file annually, with respect to each fiscal year during which payments were made as a result of such an agreement or arrangement, a report with the Secretary, signed by its president and treasurer or corresponding principal officers, containing a statement (A) of its receipts of any kind from employers on account of labor relations advice or services, designating the sources thereof, and (B) of its disbursements of any kind, in connection with such services and the purposes thereof. In each such case such information shall be set forth in such categories as the Secretary may prescribe.

(c) Advisory or representative services exempt from filing requirements. Nothing in this section shall be construed to require any employer or other person to file a report covering the services of such person by reason of his giving or agreeing to give advice to such employer or representing or agreeing to represent such employer before any court, administrative agency, or tribunal of arbitration or engaging or agreeing to engage in collective bargaining on behalf of such employer with respect to wages, hours, or other terms or conditions of employment or the negotiation of an agreement or any question arising thereunder.

(d) Exemption from filing requirements generally. Nothing contained in this section shall be construed to require an employer to file a report under subsection (a) of this section unless he has made an expenditure, payment, loan, agreement, or arrangement of the kind described therein. Nothing contained in this section shall be construed to require any other person to file a report under subsection (b) of this section unless he was a party to an agreement or arrangement of the kind described therein.

(e) Services by and payments to regular officers, supervisors, and employees of employer. Nothing contained in this section shall be construed to require any regular officer, supervisor, or employee of an employer to file a report in connection with services rendered to such employer nor shall any employer be required to file a report covering expenditures made to any regular officer, supervisor, or employee of an employer as compensation for service as a regular officer, supervisor, or employee of such employer.

(f) Rights protected by section 158(c) of this title. Nothing contained in this section shall be construed as an amendment to, or modification of the rights protected by, section 158(c) of this title.

(g) Definition. The term "interfere with, restrain, or coerce" as used in this section means interference, restraint, and coercion which, if done with respect to the exercise of rights guaranteed in section 157 of this title, would, under section 158(a) of this title, constitute an unfair labor practice.

§204.   (§434) Exemption of attorney-client communications

Nothing contained in this chapter shall be construed to require an attorney who is a member in good standing of the bar of any State, to include in any report required to be filed pursuant to the provisions of this chapter any information which was lawfully communicated to such attorney by any of his clients in the course of a legitimate attorney-client relationship.

§205.   (§435) Reports and documents as public information

(a) Publication; statistical and research purposes. The contents of the reports and documents filed with the Secretary pursuant to sections 431, 432, 433, and 441 of this title shall be public information, and the Secretary may publish any information and data which he obtains pursuant to the provisions of this subchapter. The Secretary may use the information and data for statistical and research purposes, and compile and publish such studies, analyses, reports, and surveys based thereon as he may deem appropriate.

(b) Inspection and examination of information and data. The Secretary shall by regulation make reasonable provision for the inspection and examination, on the request of any person, of the information and data contained in any report or other document filed with him pursuant to section 431, 432, 433, or 441, of this title.

(c) Copies of reports or documents; availability to State agencies. The Secretary shall by regulation provide for the furnishing by the Department of Labor of copies of reports or other documents filed with the Secretary pursuant to this subchapter, upon payment of a charge based upon the cost of the service. The Secretary shall make available without payment of a charge, or require any person to furnish, to such State agency as is designated by law or

by the Governor of the State in which such person has his principal place of business or headquarters, upon request of the Governor of such State, copies of any reports and documents filed by such person with the Secretary pursuant to section 431, 432, 433, or 441 of this title, or of information and data contained therein. No person shall be required by reason of any law of any State to furnish to any officer or agency of such State any information included in a report filed by such person with the Secretary pursuant to the provisions of this subchapter, if a copy of such report, or of the portion thereof containing such information, is furnished to such officer or agency. All moneys received in payment of such charges fixed by the Secretary pursuant to this subsection shall be deposited in the general fund of the Treasury.

§206. (§436) Retention of records

Every person required to file any report under this Subchapter shall maintain records of the matters required to be reported which will provide in sufficient detail the necessary basic information and data from which the documents filed with the Secretary may be verified, explained, or clarified, and checked for accuracy and completeness, and shall include vouchers, worksheets, receipts, and applicable resolutions, and shall keep such records available for examination for a period of not less than five years after the filing of the documents based on the information which they contain.

§207. (§437) Time for making reports

(a) Each labor organization shall file the initial report required under section 431(a) of this title within ninety days after the date on which it first becomes subject to this chapter.

(b) Each person required to file a report under section 431(b), 432, 433(a), the second sentence of 433(b), or section 441 of this title shall file such report within ninety days after the end of each of its fiscal years; except that where such person is subject to section 431(b), 432, 433(a), the second sentence of 433(b), or section 441 of this title, as the case may be, for only a portion of such a fiscal year (because September 14, 1959, occurs during such person's fiscal year or such person becomes subject to this chapter during its fiscal year) such person may consider that portion as the entire fiscal year in making such report.

§208. (§438) Rules and regulations; simplified reports

The Secretary shall have authority to issue, amend, and rescind rules and regulations prescribing the form and publication of reports required to be filed under this subchapter and such other reasonable rules and regulations (including rules prescribing reports concerning trusts in which a labor organization is interested) as he may find necessary to prevent the circumvention or evasion of such reporting requirements. In exercising his power under this section the Secretary shall prescribe by general rule simplified reports for labor organizations or employers for whom he finds that by virtue of their size a detailed report would be unduly burdensome, but the Secretary may revoke such provision for simplified forms of any labor organization or employer if he determines, after such investigation as he deems proper and due notice and opportunity for a hearing, that the purposes of this section would be served thereby.

§209. (§439) Violations and penalties

(a) Willful violations of provisions of subchapter. Any person who willfully violates this subchapter shall be fined not more than $10,000 or imprisoned for not more than one year, or both.

(b) False statements or representation of fact with knowledge of falsehood. Any person who makes a false statement or representation of a material fact, knowing it to be false, or who knowingly fails to disclose a material fact, in any document, report, or other information required under the provisions of this subchapter shall be fined not more than $10,000 or imprisoned for not more than one year, or both.

(c) False entry in or willful concealment, etc., of books and records. Any person who willfully makes a false entry in or willfully conceals, withholds, or destroys any books, records, reports, or statements required to be kept by any provision of this subchapter shall be fined not more than $10,000 or imprisoned for not more than one year, or both.

(d) Personal responsibility of individuals required to sign reports. Each individual required to sign reports under sections 431 and 433 of this title shall be personally responsible for the filing of such reports and for any statement contained therein which he knows to be false.

§210.   (§440) Civil action for enforcement by Secretary; jurisdiction

Whenever it shall appear that any person has violated or is about to violate any of the provisions of this subchapter, the Secretary may bring a civil action for such relief (including injunctions) as may be appropriate. Any such action may be brought in the district court of the United States where the violation occurred or, at the option of the parties, in the United States District Court for the District of Columbia.

§211.   (§441) Surety company reports; contents; waiver or modification of requirements respecting contents of reports

Each surety company which issues any bond required by this chapter or the Employee Retirement Income Security Act of 1974 [29 U.S.C. §1001 et seq.] shall file annually with the Secretary, with respect to each fiscal year during which any such bond was in force, a report, in such form and detail as he may prescribe by regulation, filed by the president and treasurer or corresponding principal officers of the surety company, describing its bond experience under each such chapter or Act, including information as to the premiums received, total claims paid, amounts recovered by way of subrogation, administrative and legal expenses and such related data and information as the Secretary shall determine to be necessary in the public interest and to carry out the policy of the chapter. Notwithstanding the foregoing, if the Secretary finds that any such specific information cannot be practicably ascertained or would be uninformative, the Secretary may modify or waive the requirement for such information.

TITLE III. TRUSTEESHIPS

§301.   (§461) Reports

(a) Filing and contents; Annual financial report. Every labor organization which has or assumes trusteeship over any subordinate labor organization shall file with the Secretary within thirty days after September 14, 1959 or the imposition of any such trusteeship, and semiannually thereafter, a report, signed by its president and treasurer or corresponding principal officers, as well as by the trustees of such subordinate labor organization, containing the following information: (1) the name and address of the subordinate organization; (2) the date of establishing the trusteeship; (3) a

detailed statement of the reason or reasons for establishing or continuing the trusteeship; and (4) the nature and extent of participation by the membership of the subordinate organization in the selection of delegates to represent such organization in regular or special conventions or other policy-determining bodies and in the election of officers of the labor organization which has assumed trusteeship over such subordinate organization. The initial report shall also include a full and complete account of the financial condition of such subordinate organization as of the time trusteeship was assumed over it. During the continuance of a trusteeship the labor organization which has assumed trusteeship over a subordinate labor organization shall file on behalf of the subordinate labor organization the annual financial report required by section 431(b) of this title signed by the president and treasurer or corresponding principal officers of the labor organization which has assumed such trusteeship and the trustees of the subordinate labor organization.

(b) Applicability of other laws. The provisions of sections 431(c), 435, 436, 438, and 440 of this title shall be applicable to reports filed under this subchapter.

(c) Penalty for violations. Any person who willfully violates this section shall be fined not more than $10,000 or imprisoned for not more than one year, or both.

(d) False statements and entries; failure to disclose material facts, withholding, concealing or destroying documents, books, records, reports, or statements; penalty. Any person who makes a false statement or representation of a material fact, knowing it to be false, or who knowingly fails to disclose a material fact, in any report required under the provisions of this section or willfully makes any false entry in or willfully withholds, conceals, or destroys any documents, books, records, reports, or statements upon which such report is based, shall be fined not more than $10,000 or imprisoned for not more than one year, or both.

(e) Personal liability. Each individual required to sign a report under this section shall be personally responsible for the filing of such report and for any statement contained therein which he knows to be false.

§302. (§462) Purposes for establishment of trusteeship

Trusteeships shall be established and administered by a labor organization over a subordinate body only in accordance with the constitution and bylaws of the organization which has assumed trusteeship over the subordinate body and for the purpose of correcting corruption or financial malpractice, assuring the performance of collective bargaining agreements or other duties of a bargaining representative, restoring democratic procedures, or otherwise carrying out the legitimate objects of such labor organization.

§303.   (§463) Unlawful acts relating to labor organization under trusteeship

(a) During any period when a subordinate body of a labor organization is in trusteeship, it shall be unlawful (1) to count the vote of delegates from such body in any convention or election of officers of the labor organization unless the delegates have been chosen by secret ballot in an election in which all the members in good standing of such subordinate body were eligible to participate, or (2) to transfer to such organization any current receipts or other funds of the subordinate body except the normal per capita tax and assessments payable by subordinate bodies not in trusteeship: *Provided,* That nothing herein contained shall prevent the distribution of the assets of a labor organization in accordance with its constitution and bylaws upon the bona fide dissolution thereof.

(b) Any person who willfully violates this section shall be fined not more than $10,000 or imprisoned for not more than one year, or both.

§304.   (§464) Civil action for enforcement

(a) Complaint; investigation; commencement of action by Secretary, member or subordinate body of labor organization; jurisdiction. Upon the written complaint of any member or subordinate body of a labor organization alleging that such organization has violated the provisions of this subchapter (except section 461 of this title) the Secretary shall investigate the complaint and if the Secretary finds probable cause to believe that such violation has occurred and has not been remedied he shall, without disclosing the identity of the complainant, bring a civil action in any district court of the United States having jurisdiction of the labor organization for such relief (including injunctions) as may be appropriate. Any member of subordinate body of a labor organization affected by any violation of this subchapter (except section 461 of this title) may bring a civil action in any district court of the United States having jurisdiction of the labor organization for such relief (including injunctions) as may be appropriate.

(b) Venue. For the purpose of actions under this section, district courts of the United States shall be deemed to have jurisdiction of a labor organization (1) in the district in which the principal office of such labor organization is located, or (2) in any district in which its duly authorized officers or agents are engaged in conducting the affairs of the trusteeship.

(c) Presumptions of validity or invalidity of trusteeship. In any proceeding pursuant to this section a trusteeship established by a labor organization in conformity with the procedural requirements of its constitution and bylaws and authorized or ratified after a fair hearing either before the executive board or before such other body as may be provided in accordance with its constitution or bylaws shall be presumed valid for a period of eighteen months from the date of its establishment and shall not be subject to attack during such period except upon clear and convincing proof that the trusteeship was not established or maintained in good faith for a purpose allowable under section 462 of this title. After the expiration of eighteen months the trusteeship shall be presumed invalid in any such proceeding and its discontinuance shall be decreed unless the labor organization shall show by clear and convincing proof that the continuation of the trusteeship is necessary for a purpose allowable under section 462 of this title. In the latter event the court may dismiss the complaint or retain jurisdiction of the cause on such conditions and for such period as it deems appropriate.

§305.   (§465) Report to Congress

The Secretary shall submit to the Congress at the expiration of three years from September 14, 1959, a report upon the operation of this subchapter.

§306.   (§466) Additional rights and remedies; exclusive jurisdiction of district court; res judicata

The rights and remedies provided by this Subchapter shall be in addition to any and all other rights and remedies at law or in equity: *Provided,* That upon the filing of a complaint by the Secretary the jurisdiction of the district court over such trusteeship shall be exclusive and the final judgment shall be res judicata.

Title IV. Elections

§401.   (§481) Terms of office and election procedures

(a) Officers of national or international labor organizations; manner of election. Every national or international labor organization, except a federation of national or international labor organization, shall elect its officers not less often than once every five years either by secret ballot among the members in good standing or at a convention of delegates chosen by secret ballot.

(b) Officers of local labor organizations; manner of election. Every local labor organization shall elect its officers not less often than once every three years by secret ballot among the members in good standing.

(c) Requests for distribution of campaign literature; civil action for enforcement; jurisdiction; inspection of membership lists; adequate safeguards to insure fair election. Every national or international labor organization, except a federation of national or international labor organizations, and every local labor organization, and its officers, shall be under a duty, enforceable at the suit of any bona fide candidate for office in such labor organization in the district court of the United States in which such labor organization maintains its principal office, to comply with all reasonable requests of any candidate to distribute by mail or otherwise at the candidate's expense campaign literature in aid of such person's candidacy to all members in good standing of such labor organization and to refrain from discrimination in favor of or against any candidate with respect to the use of lists of members, and whenever such labor organizations or its officers authorize the distribution by mail or otherwise to members of campaign literature on behalf of any candidate or of the labor organization itself with reference to such election, similar distribution at the request of any other bona fide candidate shall be made by such labor organization and its officers, with equal treatment as to the expense of such distribution. Every bona fide candidate shall have the right, once within 30 days prior to an election of a labor organization in which he is a candidate, to inspect a list containing the names and last known addresses of all members of the labor organization who are subject to a collective bargaining agreement requiring membership therein as a condition of employment, which list shall be maintained and kept at the principal office of such labor organization by a designated official thereof. Adequate safeguards to insure a fair election shall be provided, including the right of any candidate to have an observer at the polls and at the counting of the ballots.

(d) Officers of intermediate bodies; manner of election. Officers of intermediate bodies, such as general committees, system boards, joint boards, or joint councils, shall be elected not less often than once every four years by secret ballot among the members in good standing or by labor organization officers representative of such members who have been elected by secret ballot.

(e) Nomination of candidates; eligibility; notice of election; voting rights; counting and publication of results; preservation of ballots and records. In any election required by this section which is to be held by secret ballot a reasonable opportunity shall be given for the nomination of candidates and every member in good standing shall be eligible to be a candidate and to hold office (subject to section 504 of this title and to reasonable qualifications uniformly imposed) and shall have the right to vote for or otherwise support the candidate or candidates of his choice, without being subject to penalty, discipline, or improper interference or reprisal of any kind by such organization or any member thereof. Not less than fifteen days prior to the election notice thereof shall be mailed to each member at his last known home address. Each member in good standing shall be entitled to one vote. No member whose dues have been withheld by his employer for payment to such organization pursuant to his voluntary authorization provided for in a collective bargaining agreement shall be declared ineligible to vote or be a candidate for office in such organization by reason of alleged delay or default in the payment of dues. The votes cast by members of each local labor organization shall be counted, and the results published, separately. The election officials designated in the constitution and bylaws or the secretary, if no other official is designated, shall preserve for one year the ballots and other records pertaining to the election. The election shall be conducted in accordance with the constitution and bylaws of such organization insofar as they are not inconsistent with the provisions of this subchapter.

(f) Election of officers by convention of delegates; manner of conducting convention; preservation of records. When officers are chosen by a convention of delegates elected by secret ballot, the convention shall be conducted in accordance with the constitution and bylaws of the labor organization insofar as they are not inconsistent with the provisions of this subchapter. The officials designated in the constitution and bylaws or the secretary, if no other is designated, shall preserve for one year the credentials of the delegates and all minutes and other records of the convention pertaining to the election of officers.

(g) Use of dues, assessments or similar levies, and funds of employer for promotion of candidacy of person. No moneys received by any labor organization by way of dues, assessment, or similar levy, and no moneys

of an employer shall be contributed or applied to promote the candidacy of any person in any election subject to the provisions of this subchapter. Such moneys of a labor organization may be utilized for notices, factual statements of issues not involving candidates, and other expenses necessary for the holding of an election.

(h) Removal of officers guilty of serious misconduct. If the Secretary, upon application of any member of a local labor organization, finds after hearing in accordance with subchapter II of chapter 5 of Title 5 that the constitution and bylaws of such labor organization do not provide an adequate procedure for the removal of an elected officer guilty of serious misconduct, such officer may be removed, for cause shown and after notice and hearing, by the members in good standing voting in a secret ballot, conducted by the officers of such labor organization in accordance with its constitution and bylaws insofar as they are not inconsistent with the provisions of this subchapter.

(i) Rules and regulations for determining adequacy of removal procedures. The Secretary shall promulgate rules and regulations prescribing minimum standards and procedures for determining the adequacy of the removal procedures to which reference is made in subsection (h) of this section.

§402.   (§482) Enforcement

(a) Filing of complaint; presumption of validity of challenged election. A member of a labor organization —

(1) who has exhausted the remedies available under the constitution and bylaws of such organization and of any parent body, or

(2) who has invoked such available remedies without obtaining a final decision within three calendar months after their invocation, may file a complaint with the Secretary within one calendar month thereafter alleging the violation of any provision of section 481 of this title (including violation of the constitution and bylaws of the labor organization pertaining to the election and removal of officers). The challenged election shall be presumed valid pending a final decision thereon (as hereinafter provided) and in the interim the affairs of the organization shall be conducted by the officers elected or in such other manner as its constitution and bylaws may provide.

(b) Investigation of complaint; commencement of civil action by Secretary; jurisdiction; preservation of assets. The Secretary shall investigate such complaint and, if he finds probable cause to believe that a violation of this subchapter has occurred and has not been remedied, he shall, within sixty days

after the filing of such complaint, bring a civil action against the labor organization as an entity in the district court of the United States in which such labor organization maintains its principal office to set aside the invalid election, if any, and to direct the conduct of an election or hearing and vote upon the removal of officers under the supervision of the Secretary and in accordance with the provisions of this subchapter and such rules and regulations as the Secretary may prescribe. The court shall have power to take such action as it deems proper to preserve the assets of the labor organization.

   (c) Declaration of void election; order for new election; certification of election to court; decree; certification of result of vote for removal of officers. If, upon a preponderance of the evidence after a trial upon the merits, the court finds—

   (1) that an election has not been held within the time prescribed by section 481 of this title, or

   (2) that the violation of section 481 of this title may have affected the outcome of an election,

the court shall declare the election, if any, to be void and direct the conduct of a new election under supervision of the Secretary and, so far as lawful and practicable, in conformity with the constitution and bylaws of the labor organization. The Secretary shall promptly certify to the court the names of the persons elected, and the court shall thereupon enter a decree declaring such persons to be the officers of the labor organization. If the proceeding is for the removal of officers pursuant to subsection (h) of section 481 of this title, the Secretary shall certify the results of the vote and the court shall enter a decree declaring whether such persons have been removed as officers of the labor organization.

   (d) Review of orders; stay of order directing election. An order directing an election, dismissing a complaint, or designating elected officers of a labor organization shall be appealable in the same manner as the final judgment in a civil action, but an order directing an election shall not be stayed pending appeal.

§403.   (§483) Application of other laws; existing rights and remedies; exclusiveness of remedy for challenging election

   No labor organization shall be required by law to conduct elections of officers with greater frequency or in a different form or manner than is required by its own constitution or bylaws, except as otherwise provided by this subchapter. Existing rights and remedies to enforce the constitution and bylaws of a labor organization with respect to elections prior to the conduct thereof shall not be affected by the provisions of this subchapter. The remedy provided by this subchapter for challenging an election already conducted shall be exclusive.

TITLE V. SAFEGUARDS FOR LABOR ORGANIZATIONS

§501.   (§501) Fiduciary responsibility of officers of labor organizations

(a) Duties of officers; exculpatory provisions and resolutions void. The officers, agents, shop stewards, and other representatives of a labor organization occupy positions of trust in relation to such organization and its members as a group. It is, therefore, the duty of each such person, taking into account the special problems and functions of a labor organization, to hold its money and property solely for the benefit of the organization and its members and to manage, invest, and expend the same in accordance with its constitution and bylaws and any resolutions of the governing bodies adopted thereunder, to refrain from dealing with such organization as an adverse party or in behalf of an adverse party in any matter connected with his duties and from holding or acquiring any pecuniary or personal interest which conflicts with the interests of such organization, and to account to the organization for any profit received by him in whatever capacity in connection with transactions conducted by him or under his direction on behalf of the organization. A general exculpatory provision in the constitution and bylaws of such a labor organization or a general exculpatory resolution of a governing body purporting to relieve any such person of liability for breach of the duties declared by this section shall be void as against public policy.

(b) Violation of duties; action by member after refusal or failure by labor organization to commence proceedings; jurisdiction; leave of court; counsel fees and expenses. When any officer, agent, shop steward, or representative of any labor organization is alleged to have violated the duties declared in subsection (a) of this section and the labor organization or its governing board or officers refuse or fail to sue or recover damages or secure an accounting or other appropriate relief within a reasonable time after being requested to do so by any member of the labor organization, such member may sue such officer, agent, shop steward, or representative in any district court of the United States or in any State court of competent jurisdiction to recover damages or secure an accounting or other appropriate relief for the benefit of the labor organization. No such proceeding shall be brought except upon leave of the court obtained upon verified application and for good cause shown, which application may be made ex parte. The trial judge may allot a reasonable part of the recovery in

any action under this subsection to pay the fees of counsel prosecuting the suit at the instance of the member of the labor organization and to compensate such member for any expenses necessarily paid or incurred by him in connection with the litigation.

(c) Embezzlement of assets; penalty. Any person who embezzles, steals, or unlawfully and willfully abstracts or converts to his own use, or the use of another, any of the moneys, funds, securities, property, or other assets of a labor organization of which he is an officer, or by which he is employed, directly or indirectly, shall be fined not more than $10,000 or imprisoned for not more than five years, or both.

§502. (§502) Bonding of officers and employees of labor organizations; amount, form, and placement of bonds; penalty for violation

(a) Every officer, agent, shop steward, or other representative or employee of any labor organization (other than a labor organization whose property and annual financial receipts do not exceed $5,000 in value), or of a trust in which a labor organization is interested, who handles funds or other property thereof shall be bonded to provide protection against loss by reason of acts of fraud or dishonesty on his part directly or through connivance with others. The bond of each such person shall be fixed at the beginning of the organization's fiscal year and shall be in an amount not less than 10 per centum of the funds handled by him and his predecessor or predecessors, if any, during the preceding fiscal year, but in no case more than $500,000. If the labor organization or the trust in which a labor organization is interested does not have a preceding fiscal year, the amount of the bond shall be, in the case of a local labor organization, not less than $1,000, and in the case of any other labor organization or of a trust in which a labor organization is interested, not less than $10,000. Such bonds shall be individual or schedule in form, and shall have a corporate surety company as surety thereon. Any person who is not covered by such bonds shall not be permitted to receive, handle, disburse, or otherwise exercise custody or control of the funds or other property of a labor organization or of a trust in which a labor organization is interested. No such bond shall be placed through an agent or broker or with a surety company in which any labor organization or any officer, agent, shop steward, or other representative of a labor organization has any direct or indirect interest. Such surety company shall be a corporate surety which holds a grant of authority from the Secretary of the Treasury under sections 9304-9308 of Title 31, as an acceptable surety on Federal bonds: *Provided,* That when in the opinion of the Secretary a labor organization has made other bonding arrangements which would provide the protection required by this section at comparable cost or less, he may exempt such labor organization from placing a bond through a surety company holding such grant of authority.

(b) Any person who willfully violates this section shall be fined not more than $10,000 or imprisoned for not more than one year, or both.

§503.   (§503) Financial transactions between labor organization and officers and employees

(a) Direct and indirect loans. No labor organization shall make directly or indirectly any loan or loans to any officer or employee of such organization which results in a total indebtedness on the part of such officer or employee to the labor organization in excess of $2,000.

(b) Direct or indirect payment of fines. No labor organization or employer shall directly or indirectly pay the fine of any officer or employee convicted of any willful violation of this Act.

(c) Penalty for violations. Any person who willfully violates this section shall be fined not more than $5,000 or imprisoned for not more than one year, or both.

§504.   (§504) Prohibition against certain persons holding office

(a) Membership in Communist Party; persons convicted of robbery, bribery, etc. No person who is or has been a member of the Communist Party or who has been convicted of, or served any part of a prison term resulting from his conviction of, robbery, bribery, extortion, embezzlement, grand larceny, burglary, arson, violation of narcotics laws, murder, rape, assault with intent to kill, assault which inflicts grievous bodily injury, or a violation of subchapter III or IV of this chapter, any felony involving abuse or misuse of such person's position or employment in a labor organization or employee benefit plan to seek or obtain an illegal gain at the expense of the members of the labor organization or the beneficiaries of the employee benefit plan, or conspiracy to commit any such crimes or attempt to commit any such crimes, or a crime in which any of the foregoing crimes is an element, shall serve or be permitted to serve —

(1) as a consultant or adviser to any labor organization,

(2) as an officer, director, trustee, member of any executive board or similar governing body, business agent, manager, organizer, employee, or representative in any capacity of any labor organization,

(3) as a labor relations consultant or adviser to a person engaged in an industry or activity affecting commerce, or as an officer, director, agent, or employee of any group or association of employers dealing with any labor organization, or in a position having specific collective bargaining authority or direct responsibility in the area of labor-management relations in any corporation or association engaged in an industry or activity affecting commerce, or

(4) in a position which entitles its occupant to a share of the proceeds of, or as an officer or executive or administrative employee of, any entity whose activities are in whole or substantial part devoted to providing goods or services to any labor organization, or

(5) in any capacity, other than in his capacity as a member of such labor organization, that involves decisionmaking authority concerning, or decisionmaking authority over, or custody of, or control of the moneys, funds, assets, or property of any labor organization,

during or for the period of thirteen years after such conviction or after the end of such imprisonment, whichever is later, unless the sentencing court on the motion of the person convicted sets a lesser period of at least three years after such conviction or after the end of such imprisonment, whichever is later, or unless prior to the end of such period, in the case of a person so convicted or imprisoned, (A) his citizenship rights, having been revoked as a result of such conviction, have been fully restored, or (B) if the offense is a Federal offense, the sentencing judge or, if the offense is a State or local offense, the United States district court for the district in which the offense was committed, pursuant to sentencing guidelines and policy statements under section 994(a) of Title 28, determines that such person's service in any capacity referred to in clauses (1) through (5) would not be contrary to the purposes of this chapter. Prior to making any such determination the court shall hold a hearing and shall give notice of such proceeding by certified mail to the Secretary of Labor and to State, county, and Federal prosecuting officials in the jurisdiction or jurisdictions in which such person was convicted. The court's determination in any such proceeding shall be final. No person shall knowingly hire, retain, employ, or otherwise place any other person to serve in any capacity in violation of this subsection.

(b) *Penalty for violations.* Any person who willfully violates this section shall be fined not more than $10,000 or imprisoned for not more than five years, or both.

(c) *Definitions.* For the purpose of this section —

(1) A person shall be deemed to have been "convicted" and under the disability of "conviction" from the date of the judgment of the trial court, regardless of whether that judgment remains under appeal.

(2) A period of parole shall not be considered as part of a period of imprisonment.

(d) *Salary of persons barred from labor organization office during appeal of conviction.* Whenever any person —

(1) by operation of this section, has been barred from office or other position in a labor organization as a result of a conviction, and

(2) has filed an appeal of that conviction,

any salary which would be otherwise due such person by virtue of such office or position, shall be placed in escrow by the individual employer or organization responsible for payment of such salary. Payment of such salary into escrow shall continue for the duration of the appeal or for the period of time during which such salary would be otherwise due, whichever period is shorter. Upon the final reversal of such person's conviction on appeal, the amounts in escrow shall be paid to such person. Upon the final sustaining of such person's conviction on appeal, the amounts in escrow shall be returned to the individual employer or organization responsible for payment of those amounts. Upon final reversal of such person's conviction, such person shall no longer be barred by this statute from assuming any position from which such person was previously barred.

TITLE VI. MISCELLANEOUS PROVISIONS

§601.   (§521) Investigations by Secretary; applicability of other laws

(a) The Secretary shall have power when he believes it necessary in order to determine whether any person has violated or is about to violate any provision of this chapter (except subchapter II of this chapter) to make an investigation and in connection therewith he may enter such places and inspect such records and accounts and question such persons as he may deem necessary to enable him to determine the facts relative thereto. The Secretary may report to interested persons or officials concerning the facts required to be shown in any report required by this chapter and concerning the reasons for failure or refusal to file such a report or any other matter which he deems to be appropriate as a result of such an investigation.

(b) For the purpose of any investigation provided for in this chapter, the provisions of sections 49 and 50 of title 15 (relating to the attendance of witnesses and the production of books, papers, and documents), are made applicable to the jurisdiction, powers, and duties of the Secretary or any officers designated by him.

§602.   (§522) Extortionate picketing; penalty for violation

(a) It shall be unlawful to carry on picketing on or about the premises of any employer for the purpose of, or as part of any conspiracy or in furtherance of any plan or purpose for, the personal profit or enrichment of any individual (except a bona fide increase in wages or other employee benefits) by taking or obtaining any money or other thing of value from such employer against his will or with his consent.

(b) Any person who willfully violates this section shall be fined not more than $10,000 or imprisoned not more than twenty years, or both.

§603.   (§523) Retention of rights under other Federal and State laws

(a) Except as explicitly provided to the contrary, nothing in this chapter shall reduce or limit the responsibilities of any labor organization or any officer, agent, shop steward, or other representative of a labor organization, or of any trust in which a labor organization is interested, under any other Federal law or under the laws of any State, and, except as explicitly provided to the contrary, nothing in this chapter shall take away any right or bar any remedy to which members of a labor organization are entitled under such other Federal law or law of any State.

(b) Nothing contained in this chapter and section 186(a)-(c) of this title shall be construed to supersede or impair or otherwise affect the provisions of the Railway Labor Act, as amended [45 U.S.C. §151 et seq.], or any of the obligations, rights, benefits, privileges, or immunities of any carrier, employee, organization, representative, or person subject thereto; nor shall anything contained in this chapter be construed to confer any rights, privileges, immunities, or defenses upon employers, or to impair or otherwise affect the rights of any person under the National Labor Relations Act, as amended [29 U.S.C. §151 et seq.].

§604.   (§524) Effect on State laws

Nothing in this chapter shall be construed to impair or diminish the authority of any State to enact and enforce general criminal laws with respect to robbery, bribery, extortion, embezzlement, grand larceny, burglary, arson, violation of narcotics laws, murder, rape, assault with intent to kill, or assault which inflicts grievous bodily injury, or conspiracy to commit any of such crimes.

§2201. (§524a) Elimination of racketeering activities threat; State legislation governing collective bargaining representative*

Notwithstanding this or any other Act regulating labor-management relations, each State shall have the authority to enact and enforce, as part of a comprehensive statutory system to eliminate the threat of pervasive racketeering activity in an industry that is, or over time has been, affected by such activity, a provision of law that applies equally to employers, employees, and collective bargaining representatives, which provision of law governs service in any position in a local labor organization which acts or seeks to act in that State as a collective bargaining representative pursuant to the National Labor Relations Act [29 U.S.C. §151 et seq.], in the industry that is subject to that program.*

§605. (§525) Service of process

For the purposes of this chapter, service of summons, subpena, or other legal process of a court of the United States upon an officer or agent of a labor organization in his capacity as such shall constitute service upon the labor organization.

§606. (§526) Applicability of administrative procedure provisions

The provisions of subchapter II of chapter 5, and chapter 7, of title 5 shall be applicable to the issuance, amendment, or rescission of any rules or regulations, or any adjudication authorized or required pursuant to the provisions of this chapter.

§607. (§527) Cooperation with other agencies and departments

In order to avoid unnecessary expense and duplication of functions among Government agencies, the Secretary may make such arrangements or agreements for cooperation or mutual assistance in the performance of his functions under this chapter and the functions of any such agency as he may find to be practicable and consistent with law. The Secretary may utilize

---

* This section was added by Pub. L. 98-473, Title II, §2201, Oct. 12, 1984, 98 Stat. 2192.

the facilities or services of any department, agency, or establishment of the United States or of any State or political subdivision of a State, including the services of any of its employees, with the lawful consent of such department, agency, or establishment; and each department, agency, or establishment of the United States is authorized and directed to cooperate with the Secretary and, to the extent permitted by law, to provide such information and facilities as he may request for his assistance in the performance of his functions under this chapter. The Attorney General or his representative shall receive from the Secretary for appropriate action such evidence developed in the performance of his functions under this chapter as may be found to warrant consideration for criminal prosecution under the provisions of this chapter or other Federal law.

§608.   (§528) Criminal contempt

No person shall be punished for any criminal contempt allegedly committed outside the immediate presence of the court in connection with any civil action prosecuted by the Secretary or any other person in any court of the United States under the provisions of this chapter unless the facts constituting such criminal contempt are established by the verdict of the jury in a proceeding in the district court of the United States, which jury shall be chosen and empaneled in the manner prescribed by the law governing trial juries in criminal prosecutions in the district courts of the United States.

§609.   (§529) Prohibition on certain discipline by labor organization

It shall be unlawful for any labor organization, or any officer, agent, shop steward, or other representative of a labor organization, or any employee thereof to fine, suspend, expel, or otherwise discipline any of its members for exercising any right to which he is entitled under the provisions of this chapter. The provisions of section 412 of this title shall be applicable in the enforcement of this section.

§610.   (§530) Deprivation of rights by violence; penalty

It shall be unlawful for any person through the use of force or violence, or threat of the use of force or violence, to restrain, coerce, or intimidate, or attempt to restrain, coerce, or intimidate any member of a labor organization for the purpose of interfering with or preventing the exercise of any right to which he is entitled under the provisions of this chapter. Any person who willfully violates this section shall be fined not more than $1,000 or imprisoned for not more than one year, or both.

§611.   (§531) Separability of provisions

If any provision of this chapter, or the application of such provision to any person or circumstances, shall be held invalid, the remainder of this chapter or the application of such provision to persons or circumstances other than those as to which it is held invalid, shall not be affected thereby.

Federal Arbitration Act — Selected Provisions[*]
61 Stat. 669 (1947), as amended, 9 U.S.C. §§1 et seq.

§1. "Maritime transactions" and "commerce" defined; exceptions to operation of title

"Maritime transactions", as herein defined, means charter parties, bills of lading of water carriers, agreements relating to wharfage, supplies furnished vessels or repairs to vessels, collisions, or any other matters in foreign commerce which, if the subject of controversy, would be embraced within admiralty jurisdiction; "commerce", as herein defined, means commerce among the several States or with foreign nations, or in any Territory of the United States or in the District of Columbia, or between any such Territory and another, or between any such Territory and any State or foreign nation, or between the District of Columbia and any State or Territory or foreign nation, but nothing herein contained shall apply to contracts of employment of seamen, railroad employees, or any other class of workers engaged in foreign or interstate commerce.[*]

§2. Validity, irrevocability and enforcement of agreements to arbitrate

A written provision in any maritime transaction or a contract evidencing a transaction involving commerce to settle by arbitration a controversy thereafter arising out of such contract or transaction, or the refusal to perform the whole or any part thereof, or an agreement in writing to submit to arbitration an existing controversy arising out of such a contract, transaction, or refusal, shall be valid, irrevocable, and enforceable, save upon such grounds as exist at law or in equity for the revocation of any contract.

§3. Stay of proceedings where issue therein referable to arbitration

If any suit or proceeding be brought in any of the courts of the United States upon any issue referable to arbitration under an agreement in writing for such arbitration, the court in which such suit is pending, upon being satisfied that the issue involved in such suit or proceeding is referable to arbitration under such an agreement, shall on application of one of the parties

---

* [This law is derived from Act of Feb. 12, 1925, c.213, 43 Stat. 883. — EDS.]

stay the trial of the action until such arbitration has been had in accordance with the terms of the agreement, providing the applicant for the stay is not in default in proceeding with such arbitration.

§4. Failure to arbitrate under agreement; petition to United States court having jurisdiction for order to compel arbitration; notice and service thereof; hearing and determination

A party aggrieved by the alleged failure, neglect, or refusal of another to arbitrate under a written agreement for arbitration may petition any United States district court which, save for such agreement, would have jurisdiction under Title 28, in a civil action or in admiralty of the subject matter of a suit arising out of the controversy between the parties, for an order directing that such arbitration proceed in the manner provided for in such agreement. . . .

§5. Appointment of arbitrators or umpire

If in the agreement provision be made for a method of naming or appointing an arbitrator or arbitrators or an umpire, such method shall be followed; but if no method be provided therein, or if a method be provided and any party thereto shall fail to avail himself of such method, or if for any other reason there shall be a lapse in the naming of an arbitrator or arbitrators or umpire, or in filling a vacancy, then upon the application of either party to the controversy the court shall designate and appoint an arbitrator or arbitrators or umpire, as the case may require, who shall act under the said agreement with the same force and effect as if he or they had been specifically named therein; and unless otherwise provided in the agreement the arbitration shall be by a single arbitrator.

[Sections 6-8, 9 U.S.C. §§6-8, are omitted.]

§9. Award of arbitrators; confirmation; jurisdiction; procedure

If the parties in their agreement have agreed that a judgment of the court shall be entered upon the award made pursuant to the arbitration, and shall specify the court, then at any time within one year after the award is made any party to the arbitration may apply to the court so specified for an order confirming the award, and thereupon the court must grant such an order unless the award is vacated, modified, or corrected as prescribed in sections 10 and 11 of this title. If no court is specified in the agreement of the parties, then such application may be made to the United States court in and for the district within which such award was made. . . .

§10. Same; vacation; grounds; rehearing

(a) In any of the following cases the United States court in and for the district wherein the award was made may make an order vacating the award upon the application of any party to the arbitration —

(1) where the award was procured by corruption, fraud, or undue means;

(2) where there was evident partiality or corruption in the arbitrators, or either of them;

(3) where the arbitrators were guilty of misconduct in refusing to postpone the hearing, upon sufficient cause shown, or in refusing to hear evidence pertinent and material to the controversy; or of any other misbehavior by which the rights of any party have been prejudiced; or

(4) where the arbitrators exceeded their powers, or so imperfectly executed them that a mutual, final, and definite award upon the subject matter submitted was not made.

(b) If an award is vacated and the time within which the agreement required the award to be made has not expired, the court may, in its discretion, direct a rehearing by the arbitrators.

(c) The United States district court for the district wherein an award was made that was issued pursuant to section 580 of title 5 may make an order vacating the award upon the application of a person, other than a party to the arbitration, who is adversely affected or aggrieved by the award, if the use of arbitration or the award is clearly inconsistent with the factors set forth in section 572 of title 5.[*]

§11. Same; modification or correction; grounds; order

In either of the following cases the United States court in and for the district wherein the award was made may make an order modifying or correcting the award upon the application of any party to the arbitration —

(a) Where there was an evident material miscalculation of figures or an evident material mistake in the description of any person, thing, or property referred to in the award.

---

[*] As added by Pub. L. 101-552 (1990) and redesignated as subsection "c" by Pub. L. 107-169 (2002).

(b) Where the arbitrators have awarded upon a matter not submitted to them, unless it is a matter not affecting the merits of the decision upon the matter submitted.

(c) Where the award is imperfect in matter of form not affecting the merits of the controversy.

The order may modify and correct the award, so as to effect the intent thereof and promote justice between the parties.

§12. Notice of motions to vacate or modify; service; stay of proceedings

Notice of a motion to vacate, modify, or correct an award must be served upon the adverse party or his attorney within three months after the award is filed or delivered. . . . For the purposes of the motion any judge who might make an order to stay the proceedings in an action brought in the same court may make an order, to be served with the notice of motion, staying the proceedings of the adverse party to enforce the award.

[Sections 13-16 of Chapter 1 and Chapters 2-3 are omitted.]

United States Bankruptcy Code — Selected Provisions[*]
92 Stat. 2549 (1978), as amended, 11 U.S.C. §§101 et seq.

§1113.   Rejection of collective bargaining agreements[**]

(a) The debtor in possession, or the trustee if one has been appointed under the provisions of this chapter, other than a trustee in a case covered by subchapter IV of this chapter and by title I of the Railway Labor Act, may assume or reject a collective bargaining agreement only in accordance with the provisions of this section.[*][**]'

(b)(1) Subsequent to filing a petition and prior to filing an application seeking rejection of a collective bargaining agreement, the debtor in possession or trustee (hereinafter in this section, "trustee" shall include a debtor in possession), shall—

(A) make a proposal to the authorized representative of the employees covered by such agreement, based on the most complete and reliable information available at the time of such proposal, which provides for those necessary modifications in the employees benefits and protections that are necessary to permit the reorganization of the debtor and assures that all creditors, the debtor and all of the affected parties are treated fairly and equitably; and

(B) provide, subject to subsection (d)(3), the representative of the employees with such relevant information as is necessary to evaluate the proposal.

(2) During the period beginning on the date of the making of a proposal provided for in paragraph (1) and ending on the date of the hearing provided for in subsection (d)(1), the trustee shall meet, at reasonable times, with the authorized representative to confer in good faith in attempting to reach mutually satisfactory modifications of such agreement.

(c) The court shall approve an application for rejection of a collective bargaining agreement only if the court finds that—

(1) the trustee has, prior to the hearing, made a proposal that fulfills the requirements of subsection (b)(1);

(2) the authorized representative of the employees has refused to accept such proposal without good cause; and

(3) the balance of the equities clearly favors rejection of such agreement.

---

[*] [Section references are to the United States Code. — Eds.]
[**] Added by Pub. L. 98-353, Title III, §541(a), July 10, 1984, 98 Stat. 390.

(d)(1) Upon the filing of an application for rejection the court shall schedule a hearing to be held not later than fourteen days after the date of the filing of such application. All interested parties may appear and be heard at such hearing. Adequate notice shall be provided to such parties at least ten days before the date of such hearing. The court may extend the time for the commencement of such hearing for a period not exceeding seven days where the circumstances of the case, and the interests of justice require such extension, or for additional periods of time to which the trustee and representative agree.

(2) The court shall rule on such application for rejection within thirty days after the date of the commencement of the hearing. In the interests of justice, the court may extend such time for ruling for such additional period as the trustee and the employees' representative may agree to. If the court does not rule on such application within thirty days after the date of the commencement of the hearing, or within such additional time as the trustee and the employees' representative may agree to, the trustee may terminate or alter any provisions of the collective bargaining agreement pending the ruling of the court on such application.

(3) The court may enter such protective orders, consistent with the need of the authorized representative of the employee (sic) to evaluate the trustee's proposal and the application for rejection, as may be necessary to prevent disclosure of information provided to such representative where such disclosure could compromise the position of the debtor with respect to its competitors in the industry in which it is engaged.

(e) If during a period when the collective bargaining agreement continues in effect, and if essential to the continuation of the debtor's business, or in order to avoid irreparable damage to the estate, the court, after notice and a hearing, may authorize the trustee to implement interim changes in the terms, conditions, wages, benefits, or work rules provided by a collective bargaining agreement. Any hearing under this paragraph shall be scheduled in accordance with the needs of the trustee. The implementation of such interim changes shall not render the application for rejection moot.

(f) No provision of this title shall be construed to permit a trustee to unilaterally terminate or alter any provisions of a collective bargaining agreement prior to compliance with the provisions of this section.

§1114. Payment of insurance benefits to retired employees

(a) For purposes of this section, the term "retiree benefits" means payments to any entity or person for the purpose of providing or reimbursing payments for retired employees and their spouses and dependents, for medical, surgical, or hospital care benefits, or benefits in the event of sickness, accident, disability, or death under any plan, fund, or program (through the purchase of insurance or otherwise) maintained or established in whole or in part by the debtor prior to filing a petition commencing a case under this title.

(b)(1) For purposes of this section, the term "authorized representative" means the authorized representative designated pursuant to subsection (c) for persons receiving any retiree benefits covered by a collective bargaining agreement or subsection (d) in the case of persons receiving retiree benefits not covered by such an agreement.

(2) Committees of retired employees appointed by the court pursuant to this section shall have the same rights, powers, and duties as committees appointed under sections 1102 and 1103 of this title for the purpose of carrying out the purposes of sections 1114 and 1129(a)(13) and, as permitted by the court, shall have the power to enforce the rights of persons under this title as they relate to retiree benefits.

(c)(1) A labor organization shall be, for purposes of this section, the authorized representative of those persons receiving any retiree benefits covered by any collective bargaining agreement to which that labor organization is signatory, unless (A) such labor organization elects not to serve as the authorized representative of such persons, or (B) the court, upon a motion by any party in interest, after notice and hearing, determines that different representation of such persons is appropriate.

(2) In cases where the labor organization referred to in paragraph (1) elects not to serve as the authorized representative of those persons receiving any retiree benefits covered by any collective bargaining agreement to which that labor organization is signatory, or in cases where the court, pursuant to paragraph (1) finds different representation of such persons appropriate, the court, upon a motion by any party in interest, and after notice and a hearing, shall appoint a committee of retired employees if the debtor seeks to modify or not pay the retiree benefits or if the court otherwise determines that it is appropriate, from among such persons, to serve as the authorized representative of such persons under this section.

(d) The court, upon a motion by any party in interest, and after notice and a hearing, shall appoint a committee of retired employees if the debtor seeks to modify or not pay the retiree benefits or if the court otherwise determines that it is appropriate, to serve as the authorized representative, under this section, of those persons receiving any retiree benefits not covered by a collective bargaining agreement.

(e)(1) Notwithstanding any other provision of this title, the debtor in possession, or the trustee if one has been appointed under the provisions of this chapter (hereinafter in this section "trustee" shall include a debtor in possession), shall timely pay and shall not modify any retiree benefits, except that —

       (A) the court, on motion of the trustee or authorized representative, and after notice and a hearing, may order modification of such payments, pursuant to the provisions of subsections (g) and (h) of this section, or

       (B) the trustee and the authorized representative of the recipients of those benefits may agree to modification of such payments,
after which such benefits as modified shall continue to be paid by the trustee.

(2) Any payment for retiree benefits required to be made before a plan confirmed under section 1129 of this title is effective has the status of an allowed administrative expense as provided in section 503 of this title.

(f)(1) Subsequent to filing a petition and prior to filing an application seeking modification of the retiree benefits, the trustee shall —

       (A) make a proposal to the authorized representative of the retirees, based on the most complete and reliable information available at the time of such proposal, which provides for those necessary modifications in the retiree benefits that are necessary to permit the reorganization of the debtor and assures that all creditors, the debtor and all of the affected parties are treated fairly and equitably; and

       (B) provide, subject to subsection (k)(3), the representative of the retirees with such relevant information as is necessary to evaluate the proposal.

(2) During the period beginning on the date of the making of a proposal provided for in paragraph (1), and ending on the date of the hearing provided for in subsection (k)(1), the trustee shall meet, at reasonable times, with the authorized representative to confer in good faith in attempting to reach mutually satisfactory modifications of such retiree benefits.

(g) The court shall enter an order providing for modification in the payment of retiree benefits if the court finds that —

       (1) the trustee has, prior to the hearing, made a proposal that fulfills the requirements of subsection (f);

       (2) the authorized representative of the retirees has refused to accept such proposal without good cause; and

(3) such modification is necessary to permit the reorganization of the debtor and assures that all creditors, the debtor, and all of the affected parties are treated fairly and equitably, and is clearly favored by the balance of the equities;

except that in no case shall the court enter an order providing for such modification which provides for a modification to a level lower than that proposed by the trustee in the proposal found by the court to have complied with the requirements of this subsection and subsection (f): *Provided, however,* That at any time after an order is entered providing for modification in the payment of retiree benefits, or at any time after an agreement modifying such benefits is made between the trustee and the authorized representative of the recipients of such benefits, the authorized representative may apply to the court for an order increasing those benefits which order shall be granted if the increase in retiree benefits sought is consistent with the standard set forth in paragraph (3): *Provided further,* That neither the trustee nor the authorized representative is precluded from making more than one motion for a modification order governed by this subsection.

(h)(1) Prior to a court issuing a final order under subsection (g) of this section, if essential to the continuation of the debtor's business, or in order to avoid irreparable damage to the estate, the court, after notice and a hearing, may authorize the trustee to implement interim modifications in retiree benefits.

(2) Any hearing under this subsection shall be scheduled in accordance with the needs of the trustee.

(3) The implementation of such interim changes does not render the motion for modification moot.

(i) No retiree benefits paid between the filing of the petition and the time a plan confirmed under section 1129 of this title becomes effective shall be deducted or offset from the amounts allowed as claims for any benefits which remain unpaid, or from the amounts to be paid under the plan with respect to such claims for unpaid benefits, whether such claims for unpaid benefits are based upon or arise from a right to future unpaid benefits or from any benefits not paid as a result of modifications allowed pursuant to this section.

(j) No claim for retiree benefits shall be limited by section 502(b)(7) of this title.

(k)(1) Upon the filing of an application for modifying retiree benefits, the court shall schedule a hearing to be held not later than fourteen days after the date of the filing of such application. All interested parties may appear and be heard at such hearing. Adequate notice shall be provided to such parties at least ten days before the date of such hearing. The court may extend the time for the commencement of such hearing for a period not exceeding seven days where the circumstances of the case, and the interests of justice require such extension, or for additional periods of time to which the trustee and the authorized representative agree.

(2) The court shall rule on such application for modification within ninety days after the date of the commencement of the hearing. In the interests of justice, the court may extend such time for ruling for such additional period as the trustee and the authorized representative may agree to. If the court does not rule on such application within ninety days after the date of the commencement of the hearing, or within such additional time as the trustee and the authorized representative may agree to, the trustee may implement the proposed modifications pending the ruling of the court on such application.

(3) The court may enter such protective orders, consistent with the need of the authorized representative of the retirees to evaluate the trustee's proposal and the application for modification, as may be necessary to prevent disclosure of information provided to such representative where such disclosure could compromise the position of the debtor with respect to its competitors in the industry in which it is engaged.

(*l*) This section shall not apply to any retiree, or the spouse or dependents of such retiree, if such retiree's gross income for the twelve months preceding the filing of the bankruptcy petition equals or exceeds $250,000, unless such retiree can demonstrate to the satisfaction of the court that he is unable to obtain health, medical, life, and disability coverage for himself, his spouse, and his dependents who would otherwise be covered by the employer's insurance plan, comparable to the coverage provided by the employer on the day before the filing of a petition under this title.

§1167.   Collective bargaining agreements

Notwithstanding section 365 of this title, neither the court nor the trustee may change the wages or working conditions of employees of the debtor established by a collective bargaining agreement that is subject to the Railway Labor Act except in accordance with section 6 of such Act.

Selected Forms

National Labor Relations Board

Form NLRB-501   Charge Against Employer
Form NLRB-502   Petition
Form NLRB-508   Charge Against Labor Organization or Its Agents

National Mediation Board

Form NMB-1   Application for Investigation of Representation Dispute
Form NMB-2   Application for Mediation Services

Please Review the Following Important Information Before Filling Out a Charge Form!

- Please call an Information Officer in the Regional Office nearest you for assistance in filing a charge. The Information Officer will be happy to answer your questions about the charge form or to draft the charge on your behalf. Seeking assistance from an Information Officer may help you to avoid having the processing of your charge delayed or your charge dismissed because of mistakes made in completing the form.
- Please be advised that not every workplace action that you may view as unfair constitutes an unfair labor practice within the jurisdiction of the National Labor Relations Act (NLRA). Please click on the Help Desk button for more information on matters covered by the NLRA.
- The section of the charge form called, "Basis of Charge," seeks only a brief description of the alleged unfair labor practice. You should **NOT** include a detailed recounting of the evidence in support of the charge or a list of the names and telephone numbers of witnesses.
- After completing the charge form, be sure to sign and date the charge and mail or deliver the completed form to the appropriate Regional Office.
- A charge should be filed with the Regional Office which has jurisdiction over the geographic area of the United States where the unfair labor practice occurred. For example, an unfair labor practice charge alleging that an employer unlawfully discharged an employee would usually be filed with the Regional Office having jurisdiction over the worksite where the employee was employed prior to his/her discharge. An Information Officer will be pleased to assist you in locating the appropriate Regional Office in which to file your charge.
- The NLRB's Rules and Regulations state that it is the responsibility of the individual, employer or union filing a charge to timely and properly serve a copy of the charge on the person, employer or union against whom such charge is made.
- By statute, only charges filed and served within **six (6) months** of the date of the event or conduct, which is the subject of that charge, will be processed by the NLRB.

FORM EXEMPT UNDER 44 U.S.C 3512

INTERNET FORM NLRB-501 (2-08)	UNITED STATES OF AMERICA NATIONAL LABOR RELATIONS BOARD **CHARGE AGAINST EMPLOYER**	**DO NOT WRITE IN THIS SPACE**	
		Case	Date Filed

INSTRUCTIONS:
File an original with NLRB Regional Director for the region in which the alleged unfair labor practice occurred or is occurring.

1. EMPLOYER AGAINST WHOM CHARGE IS BROUGHT

a. Name of Employer	b. Tel. No.
	c. Cell No.
	f. Fax No.
d. Address *(Street, city, state, and ZIP code)* e. Employer Representative	g. e-Mail
	h. Number of workers employed
i. Type of Establishment *(factory, mine, wholesaler, etc.)* j. Identify principal product or service	

k. The above-named employer has engaged in and is engaging in unfair labor practices within the meaning of section 8(a), subsections (1) and *(list subsections)* _____ of the National Labor Relations Act, and these unfair labor practices are practices affecting commerce within the meaning of the Act, or these unfair labor practices are unfair practices affecting commerce within the meaning of the Act and the Postal Reorganization Act.

2. Basis of the Charge *(set forth a clear and concise statement of the facts constituting the alleged unfair labor practices)*

3. Full name of party filing charge *(if labor organization, give full name, including local name and number)*

4a. Address *(Street and number, city, state, and ZIP code)*	4b. Tel. No.
	4c. Cell No.
	4d. Fax No.
	4e. e-Mail

5. Full name of national or international labor organization of which it is an affiliate or constituent unit *(to be filled in when charge is filed by a labor organization)*

6. DECLARATION	Tel. No.
I declare that I have read the above charge and that the statements are true to the best of my knowledge and belief.	Office, if any, Cell No.
By _____ _____ (signature of representative or person making charge) (Print/type name and title or office, if any)	Fax No.
	e-Mail
Address _____ (date)	

WILLFUL FALSE STATEMENTS ON THIS CHARGE CAN BE PUNISHED BY FINE AND IMPRISONMENT (U.S. CODE, TITLE 18, SECTION 1001)

PRIVACY ACT STATEMENT

Solicitation of the information on this form is authorized by the National Labor Relations Act (NLRA), 29 U.S.C. § 151 *et seq.* The principal use of the information is to assist the National Labor Relations Board (NLRB) in processing unfair labor practice and related proceedings or litigation. The routine uses for the information are fully set forth in the Federal Register, 71 Fed. Reg. 74942-43 (Dec. 13, 2006). The NLRB will further explain these uses upon request. Disclosure of this information to the NLRB is voluntary; however, failure to supply the information will cause the NLRB to decline to invoke its processes.

PLEASE REVIEW THE FOLLOWING
IMPORTANT INFORMATION
BEFORE FILLING OUT A PETITION FORM!

- Please call an Information Officer in the Regional Office nearest you for assistance in filing a petition. The Information Officer will be happy to answer your questions about the petition form or to draft the petition on your behalf.
- Check one of the boxes listed under Question 1 representing the purpose of the petition: RC-a union desires to be certified as the bargaining representative of employees; RM-an employer seeks an election because one or more individuals or unions have sought recognition as the bargaining representative, or based on a reasonable belief supported by objective considerations that the currently recognized union has lost its majority status; RD-employees seek to remove the currently recognized union as the bargaining representative; UD-employees desire an election to restrict the union's right to maintain a union shop clause; UC-a labor organization or an employer seeks clarification of the existing bargaining unit; or AC-a labor organization or an employer seeks an amendment of a certification issued in a prior Board case.
- Under Question 5, please carefully describe the bargaining unit involved in the petition, listing the job classifications included in the unit and the job classifications excluded from the unit.
- After completing the petition form, be sure to sign and date the petition and mail, fax or hand deliver the completed petition form to the appropriate Regional Office.
- The filing of a petition seeking certification or decertification of a union should be accompanied by a sufficient showing of interest to support such a petition—i.e., a showing that 30% or more of the employees in the bargaining unit seek to be represented by the union or seek to decertify the currently recognized union. If the original showing is not sent to the Region with the filing of the petition, a party must deliver the original showing of interest to the Region within **48 hours** after the filing of the petition, but in no event later than the last day on which a petition may be timely filed.
- Be sure to include telephone and fax numbers of the parties since this will be a significant aid to the processing of the petition.
- Be sure to include the name and address of any other labor organization or individuals known to have a representative interest in any of the employees in the unit described in Question 5 of the petition.
- A petition should be filed with the Regional Office where the bargaining unit exists. If the bargaining unit exists in two or more Regions, it can be filed in any of such Regions. An Information Officer will be happy to assist you in locating the appropriate Regional Office in which to file your petition.

FORM EXEMPT UNDER 44 U.S.C.

INTERNET FORM NLRB-502 (2-08)	UNITED STATES GOVERNMENT NATIONAL LABOR RELATIONS BOARD **PETITION**	**DO NOT WRITE IN THIS SPACE**	
		Case No.	Date Filed

INSTRUCTIONS: Submit an original of this Petition to the NLRB Regional Office in the Region in which the employer concerned is located.

The Petitioner alleges that the following circumstances exist and requests that the NLRB proceed under its proper authority pursuant to Section 9 of the NLRA.

1. PURPOSE OF THIS PETITION (if box RC, RM, or RD is checked and a charge under Section 8(b)(7) of the Act has been filed involving the Employer named herein, the statement following the description of the type of petition shall not be deemed made.) (Check One)

☐ **RC-CERTIFICATION OF REPRESENTATIVE** - A substantial number of employees wish to be represented for purposes of collective bargaining by Petitioner and Petitioner desires to be certified as representative of the employees.

☐ **RM-REPRESENTATION (EMPLOYER PETITION)** - One or more individuals or labor organizations have presented a claim to Petitioner to be recognized as the representative of employees of Petitioner.

☐ **RD-DECERTIFICATION (REMOVAL OF REPRESENTATIVE)** - A substantial number of employees assert that the certified or currently recognized bargaining representative is no longer their representative.

☐ **UD-WITHDRAWAL OF UNION SHOP AUTHORITY (REMOVAL OF OBLIGATION TO PAY DUES)** - Thirty percent (30%) or more of employees in a bargaining unit covered by an agreement between their employer and a labor organization desire that such authority be rescinded.

☐ **UC-UNIT CLARIFICATION**- A labor organization is currently recognized by Employer, but Petitioner seeks clarification of placement of certain employees:
(Check one) ☐ In unit not previously certified. ☐ In unit previously certified in Case No. _____

☐ **AC-AMENDMENT OF CERTIFICATION**- Petitioner seeks amendment of certification issued in Case No. _____
Attach statement describing the specific amendment sought.

2. Name of Employer	Employer Representative to contact	Tel. No.
3. Address(es) of Establishment(s) involved (Street and number, city, State, ZIP code)		Fax No.

4a. Type of Establishment (Factory, mine, wholesaler, etc.)	4b. Identify principal product or service	Cell No.
		e-Mail

5. Unit Involved (In UC petition, describe **present** bargaining unit and attach description of proposed clarification.)		6a. Number of Employees in Unit:
Included		Present
Excluded		Proposed (By UC/AC)
		6b. Is this petition supported by 30% or more of the employees in the unit?* ☐ Yes ☐ No *Not applicable in RM, UC, and AC

(If you have checked box RC in 1 above, check and complete EITHER item 7a or 7b, whichever is applicable)

7a. ☐ Request for recognition as Bargaining Representative was made on (Date) _____ and Employer declined recognition on or about (Date) _____ (If no reply received, so state).

7b. ☐ Petitioner is currently recognized as Bargaining Representative and desires certification under the Act.

8. Name of Recognized or Certified Bargaining Agent (If none, so state.)		Affiliation	
Address	Tel. No.	Date of Recognition or Certification	
	Cell No.	Fax No.	e-Mail

9. Expiration Date of Current Contract. If any (Month, Day, Year)	10. If you have checked box UD in 1 above, show here the date of execution of agreement granting union shop (Month, Day and Year)

11a. Is there now a strike or picketing at the Employer's establishment(s) Involved? Yes ☐ No ☐	11b. If so, approximately how many employees are participating?

11c. The Employer has been picketed by or on behalf of (Insert Name) _____ , a labor organization, of (Insert Address) _____ Since (Month, Day, Year) _____

12. Organizations or individuals other than Petitioner (and other than those named in items 8 and 11c), which have claimed recognition as representatives and other organizations and individuals known to have a representative interest in any employees in unit described in item 5 above. (If none, so state)

Name	Address	Tel. No.	Fax No.
		Cell No.	e-Mail

13. Full name of party filing petition (If labor organization, give full name, including local name and number)			
14a. Address (street and number, city, state, and ZIP code)	14b. Tel. No. EXT	14c. Fax No.	
	14d. Cell No.	14e. e-Mail	

15. Full name of national or international labor organization of which Petitioner is an affiliate or constituent (to be filled in when petition is filed by a labor organization)

I declare that I have read the above petition and that the statements are true to the best of my knowledge and belief.

Name (Print)	Signature	Title (if any)
Address (street and number, city, state, and ZIP code)	Tel. No.	Fax No.
	Cell No.	eMail

WILLFUL FALSE STATEMENTS ON THIS PETITION CAN BE PUNISHED BY FINE AND IMPRISONMENT (U.S. CODE, TITLE 18, SECTION 1001)

PRIVACY ACT STATEMENT

Solicitation of the information on this form is authorized by the National Labor Relations Act (NLRA), 29 U.S.C. § 151 *et seq.* The principal use of the information is to assist the National Labor Relations Board (NLRB) in processing unfair labor practice and related proceedings or litigation. The routine uses for the information are fully set forth in the Federal Register, 71 Fed. Reg. 74942-43 (Dec. 13, 2006). The NLRB will further explain these uses upon request. Disclosure of this information to the NLRB is voluntary; however, failure to supply the information will cause the NLRB to decline to invoke its processes.

Please Review the Following
Important Information
Before Filling Out a Charge Form!

- Please call an Information Officer in the Regional Office nearest you for assistance in filing a charge. The Information Officer will be happy to answer your questions about the charge form or to draft the charge on your behalf. Seeking assistance from an Information Officer may help you to avoid having the processing of your charge delayed or your charge dismissed because of mistakes made in completing the form.

- Please be advised that not every workplace action that you may view as unfair constitutes an unfair labor practice within the jurisdiction of the National Labor Relations Act (NLRA). Please click on the Help Desk button for more information on matters covered by the NLRA.

- The section of the charge form called, "Basis of Charge," seeks only a brief description of the alleged unfair labor practice. You should **NOT** include a detailed recounting of the evidence in support of the charge or a list of the names and telephone numbers of witnesses.

- After completing the charge form, be sure to sign and date the charge and mail or deliver the completed form to the appropriate Regional Office.

- A charge should be filed with the Regional Office which has jurisdiction over the geographic area of the United States where the unfair labor practice occurred. For example, an unfair labor practice charge alleging that an employer unlawfully discharged an employee would usually be filed with the Regional Office having jurisdiction over the worksite where the employee was employed prior to his/her discharge. An Information Officer will be pleased to assist you in locating the appropriate Regional Office in which to file your charge.

- The NLRB's Rules and Regulations state that it is the responsibility of the individual, employer or union filing a charge to timely and properly serve a copy of the charge on the person, employer or union against whom such charge is made.

- By statute, only charges filed and served within **six (6) months** of the date of the event or conduct, which is the subject of that charge, will be processed by the NLRB.

INTERNET FORM NLRB-508 (2-08)	UNITED STATES OF AMERICA NATIONAL LABOR RELATIONS BOARD CHARGE AGAINST LABOR ORGANIZATION OR ITS AGENTS	FORM EXEMPT UNDER 44 U.S.C 3512

DO NOT WRITE IN THIS SPACE

Case | Date Filed

INSTRUCTIONS: File an original with NLRB Regional Director for the region in which the alleged unfair labor practice occurred or is occurring.

1. LABOR ORGANIZATION OR ITS AGENTS AGAINST WHICH CHARGE IS BROUGHT

a. Name

b. Union Representative to contact

c. Address (Street, city, state, and ZIP code)

d. Tel. No. | e. Cell No.

f. Fax No. | g. e-Mail

h. The above-named organization(s) or its agents has (have) engaged in and is (are) engaging in unfair labor practices within the meaning of section 8(b), subsection(s) (list subsections) _____ of the National Labor Relations Act, and these unfair labor practices are unfair practices affecting commerce within the meaning of the Act, or these unfair labor practices are unfair practices affecting commerce within the meaning of the Act and the Postal Reorganization Act.

2. Basis of the Charge (set forth a clear and concise statement of the facts constituting the alleged unfair labor practices)

3. Name of Employer

4a. Tel. No. | b. Cell No.

c. Fax No. | d. e-Mail

5. Location of plant involved (street, city, state and ZIP code)

6. Employer representative to contact

7. Type of establishment (factory, mine, wholesaler, etc.) | 8. Identify principal product or service | 9. Number of workers employed

10. Full name of party filing charge

11a. Tel. No. | b. Cell No.

c. Fax No. | d. e-Mail

11. Address of party filing charge (street, city, state and ZIP code.)

12. DECLARATION

I declare that I have read the above charge and that the statements therein are true to the best of my knowledge and belief.

By _____ (signature of representative or person making charge) (Print/type name and title or office, if any)

Tel. No.

Cell No.

Fax No.

e-Mail

Address _____ (date) _____

WILLFUL FALSE STATEMENTS ON THIS CHARGE CAN BE PUNISHED BY FINE AND IMPRISONMENT (U.S. CODE, TITLE 18, SECTION 1001)

PRIVACY ACT STATEMENT

Solicitation of the information on this form is authorized by the National Labor Relations Act (NLRA), 29 U.S.C. § 151 et seq. The principal use of the information is to assist the National Labor Relations Board (NLRB) in processing unfair labor practice and related proceedings or litigation. The routine uses for the information are fully set forth in the Federal Register, 71 Fed. Reg. 74942-43 (Dec. 13, 2006). The NLRB will further explain these uses upon request. Disclosure of this information to the NLRB is voluntary; however, failure to supply the information will cause the NLRB to decline to invoke its processes.

Form NMB - 1 OMB No. 3140-0001 (Expiration Date 8/31/2017)

Application for Investigation of Representation Dispute

Date: _____

TO THE NATIONAL MEDIATION BOARD, Washington, D. C. 20005: A dispute has arisen among the employees of:

Name of Carrier:		Address:	
Contact:		City, State, Zip Code:	
Telephone Number:		Fax Number:	
E-Mail			

as to who is the representative of these employees designated and authorized in accordance with the requirements of the Railway Labor Act. The undersigned, one of the parties to the dispute, hereby requests the National Mediation Board to investigate this dispute, and to certify the name or names of the individuals or organizations authorized to represent the employees involved in accordance with Section 2, Ninth, of the Act.

PARTIES TO DISPUTE

Petitioning organization or representative:	
Organization holding existing agreement, if any:	Date:
Other organization or representatives involved in dispute:	

CRAFT OR CLASS of Employees Involved – (If more than one craft or class, use a separate application)

Craft or Class	Number of Employees

Federal Law prohibits knowingly and willfully making materially false, fictitious, or fraudulent statements or representations in any matter within the jurisdiction of the U.S. Government. 18 U.S.C. § 1001. This includes the information provided on this application as well as the accompanying showing of interest.

EVIDENCE OF REPRESENTATION – this application is supported by:

	At least 50%

I declare that the information submitted is true to the best of my knowledge

Name and Signature:			
Title:			
Address:		Telephone:	
City, State, Zip Code:		Fax:	
E-Mail			

Instructions: Continue to page 2.
Form NMB - 1 OMB No. 3140-0001 (Expiration Date 08/31/2017)

Application for Investigation of Representation Dispute

APPLICANT NOTICE OF APPEARANCE

The _____ hereby enters the following names, addresses,
(Applicant Organization)

phone numbers, fax numbers, and email addresses for the individual(s) designated as the representative(s)

of _____ in connection with the Application for Investigation
(Applicant Organization)

of Representation Dispute:

Name & Title:		Telephone:	
Address:		Fax:	
City, State, Zip Code		Email:	
		Alternate Telephone:	

Name & Title:		Telephone:	
Address:		Fax:	
City, State, Zip Code		Email:	
		Alternate Telephone:	

Name & Title:		Telephone:	
Address:		Fax:	
City, State, Zip Code		Email:	
		Alternate Telephone:	

Filing Instructions: File this application in duplicate.   **Additional Sheets:** Use and attach additional sheets as needed.

According to the Paperwork Reduction Act of 1995, no persons are required to respond to a collection of information unless it displays a valid OMB control Number. The valid OMB control number for this information collection is 3140-0001. The time required to complete this information collection is estimated to average 15 minutes per response, including the time to review instructions, search existing data resources, gather the data needed, and complete and review the information collection.

Form NMB-2 OMB No. 3140-0002 (Expiration Date 08/31/2016)

Mail to:
Mediation Department
National Mediation board
1301 k Street NW, Suite 250 E.
Washington, DC 20005

Or fax to:
Mediation – 202-692-5084

email:mediation@nmb.gov

Application for Mediation Services

TO THE NATIONAL MEDIATION BOARD, Washington, D. C. 20005: A dispute has arisen between the parties shown below which has not been adjusted between them, and the services of the National Mediation Board under Section 5, First, of the Railway Labor Act, are hereby invoked on specific questions set forth below. The approximate number of employees involved is _____ in the craft(s) or class(es) of

_____ .

THE SPECIFIC ISSUE(S) IN DISPUTE (If necessary extend question on additional sheet or attach exhibit):

PARTIES TO DISPUTE

	Carrier		Organization/Individual
Carrier Name		Organization Name	
L. R. Official/Title		Organization Official/Title	
Address		Address	
City, State and Zip Code		City, State and Zip Code	
Telephone		Telephone	
Fax		Fax	
Email		Email	

WORKING AGREEMENT

If an agreement governing rates of pay, rules, or working conditions is in effect, give name of parties thereto and date thereof. If there is no such agreement, so state _____ .

COMPLIANCE WITH RAILWAY LABOR ACT

1. If this dispute involves change in the above-mentioned agreement, attach copy of the 30-day notice served by party desiring change and insert date of notice here _____ .

2. If this dispute involves the negotiation of a new or supplemental agreement, attach copy of request made by party desiring same and insert date of request here _____ .

3. If there has been refusal to confer, so state and give reason; otherwise, give date of last conference here _____ .

Signed at _____ this _____ of _____ 20_____ .
            (City and State)   (Day)   (Month)

	Carrier Official	Organization Official
Name:		
Title:		
Signature:		

Filing Instructions: File this application in duplicate.   **Additional Sheets:** Use and attach additional sheets as needed.

Updated October 27, 2008

NLRB Regulation

AMENDMENTS TO NLRB REPRESENTATION ELECTION RULES

Subpart C — Procedure Under Section 9(c) of the Act for the Determination of Questions Concerning Representation of Employees and for Clarification of Bargaining Units and for Amendment of Certifications Under Section 9(b) of the Act

§102.60   Petitions.

(a) *Petition for certification or decertification.* A petition for investigation of a question concerning representation of employees under paragraphs (1)(A)(i) and (1)(B) of Section 9(c) of the Act (hereinafter called a petition for certification) may be filed by an employee or group of employees or any individual or labor organization acting in their behalf or by an employer. A petition under paragraph (1)(A)(ii) of Section 9(c) of the Act, alleging that the individual or labor organization which has been certified or is being currently recognized as the bargaining representative is no longer such representative (hereinafter called a petition for decertification), may be filed by any employee or group of employees or any individual or labor organization acting in their behalf. Petitions under this section shall be in writing and signed, and either shall be sworn to before a notary public, Board agent, or other person duly authorized by law to administer oaths and take acknowledgments or shall contain a declaration by the person signing it, under the penalty of perjury, that its contents are true and correct (see 28 U.S.C. 1746). One original of the petition shall be filed, and a copy served on all parties named in the petition. A person filing a petition by facsimile pursuant to §102.114(f) shall also file an original for the Agency's records, but failure to do so shall not affect the validity of the filing by facsimile, if otherwise proper. A person filing a petition electronically pursuant to §102.114(i) need not file an original. Except as provided in §102.72, such petitions shall be filed with the regional director for the Region wherein the bargaining unit exists, or, if the bargaining unit exists in two or more Regions, with the regional director for any of such Regions. A certificate of service on all parties named in the petition shall also be filed with the regional director when the petition is filed. Along with the petition, the petitioner shall serve the Agency's description of procedures in representation cases and the Agency's Statement of Position form on all parties named in the petition. Prior to the transfer of the record to the Board, the petition may be withdrawn only with the consent of the regional director with whom such petition was filed. After the transfer of the record to the Board, the petition may be withdrawn only with the consent of the Board. Whenever the regional director or the Board, as the case may be, approves the withdrawal of any petition, the case shall be closed.

(b) *Petition for clarification of bargaining unit or petition for amendment of certification.* A petition for clarification of an existing bargaining unit or a petition for amendment of certification, in the absence of a question of representation, may be filed by a labor organization or by an employer. Where applicable the same procedures set forth in paragraph (a) of this section shall be followed.

§102.61   Contents of petition for certification; contents of petition for decertification; contents of petition for clarification of bargaining unit; contents of petition for amendment of certification.

(a) *RC Petitions.* A petition for certification, when filed by an employee or group of employees or an individual or labor organization acting in their behalf, shall contain the following:

(1) The name of the employer.

(2) The address of the establishments involved.

(3) The general nature of the employer's business.

(4) A description of the bargaining unit which the petitioner claims to be appropriate.

(5) The names and addresses of any other persons or labor organizations who claim to represent any employees in the alleged appropriate unit, and brief descriptions of the contracts, if any, covering the employees in such unit.

(6) The number of employees in the alleged appropriate unit.

(7) A statement that a substantial number of employees in the described unit wish to be represented by the petitioner. Evidence supporting the statement shall be filed with the petition in accordance with paragraph (f) of this section, but shall not be served on any party.

(8) A statement that the employer declines to recognize the petitioner as the representative within the meaning of Section 9(a) of the Act

or that the labor organization is currently recognized but desires certification under the Act.

(9) The name, affiliation, if any, and address of the petitioner, and the name, title, address, telephone number, facsimile number, and email address of the individual who will serve as the representative of the petitioner and accept service of all papers for purposes of the representation proceeding.

(10) Whether a strike or picketing is in progress at the establishment involved and, if so, the approximate number of employees participating, and the date such strike or picketing commenced.

(11) Any other relevant facts.

(12) The type, date(s), time(s) and location(s) of the election sought.

(b) *RM Petitions.* A petition for certification, when filed by an employer, shall contain the following:

(1) The name and address of the petitioner, and the name, title, address, telephone number, facsimile number, and email address of the individual who will serve as the representative of the petitioner and accept service of all papers for purposes of the representation proceeding.

(2) The general nature of the petitioner's business.

(3) A brief statement setting forth that one or more individuals or labor organizations have presented to the petitioner a claim to be recognized as the exclusive representative of all employees in the unit claimed to be appropriate; a description of such unit; and the number of employees in the unit.

(4) The name or names, affiliation, if any, and addresses of the individuals or labor organizations making such claim for recognition.

(5) A statement whether the petitioner has contracts with any labor organization or other representatives of employees and, if so, their expiration date(s).

(6) Whether a strike or picketing is in progress at the establishment involved and, if so, the approximate number of employees participating, and the date such strike or picketing commenced.

(7) Any other relevant facts.

(8) Evidence supporting the statement that a labor organization has made a demand for recognition on the employer or that the employer has good faith uncertainty about majority support for an existing representative. Such evidence shall be filed together with the petition, but if the evidence reveals the names and/or number of employees who no longer wish to be represented, the evidence shall not be served on any party. However, no proof of representation on the part of the labor organization claiming a majority is required and the regional director

shall proceed with the case if other factors require it unless the labor organization withdraws its claim to majority representation.

(9) The type, date(s), time(s) and location(s) of the election sought.

(c) *RD Petitions.* Petitions for decertification shall contain the following:

(1) The name of the employer.

(2) The address of the establishments and a description of the bargaining unit involved.

(3) The general nature of the employer's business.

(4) The name and address of the petitioner and affiliation, if any, and the name, title, address, telephone number, facsimile number, and email address of the individual who will serve as the representative of the petitioner and accept service of all papers for purposes of the representation proceeding.

(5) The name or names and addresses of the individuals or labor organizations who have been certified or are being currently recognized by the employer and who claim to represent any employees in the unit involved, and the expiration date of any contracts covering such employees.

(6) An allegation that the individuals or labor organizations who have been certified or are currently recognized by the employer are no longer the representative in the appropriate unit as defined in Section 9(a) of the Act.

(7) The number of employees in the unit.

(8) A statement that a substantial number of employees in the described unit no longer wish to be represented by the incumbent representative. Evidence supporting the statement shall be filed with the petition in accordance with paragraph (f) of this section, but shall not be served on any party.

(9) Whether a strike or picketing is in progress at the establishment involved and, if so, the approximate number of employees participating, and the date such strike or picketing commenced.

(10) Any other relevant facts.

(11) The type, date(s), time(s) and location(s) of the election sought.

(d) *UC Petitions.* A petition for clarification shall contain the following:

(1) The name of the employer and the name of the recognized or certified bargaining representative.

(2) The address of the establishment involved.

(3) The general nature of the employer's business.

(4) A description of the present bargaining unit, and, if the bargaining unit is certified, an identification of the existing certification.

(5) A description of the proposed clarification.

(6) The names and addresses of any other persons or labor organizations who claim to represent any employees affected by the proposed

clarifications, and brief descriptions of the contracts, if any, covering any such employees.

(7) The number of employees in the present bargaining unit and in the unit as proposed under the clarification.

(8) The job classifications of employees as to whom the issue is raised, and the number of employees in each classification.

(9) A statement by petitioner setting forth reasons why petitioner desires clarification of unit.

(10) The name, the affiliation, if any, and the address of the petitioner, and the name, title, address, telephone number, facsimile number, and email address of the individual who will serve as the representative of the petitioner and accept service of all papers for purposes of the representation proceeding.

(11) Any other relevant facts.

(e) *AC Petitions.* A petition for amendment of certification shall contain the following:

(1) The name of the employer and the name of the certified union involved.

(2) The address of the establishment involved.

(3) The general nature of the employer's business.

(4) Identification and description of the existing certification.

(5) A statement by petitioner setting forth the details of the desired amendment and reasons therefor.

(6) The names and addresses of any other persons or labor organizations who claim to represent any employees in the unit covered by the certification and brief descriptions of the contracts, if any, covering the employees in such unit.

(7) The name, the affiliation, if any, and the address of the petitioner, and the name, title, address, telephone number, facsimile number, and email address of the individual who will serve as the representative of the petitioner and accept service of all papers for purposes of the representation proceeding.

(8) Any other relevant facts.

(f) *Provision of original signatures.* Evidence filed pursuant to paragraphs (a)(7), (b)(8), or (c)(8) of this section together with a petition that is filed by facsimile or electronically, which includes original signatures that cannot be transmitted in their original form by the method of filing of the petition, may be filed by facsimile or in electronic form provided that the original documents are received by the regional director no later than 2 days after the facsimile or electronic filing.

§102.62   Election agreements; voter list; Notice of Election.

(a) *Consent election agreements with final regional director determinations of post-election disputes.* Where a petition has been duly filed, the employer and any individual or labor organizations representing a substantial number of employees involved may, with the approval of the regional director, enter into an agreement providing for the waiver of a hearing and for an election and further providing that post-election disputes will be resolved by the regional director. Such agreement, referred to as a consent election agreement, shall include a description of the appropriate unit, the time and place of holding the election, and the payroll period to be used in determining what employees within the appropriate unit shall be eligible to vote. Such election shall be conducted under the direction and supervision of the regional director. The method of conducting such election shall be consistent with the method followed by the regional director in conducting elections pursuant to §§102.69 and 102.70 except that the rulings and determinations by the regional director of the results thereof shall be final, and the regional director shall issue to the parties a certification of the results of the election, including certifications of representative where appropriate, with the same force and effect, in that case, as if issued by the Board, and except that rulings or determinations by the regional director in respect to any amendment of such certification shall also be final.

(b) *Stipulated election agreements with discretionary Board review.* Where a petition has been duly filed, the employer and any individuals or labor organizations representing a substantial number of the employees involved may, with the approval of the regional director, enter into an agreement providing for the waiver of a hearing and for an election as described in paragraph (a) of this section and further providing that the parties may request Board review of the regional director's resolution of post-election disputes. Such agreement, referred to as a stipulated election agreement, shall also include a description of the appropriate bargaining unit, the time and place of holding the election, and the payroll period to be used in determining which employees within the appropriate unit shall be eligible to vote. Such election shall be conducted under the direction and supervision of the regional director. The method of conducting such election and the post-election procedure shall be consistent with that followed by the regional director in conducting elections pursuant to §§102.69 and 102.70.

(c) *Full consent election agreements with final regional director determinations of pre- and post-election disputes.* Where a petition has been duly filed, the employer and any individual or labor organizations representing a substantial number of the employees involved may, with the approval of the regional director, enter into an agreement, referred to as a full consent election agreement, providing that pre- and post-election disputes will be resolved by the regional director. Such agreement provides for a hearing pursuant to §§102.63, 102.64, 102.65, 102.66 and 102.67 to determine if a question of representation exists. Upon the conclusion of such a hearing, the regional director shall issue a decision. The rulings and determinations by the regional director thereunder shall be final, with the same force and effect, in that case, as if issued by the Board. Any election ordered by the regional director shall be conducted under the direction and supervision of the regional director. The method of conducting such election shall be consistent with the method followed by the regional director in conducting elections pursuant to §§102.69 and 102.70, except that the rulings and determinations by the regional director of the results thereof shall be final, and the regional director shall issue to the parties a certification of the results of the election, including certifications of representative where appropriate, with the same force and effect, in that case, as if issued by the Board, and except that rulings or determinations by the regional director in respect to any amendment of such certification shall also be final.

(d) *Voter list.* Absent agreement of the parties to the contrary specified in the election agreement or extraordinary circumstances specified in the direction of election, within 2 business days after the approval of an election agreement pursuant to paragraphs (a) or (b) of this section, or issuance of a direction of election pursuant to paragraph (c) of this section, the employer shall provide to the regional director and the parties named in the agreement or direction a list of the full names, work locations, shifts, job classifications, and contact information (including home addresses, available personal email addresses, and available home and personal cellular ("cell") telephone numbers) of all eligible voters. The employer shall also include in a separate section of that list the same information for those individuals whom the parties have agreed should be permitted to vote subject to challenge or those individuals who, according to the direction of election, will be permitted to vote subject to challenge, including, for example, individuals in the classifications or other groupings that will be permitted to vote subject to challenge. In order to be timely filed and served, the list must be received by the regional director and the parties named in the agreement or direction respectively within 2 business days after the approval of the agreement or issuance of the direction unless a longer time is specified in the agreement or direction. The list of names shall be alphabetized (overall or by department) and be in an electronic format approved by the General Counsel unless the employer certifies that it does not possess the capacity to produce the list in the required form. When feasible, the list shall be filed electronically with the regional director and served electronically on the other parties named in the agreement or direction. A certificate of service on all parties shall be filed with the regional director when the voter list is filed. The employer's failure to file or serve the list within the specified time or in proper format shall be grounds for setting aside the election whenever proper and timely objections are filed under the provisions of §102.69(a). The employer shall be estopped from objecting to the failure to file or serve the list within the specified time or in the proper format if it is responsible for the failure. The parties shall not use the list for purposes other than the representation proceeding, Board proceedings arising from it, and related matters.

(e) *Notice of election.* Upon approval of the election agreement pursuant to paragraphs (a) or (b) of this section or with the direction of election pursuant to paragraph (c) of this section, the regional director shall promptly transmit the Board's Notice of Election to the parties and their designated representatives by email, facsimile, or by overnight mail (if neither an email address nor facsimile number was provided). The employer shall post and distribute the Notice of Election in accordance with §102.67(k). The employer's failure properly to post or distribute the election notices as required herein shall be grounds for setting aside the election whenever proper and timely objections are filed under the provisions of §102.69(a). A party shall be estopped from objecting to the nonposting of notices if it is responsible for the nonposting, and likewise shall be estopped from objecting to the nondistribution of notices if it is responsible for the nondistribution.

§102.63 Investigation of petition by regional director; notice of hearing; service of notice; Notice of Petition for Election; Statement of Position; withdrawal of notice of hearing.

(a) *Investigation; notice of hearing; Notice of Petition for Election.* (1) After a petition has been filed under §102.61(a), (b), or (c), if no agreement such as that provided in §102.62 is entered into and if it appears to the regional director that there is reasonable cause to believe that a question of representation affecting commerce exists, that the policies of the Act will be effectuated, and that an election will reflect the free choice of employees in an appropriate unit, the regional director shall prepare and cause to be served upon the parties and upon any known individuals or labor organizations purporting to act as representatives of any employees directly affected by such investigation, a notice of hearing before a hearing officer at a time and place fixed therein. Except in cases presenting unusually complex issues, the regional director shall set the hearing for a date 8 days from the date of service of the notice excluding intervening Federal holidays, but if the 8th day is a weekend or Federal holiday, the regional director shall set the hearing for the following business day. The regional director may postpone the hearing for up to 2 business days upon request of a party showing special circumstances. The regional director may postpone the opening of the hearing for more than 2 business days upon request of a party showing extraordinary circumstances. A copy of the petition, a description of procedures in representation cases, a "Notice of Petition for Election", and a Statement of Position form as described in paragraphs (b)(1) through (3) of this section, shall be served with such notice of hearing. Any such notice of hearing may be amended or withdrawn before the close of the hearing by the regional director on the director's own motion.

(2) Within 2 business days after service of the notice of hearing, the employer shall post the Notice of Petition for Election in conspicuous places, including all places where notices to employees are customarily posted, and shall also distribute it electronically if the employer customarily communicates with its employees electronically. The Notice of Petition for Election shall indicate that no final decisions have been made yet regarding the appropriateness of the petitioned-for bargaining unit and whether an election shall be conducted. The employer shall maintain the posting until the petition is dismissed or withdrawn or the Notice of Petition for Election is replaced by the Notice of Election. The employer's failure properly to post or distribute the Notice of Petition for Election may be grounds for setting aside the election whenever proper and timely objections are filed under the provisions of §102.69(a). A party shall be estopped from objecting to the nonposting of notices if it is responsible for the nonposting, and likewise shall be estopped from objecting to the nondistribution of notices if it is responsible for the nondistribution.

(b)(1) *Statement of Position in RC cases.* If a petition has been filed under §102.61(a) and the regional director has issued a notice of hearing, the employer shall file with the regional director and serve on the parties named in the petition its Statement of Position such that it is received by the regional director and the parties named in the petition by the date and time specified in the notice of hearing, which shall be at noon on the business day before the opening of the hearing if the hearing is set to open 8 days from service of the notice. The regional director may set the date and time for filing and serving the Statement of Position earlier than at noon on the business day before the hearing in the event the hearing is set to open more than 8 days from service of the notice. The regional director may postpone the time for filing and serving the Statement of Position for up to 2 business days upon request of a party showing special circumstances. The regional director may postpone the time for filing and serving the Statement of Position for more than 2 business days upon request of a party showing extraordinary circumstances.

The regional director may permit the employer to amend its Statement of Position in a timely manner for good cause.

   (i) The employer's Statement of Position shall state whether the employer agrees that the Board has jurisdiction over it and provide the requested information concerning the employer's relation to interstate commerce; state whether the employer agrees that the proposed unit is appropriate, and, if the employer does not so agree, state the basis for its contention that the proposed unit is inappropriate, and state the classifications, locations, or other employee groupings that must be added to or excluded from the proposed unit to make it an appropriate unit; identify any individuals whose eligibility to vote the employer intends to contest at the pre-election hearing and the basis of each such contention; raise any election bar; state the length of the payroll period for employees in the proposed unit and the most recent payroll period ending date; state the employer's position concerning the type, date(s), time(s), and location(s) of the election and the eligibility period; and describe all other issues the employer intends to raise at the hearing.

   (ii) The Statement of Position shall also state the name, title, address, telephone number, facsimile number, and email address of the individual who will serve as the representative of the employer and accept service of all papers for purposes of the representation proceeding and be signed by a representative of the employer.

   (iii) The Statement of Position shall include a list of the full names, work locations, shifts, and job classifications of all individuals in the proposed unit as of the payroll period preceding the filing of the petition who remain employed at the time of filing, and if the employer contends that the proposed unit is inappropriate, the employer shall separately list the full names, work locations, shifts, and job classifications of all individuals that the employer contends must be added to the proposed unit to make it an appropriate unit. The employer shall also indicate those individuals, if any, whom it believes must be excluded from the proposed unit to make it an appropriate unit. The list(s) of names shall be alphabetized (overall or by department) and be in an electronic format approved by the General Counsel unless the employer certifies that it does not possess the capacity to produce the list in the required form.

(2) *Statement of Position in RM cases.* If a petition has been filed under §102.61(b) and the regional director has issued a notice of hearing, each individual or labor organization named in the petition shall file with the regional director and serve on the other parties named in the petition its Statement of Position such that it is received by the regional director

and the parties named in the petition by the date and time specified in the notice of hearing, which shall be at noon on the business day before the opening of the hearing if the hearing is set to open 8 days from service of the notice. The regional director may set the date and time for filing and serving the Statement of Position earlier than at noon on the business day before the hearing in the event the hearing is set to open more than 8 days from service of the notice. The regional director may postpone the time for filing and serving the Statement of Position for up to 2 business days upon request of a party showing special circumstances. The regional director may postpone the time for filing and serving the Statement of Position for more than 2 business days upon request of a party showing extraordinary circumstances. The regional director may permit each individual or labor organization named in the petition to amend its Statement of Position in a timely manner for good cause.

(i) *Individual or labor organization's Statement of Position.* Each individual or labor organization's Statement of Position shall state whether it agrees that the Board has jurisdiction over the employer; state whether it agrees that the proposed unit is appropriate, and, if it does not so agree, state the basis for its contention that the proposed unit is inappropriate, and state the classifications, locations, or other employee groupings that must be added to or excluded from the proposed unit to make it an appropriate unit; identify any individuals whose eligibility to vote the individual or labor organization intends to contest at the pre-election hearing and the basis of each such contention; raise any election bar; state its position concerning the type, date(s), time(s), and location(s) of the election and the eligibility period; and describe all other issues it intends to raise at the hearing.

(ii) *Identification of representative for service of papers.* Each individual or labor organization's Statement of Position shall also state the name, title, address, telephone number, facsimile number, and email address of the individual who will serve as its representative and accept service of all papers for purposes of the representation proceeding and be signed by the individual or a representative of the individual or labor organization.

(iii) *Employer's Statement of Position.* Within the time permitted for filing the Statement of Position, the employer shall file with the regional director and serve on the parties named in the petition a list of the full names, work locations, shifts, and job classifications of all individuals in the proposed unit as of the payroll period preceding the filing of the petition who remain employed at the time of filing. The list(s) of names shall be alphabetized (overall or by department) and be in an electronic format approved by the General Counsel unless the employer certifies that it does not possess the capacity to produce the list in the required form. The employer's Statement of Position shall also state whether the employer agrees that the Board has jurisdiction over it and provide the requested information concerning the employer's relation to interstate commerce; identify any individuals whose eligibility to vote the employer intends to contest at the pre-election hearing and the basis of each such contention; and state the length of the payroll period for employees in the proposed unit and the most recent payroll period ending date. The regional director may permit the employer to amend its Statement of Position in a timely manner for good cause.

(3) *Statement of Position in RD cases.* If a petition has been filed under §102.61(c) and the regional director has issued a notice of hearing, the employer and the certified or recognized representative of employees shall file with the regional director and serve on the parties named in the petition their respective Statements of Position such that they are received by the regional director and the parties named in the petition by the date and time specified in the notice of hearing, which shall be at noon on the business day before the opening of the hearing if the hearing is set to open 8 days from service of the notice. The regional director may set the date and time for filing and serving the Statement of Position earlier than at noon on the business day before the hearing in the event the hearing is set to open more than 8 days from service of the notice. The regional director may postpone the time for filing and serving the Statement of Position for up to 2 business days upon request of a party showing special circumstances. The regional director may postpone the time for filing and serving the Statement of Position for more than 2 business days upon request of a party showing extraordinary circumstances. The regional director may permit the employer and the certified or recognized representative of employees to amend their respective Statements of Position in a timely manner for good cause.

(i) The Statements of Position of the employer and the certified or recognized representative shall state each party's position concerning the Board's jurisdiction over the employer; state whether each agrees that the proposed unit is appropriate, and, if not, state the basis for the contention that the proposed unit is inappropriate, and state the classifications, locations, or other employee groupings that must be added to or excluded from the proposed unit to make it an appropriate unit; identify any individuals whose eligibility to vote each party intends to contest at the pre-election hearing and the basis of each such contention; raise any election bar; and state each party's respective positions concerning the type, date(s), time(s), and location(s) of the election and the eligibility period; and describe all other issues each party intends to raise at the hearing.

(ii) The Statements of Position shall also state the name, title, address, telephone number, facsimile number, and email address of the individual who will serve as the representative of the employer or the certified or recognized representative of the employees and accept service of all papers for purposes of the representation proceeding and be signed by a representative of the employer or the certified or recognized representative, respectively.

(iii) The employer's Statement of Position shall also include a list of the full names, work locations, shifts, and job classifications of all individuals in the proposed unit as of the payroll period preceding the filing of the petition who remain employed at the time of filing, and if the employer contends that the proposed unit is inappropriate, the employer shall separately list the full names, work locations, shifts, and job classifications of all individuals that the employer contends must be added to the proposed unit to make it an appropriate unit. The employer shall also indicate those individuals, if any, whom it believes must be excluded from the proposed unit to make it an appropriate unit. The list(s) of names shall be alphabetized (overall or by department) and be in an electronic format approved by the General Counsel unless the employer certifies that it does not possess the capacity to produce the list in the required form. The employer's Statement of Position shall also provide the requested information concerning the employer's relation to interstate commerce and state the length of the payroll period for employees in the proposed unit and the most recent payroll period ending date.

(c) *UC or AC cases.* After a petition has been filed under §102.61(d) or (e), the regional director shall conduct an investigation and, as appropriate, may issue a decision without a hearing; or prepare and cause to be served upon the parties and upon any known individuals or labor organizations purporting to act as representatives of any employees directly affected by such investigation, a notice of hearing before a hearing officer at a time and place fixed therein; or take other appropriate action. If a notice of hearing is served, it shall be accompanied by a copy of the petition. Any such notice of hearing may be amended or withdrawn before the close of the hearing by the regional director on the director's own motion. All hearing and posthearing procedure under this paragraph (c) shall be in conformance with §§102.64 through

102.69 whenever applicable, except where the unit or certification involved arises out of an agreement as provided in §102.62(a), the regional director's action shall be final, and the provisions for review of regional director's decisions by the Board shall not apply. Dismissals of petitions without a hearing shall not be governed by §102.71. The regional director's dismissal shall be by decision, and a request for review therefrom may be obtained under §102.67, except where an agreement under §102.62(a) is involved.

§102.64   Conduct of hearing.

(a) The purpose of a hearing conducted under Section 9(c) of the Act is to determine if a question of representation exists. A question of representation exists if a proper petition has been filed concerning a unit appropriate for the purpose of collective bargaining or concerning a unit in which an individual or labor organization has been certified or is being currently recognized by the employer as the bargaining representative. Disputes concerning individuals' eligibility to vote or inclusion in an appropriate unit ordinarily need not be litigated or resolved before an election is conducted. If, upon the record of the hearing, the regional director finds that a question of representation exists, the director shall direct an election to resolve the question.

(b) Hearings shall be conducted by a hearing officer and shall be open to the public unless otherwise ordered by the hearing officer. At any time, a hearing officer may be substituted for the hearing officer previously presiding. Subject to the provisions of §102.66, it shall be the duty of the hearing officer to inquire fully into all matters and issues necessary to obtain a full and complete record upon which the Board or the regional director may discharge their duties under Section 9(c) of the Act.

(c) The hearing shall continue from day to day until completed unless the regional director concludes that extraordinary circumstances warrant otherwise. The regional director may, in the director's discretion, adjourn the hearing to a different place by announcement thereof at the hearing or by other appropriate notice.

§102.65   Motions; intervention; appeals of hearing officer's ruling.

(a) All motions, including motions for intervention pursuant to paragraphs (b) and (e) of this section, shall be in writing or, if made at the hearing, may be stated orally on the record and shall briefly state the order or relief sought and the grounds for such motion. An original and two copies of written motions shall be filed and a copy thereof immediately shall be served on the other parties to the proceeding. Motions made prior to the transfer of the record to the Board shall be filed with the regional director, except that motions made during the hearing shall be filed with the hearing officer. After the transfer of the record to the Board, all motions shall be filed with the Board. Such motions shall be printed or otherwise legibly duplicated. Eight copies of such motions shall be filed with the Board. Extra copies of electronically-filed papers need not be filed. The regional director may rule upon all motions filed with him, causing a copy of the ruling to be served on the parties, or may refer the motion to the hearing officer, except that if the regional director prior to the close of the hearing grants a motion to dismiss the petition, the petitioner may obtain a review of such ruling in the manner prescribed in §102.71. The hearing officer shall rule, either orally on the record or in writing, upon all motions filed at the hearing or referred to the hearing officer as hereinabove provided, except that the hearing officer shall rule on motions to intervene and to amend the petition only as directed by the regional director, and except that all motions to dismiss petitions shall be referred for appropriate action at such time as the entire record is considered by the regional director or the Board, as the case may be. All motions, rulings, and orders shall become a part of the record, except that rulings on motions to revoke subpoenas shall become a part of the record only upon the request of the party aggrieved thereby as provided in §102.66(f).

(b) Any person desiring to intervene in any proceeding shall make a motion for intervention, stating the grounds upon which such person claims to have an interest in the proceeding. The regional director, or the hearing officer at the specific direction of the regional director, may by order permit intervention in person or by counsel or other representative to such extent and upon such terms as the regional director may deem proper, and such intervenor shall thereupon become a party to the proceeding.

(c) Rulings by the hearing officer shall not be appealed directly to the regional director, except by special permission of the regional director, but shall be considered by the regional director when the director reviews the entire record. Requests to the regional director for special permission to appeal from a ruling of the hearing officer, together with the appeal from such ruling, shall be filed promptly, in writing, and shall briefly state the reasons special permission should be granted and the grounds relied on for the appeal. The moving party shall immediately serve a copy of the request for special permission and of the appeal on the other parties and on the regional director. Any statement in opposition or other response to the request and/or to the appeal shall be filed promptly, in writing, and shall be served immediately on the other parties and on the regional director. No party shall be precluded from raising an issue at a later time because it did not seek special permission to appeal. If the regional director grants the request for special permission to appeal, the regional director may proceed forthwith to rule on the appeal. Neither the filing nor the grant of such a request shall stay the proceedings unless otherwise ordered by the regional director. As stated in §102.67, the parties may request Board review of regional director actions.

(d) The right to make motions or to make objections to rulings on motions shall not be deemed waived by participation in the proceeding.

(e)(1) A party to a proceeding may, because of extraordinary circumstances, move after the close of the hearing for reopening of the record, or move after the decision or report for reconsideration, for rehearing, or to reopen the record, but no such motion shall stay the time for filing a request for review of a decision or exceptions to a report. No motion for reconsideration, for rehearing, or to reopen the record will be entertained by the Board or by any regional director or hearing officer with respect to any matter which could have been but was not raised pursuant to any other section of these rules, except that the regional director may treat a request for review of a decision or exceptions to a report as a motion for reconsideration. A motion for reconsideration shall state with particularity the material error claimed and with respect to any finding of material fact shall specify the page of the record relied on for the motion. A motion for rehearing or to reopen the record shall specify briefly the error alleged to require a rehearing or hearing *de novo,* the prejudice to the movant alleged to result from such error, the additional evidence sought to be adduced, why it was not presented previously, and what result it would require if adduced and credited. Only newly discovered evidence — evidence which has become available only since the close of the hearing — or evidence which the regional director or the Board believes should have been taken at the hearing will be taken at any further hearing.

(2) Any motion for reconsideration or for rehearing pursuant to paragraph (e)(1) of this section shall be filed within 14 days, or such further period as may be allowed, after the service of the decision or report. Any request for an extension of time to file such a motion shall be served promptly on the other parties. A motion to reopen the record shall be filed promptly on discovery of the evidence sought to be adduced.

(3) The filing and pendency of a motion under this provision shall not unless so ordered operate to stay the effectiveness of any action taken or directed to be taken nor will a regional director or the Board delay any decision or action during the period specified in paragraph (e)(2) of this section, except that, if a motion for reconsideration based on changed circumstances or to reopen the record based on newly discovered evidence states with particularity that the granting thereof will affect the eligibility to vote of specific employees, the Board agent shall have discretion to allow such employees to vote subject to challenge even

if they are specifically excluded in the direction of election and to challenge or permit the moving party to challenge the ballots of such employees even if they are specifically included in the direction of election in any election conducted while such motion is pending. A motion for reconsideration, for rehearing, or to reopen the record need not be filed to exhaust administrative remedies.

§102.66 Introduction of evidence: rights of parties at hearing; preclusion; subpoenas; oral argument and briefs.

(a) *Rights of parties at hearing.* Any party shall have the right to appear at any hearing in person, by counsel, or by other representative, to call, examine, and cross-examine witnesses, and to introduce into the record evidence of the significant facts that support the party's contentions and are relevant to the existence of a question of representation. The hearing officer shall also have power to call, examine, and cross-examine witnesses and to introduce into the record documentary and other evidence. Witnesses shall be examined orally under oath. The rules of evidence prevailing in courts of law or equity shall not be controlling. Stipulations of fact may be introduced in evidence with respect to any issue.

(b) *Response to Statement of Position.* Issues in dispute shall be identified as follows: After a Statement of Position is received in evidence and prior to the introduction of further evidence, all other parties shall respond on the record to each issue raised in the Statement. The regional director may permit the Statement of Position to be amended in a timely manner for good cause, in which event the other parties shall respond to each amended position. The regional director may also permit responses to be amended in a timely manner for good cause. The hearing officer shall not receive evidence concerning any issue as to which parties have not taken adverse positions, except that this provision shall not preclude the receipt of evidence regarding the Board's jurisdiction over the employer or limit the regional director's discretion to direct the receipt of evidence concerning any issue, such as the appropriateness of the proposed unit, as to which the regional director determines that record evidence is necessary.

(c) *Offers of proof.* The regional director shall direct the hearing officer concerning the issues to be litigated at the hearing. The hearing officer may solicit offers of proof from the parties or their counsel as to any or all such issues. Offers of proof shall take the form of a written statement or an oral statement on the record identifying each witness the party would call to testify concerning the issue and summarizing each witness's testimony. If the regional director determines that the evidence described in an offer of proof is insufficient to sustain the proponent's position, the evidence shall not be received.

(d) *Preclusion.* A party shall be precluded from raising any issue, presenting any evidence relating to any issue, cross-examining any witness concerning any issue, and presenting argument concerning any issue that the party failed to raise in its timely Statement of Position or to place in dispute in response to another party's Statement of Position or response, except that no party shall be precluded from contesting or presenting evidence relevant to the Board's statutory jurisdiction to process the petition. Nor shall any party be precluded, on the grounds that a voter's eligibility or inclusion was not contested at the pre-election hearing, from challenging the eligibility of any voter during the election. If a party contends that the proposed unit is not appropriate in its Statement of Position but fails to specify the classifications, locations, or other employee groupings that must be added to or excluded from the proposed unit to make it an appropriate unit, the party shall also be precluded from raising any issue as to the appropriateness of the unit, presenting any evidence relating to the appropriateness of the unit, cross-examining any witness concerning the appropriateness of the unit, and presenting argument concerning the appropriateness of the unit. If the employer fails to timely furnish the lists of employees described in §§102.63(b)(1)(iii),(b)(2)(iii), or (b)(3)(iii), the employer shall be precluded from contesting the appropriateness of the proposed unit at any time and from contesting the eligibility or inclusion of any individuals at the pre-election hearing, including by presenting evidence or argument, or by cross-examination of witnesses.

(e) *Objections.* Any objection with respect to the conduct of the hearing, including any objection to the introduction of evidence, may be stated orally or in writing, accompanied by a short statement of the grounds of such objection, and included in the record. No such objection shall be deemed waived by further participation in the hearing.

(f) *Subpoenas.* The Board, or any Member thereof, shall, on the written application of any party, forthwith issue subpoenas requiring the attendance and testimony of witnesses and the production of any evidence, including books, records, correspondence, or documents, in their possession or under their control. The Executive Secretary shall have the authority to sign and issue any such subpoenas on behalf of the Board or any Member thereof. Any party may file applications for subpoenas in writing with the regional director if made prior to hearing, or with the hearing officer if made at the hearing. Applications for subpoenas may be made ex parte. The regional director or the hearing officer, as the case may be, shall forthwith grant the subpoenas requested. Any person served with a subpoena, whether ad testificandum or duces tecum, if he or she does not intend to comply with the subpoena, shall, within 5 days after the date of service of the subpoena, petition in writing to revoke the subpoena. The date of service for purposes of computing the time for filing a petition to revoke shall be the date the subpoena is received. Such petition shall be filed with the regional director who may either rule upon it or refer it for ruling to the hearing officer, except that if the evidence called for is to be produced at a hearing and the hearing has opened, the petition to revoke shall be filed with the hearing officer. Notice of the filing of petitions to revoke shall be promptly given by the regional director or hearing officer, as the case may be, to the party at whose request the subpoena was issued. The regional director or the hearing officer, as the case may be, shall revoke the subpoena if, in his opinion, the evidence whose production is required does not relate to any matter under investigation or in question in the proceedings or the subpoena does not describe with sufficient particularity the evidence whose production is required, or if for any other reason sufficient in law the subpoena is otherwise invalid. The regional director or the hearing officer, as the case may be, shall make a simple statement of procedural or other grounds for his ruling. The petition to revoke, any answer filed thereto, and any ruling thereon shall not become part of the record except upon the request of the party aggrieved by the ruling. Persons compelled to submit data or evidence are entitled to retain or, on payment of lawfully prescribed costs, to procure copies or transcripts of the data or evidence submitted by them.

(g) *Election details.* Prior to the close of the hearing, the hearing officer will:

(1) Solicit the parties' positions on the type, date(s), time(s), and location(s) of the election and the eligibility period, but shall not permit litigation of those issues;

(2) Solicit the name, address, email address, facsimile number, and phone number of the employer's on-site representative to whom the regional director should transmit the Notice of Election in the event the regional director directs an election;

(3) Inform the parties that the regional director will issue a decision as soon as practicable and that the director will immediately transmit the document to the parties and their designated representatives by email, facsimile, or by overnight mail (if neither an email address nor facsimile number was provided); and

(4) Inform the parties what their obligations will be under these rules if the director directs an election and of the time for complying with such obligations.

(h) *Oral argument and briefs.* Any party shall be entitled, upon request, to a reasonable period at the close of the hearing for oral argument, which shall be included in the stenographic report of the hearing. Post-hearing briefs shall be filed only upon special permission of the regional director and within the time and addressing the subjects permitted by the regional director. Copies of the brief shall be served on all other parties to the proceeding and a statement of such service shall be filed with the regional director together with the brief. No reply brief may be filed except upon special permission of the regional director.

(i) *Hearing officer analysis.* The hearing officer may submit an analysis of the record to the regional director but shall make no recommendations.

(j) *Witness fees.* Witness fees and mileage shall be paid by the party at whose instance the witness appears.

§102.67   Proceedings before the regional director; further hearing; action by the regional director; appeals from actions of the regional director; statement in opposition; requests for extraordinary relief; Notice of Election; voter list.

(a) *Proceedings before regional director.* The regional director may proceed, either forthwith upon the record or after oral argument, the submission of briefs, or further hearing, as the director may deem proper, to determine whether a question of representation exists in a unit appropriate for purposes of collective bargaining, and to direct an election, dismiss the petition, or make other disposition of the matter. A decision by the regional director upon the record shall set forth the director's findings, conclusions, and order or direction.

(b) *Directions of elections.* If the regional director directs an election, the direction ordinarily will specify the type, date(s), time(s), and location(s) of the election and the eligibility period. The regional director shall schedule the election for the earliest date practicable consistent with these rules. The regional director shall transmit the direction of election to the parties and their designated representatives by email, facsimile, or by overnight mail (if neither an email address nor facsimile number was provided). The regional director shall also transmit the Board's Notice of Election to the parties and their designated representatives by email, facsimile, or by overnight mail (if neither an email address nor facsimile number was provided), and it will ordinarily be transmitted simultaneously with the direction of election. If the direction of election provides for individuals to vote subject to challenge because their eligibility has not been determined, the Notice of Election shall so state, and shall advise employees that the individuals are neither included in, nor excluded from, the bargaining unit, inasmuch as the regional director has permitted them to vote subject to challenge. The election notice shall further advise employees that the eligibility or inclusion of the individuals will be resolved, if necessary, following the election.

(c) *Requests for Board review of regional director actions.* Upon the filing of a request therefor with the Board by any interested person, the Board may review any action of a regional director delegated to him under Section 3(b) of the Act except as the Board's rules provide otherwise, but such a review shall not, unless specifically ordered by the Board, operate as a stay of any action by the regional director. The request for review may be filed at any time following the action until 14 days after a final disposition of the proceeding by the regional director. No party shall be precluded from filing a request for review of the direction of election within the time provided in this paragraph because it did not file a request for review of the direction of election prior to the election.

(d) *Grounds for review.* The Board will grant a request for review only where compelling reasons exist therefor. Accordingly, a request for review may be granted only upon one or more of the following grounds:

(1) That a substantial question of law or policy is raised because of:

(i) The absence of; or

(ii) A departure from, officially reported Board precedent.

(2) That the regional director's decision on a substantial factual issue is clearly erroneous on the record and such error prejudicially affects the rights of a party.

(3) That the conduct of any hearing or any ruling made in connection with the proceeding has resulted in prejudicial error.

(4) That there are compelling reasons for reconsideration of an important Board rule or policy.

(e) *Contents of request.* A request for review must be a self-contained document enabling the Board to rule on the basis of its contents without the necessity of recourse to the record; however, the Board may, in its discretion, examine the record in evaluating the request. With respect to the ground listed in paragraph (d)(2) of this section, and other grounds where appropriate, the request must contain a summary of all evidence or rulings bearing on the issues together with page citations from the transcript and a summary of argument. Such request may not raise any issue or allege any facts not timely presented to the regional director.

(f) *Opposition to request.* Any party may, within 7 days after the last day on which the request for review must be filed, file with the Board a statement in opposition which shall be served in accordance with the requirements of paragraph (i) of this section. The Board may grant or deny the request for review without awaiting a statement in opposition.

(g) *Finality; waiver; denial of request.* The regional director's actions are final unless a request for review is granted. The parties may, at any time, waive their right to request review. Failure to request review shall preclude such parties from relitigating, in any related subsequent unfair labor practice proceeding, any issue which was, or could have been, raised in the representation proceeding. Denial of a request for review shall constitute an affirmance of the regional director's action which shall also preclude relitigating any such issues in any related subsequent unfair labor practice proceeding.

(h) *Grant of review; briefs.* The grant of a request for review shall not stay the regional director's action unless otherwise ordered by the Board. Except where the Board rules upon the issues on review in the order granting review, the appellants and other parties may, within 14 days after issuance of an order granting review, file briefs with the Board. Such briefs may be reproductions of those previously filed with the regional director and/or other briefs which shall be limited to the issues raised in the request for review. Where review has been granted, the Board may provide for oral argument or further hearing. The Board will consider the entire record in the light of the grounds relied on for review and shall make such disposition of the matter as it deems appropriate. Any request for review may be withdrawn with the permission of the Board at any time prior to the issuance of the decision of the Board thereon.

(i)(1) *Format of request.* All documents filed with the Board under the provisions of this section shall be filed in seven copies, double spaced, on 81/2- by 11-inch paper, and shall be printed or otherwise legibly duplicated. Extra copies of electronically-filed papers need not be filed. Requests for review, including briefs in support thereof and any motions under paragraph (j) of this section; statements in opposition thereto; and briefs on review shall not exceed 50 pages in length, exclusive of subject index and table of cases and other authorities cited, unless permission to exceed that limit is obtained from the Board by motion, setting forth the reasons therefor, filed not less than 5 days, including Saturdays, Sundays, and holidays, prior to the date the document is due. Where any brief filed pursuant to this section exceeds 20 pages, it shall contain a subject index with page authorities cited. A party may combine a request for review of the regional director's decision and direction of election with a request for review of a regional director's post-election decision, if the party has not previously filed a request for review of the pre-election decision. Repetitive requests will not be considered.

(2) *Service.* The party filing with the Board a request for review, a statement in opposition to a request for review, or a brief on review shall serve a copy thereof on the other parties and shall file a copy with the

regional director. A certificate of service shall be filed with the Board together with the document.

(3) *Extensions.* Requests for extensions of time to file requests for review, statements in opposition to a request for review, or briefs, as permitted by this section, shall be filed with the Board or the regional director, as the case may be. The party filing the request for an extension of time shall serve a copy thereof on the other parties and, if filed with the Board, on the regional director. A statement of such service shall be filed with the document.

(j) *Requests for extraordinary relief.* (1) A party requesting review may also move in writing to the Board for one or more of the following forms of relief:

(i) Expedited consideration of the request;

(ii) A stay of some or all of the proceedings, including the election; or

(iii) Impoundment and/or segregation of some or all of the ballots.

(2) Relief will be granted only upon a clear showing that it is necessary under the particular circumstances of the case. The pendency of a motion does not entitle a party to interim relief, and an affirmative ruling by the Board granting relief is required before the action of the regional director will be altered in any fashion.

(k) *Notice of election.* The employer shall post copies of the Board's Notice of Election in conspicuous places, including all places where notices to employees in the unit are customarily posted, at least 3 full working days prior to 12:01 a.m. of the day of the election and shall also distribute it electronically if the employer customarily communicates with employees in the unit electronically. In elections involving mail ballots, the election shall be deemed to have commenced the day the ballots are deposited by the regional office in the mail. In all cases, the notices shall remain posted until the end of the election. The term working day shall mean an entire 24-hour period excluding Saturdays, Sundays, and holidays. The employer's failure properly to post or distribute the election notices as required herein shall be grounds for setting aside the election whenever proper and timely objections are filed under the provisions of §102.69(a). A party shall be estopped from objecting to the nonposting of notices if it is responsible for the nonposting, and likewise shall be estopped from objecting to the nondistribution of notices if it is responsible for the nondistribution.

(*l*) *Voter list.* Absent extraordinary circumstances specified in the direction of election, the employer shall, within 2 business days after issuance of the direction, provide to the regional director and the parties named in such direction a list of the full names, work locations, shifts, job classifications, and contact information (including home addresses, available personal email addresses, and available home and personal cellular ("cell") telephone numbers) of all eligible voters. The employer shall also include in a separate section of that list the same information for those individuals who, according to the direction of election, will be permitted to vote subject to challenge, including, for example, individuals in the classifications or other groupings that will be permitted to vote subject to challenge. In order to be timely filed and served, the list must be received by the regional director and the parties named in the direction respectively within 2 business days after issuance of the direction of election unless a longer time is specified therein. The list of names shall be alphabetized (overall or by department) and be in an electronic format approved by the General Counsel unless the employer certifies that it does not possess the capacity to produce the list in the required form. When feasible, the list shall be filed electronically with the regional director and served electronically on the other parties named in the direction. A certificate of service on all parties shall be filed with the regional director when the voter list is filed. The employer's failure to file or serve the list within the specified time or in proper format shall be grounds for setting aside the election whenever proper and timely objections are filed under the provisions of §102.69(a). The employer shall be estopped from objecting to the failure to file or serve the list within the specified time or in the proper format if it is responsible for the failure. The parties shall not use the list for purposes other than the representation proceeding, Board proceedings arising from it, and related matters.

§102.68 Record in pre-election proceeding; what constitutes; transmission to Board.

The record in a proceeding conducted pursuant to the foregoing section shall consist of: the petition, notice of hearing with affidavit of service thereof, statements of position, responses to statements of position, offers of proof made at the pre-election hearing, motions, rulings, orders, the stenographic report of the hearing and of any oral argument before the regional director, stipulations, exhibits, affidavits of service, and any briefs or other legal memoranda submitted by the parties to the regional director or to the Board, and the decision of the regional director, if any. Immediately upon issuance of an order granting a request for review by the Board, the regional director shall transmit the record to the Board.

**§102.69 Election procedure; tally of ballots; objections;
certification by regional director; hearings; hearing
officer reports on objections and challenges; exceptions to hearing officer reports; regional director
decisions on objections and challenges.**

(a) *Election procedure; tally; objections.* Unless otherwise directed by
the Board, all elections shall be conducted under the supervision of the regional director in whose Region the proceeding is pending. All elections shall be
by secret ballot. Whenever two or more labor organizations are included as
choices in an election, either participant may, upon its prompt request to and
approval thereof by the regional director, whose decision shall be final, have
its name removed from the ballot, except that in a proceeding involving an
employer-filed petition or a petition for decertification, the labor organization
certified, currently recognized, or found to be seeking recognition may not
have its name removed from the ballot without giving timely notice in writing
to all parties and the regional director, disclaiming any representation interest
among the employees in the unit. A pre-election conference may be held at
which the parties may check the list of voters and attempt to resolve any
questions of eligibility or inclusions in the unit. When the election is conducted manually, any party may be represented by observers of its own selection, subject to such limitations as the regional director may prescribe. Any
party and Board agents may challenge, for good cause, the eligibility of any
person to participate in the election. The ballots of such challenged persons
shall be impounded. Upon the conclusion of the election the ballots will be
counted and a tally of ballots prepared and immediately made available to the
parties. Within 7 days after the tally of ballots has been prepared, any party
may file with the regional director an original and five copies of objections to
the conduct of the election or to conduct affecting the results of the election
which shall contain a short statement of the reasons therefor and a written
offer of proof in the form described in §102.66(c) insofar as applicable, except
that the regional director may extend the time for filing the written offer of
proof in support of the election objections upon request of a party showing
good cause. Such filing(s) must be timely whether or not the challenged
ballots are sufficient in number to affect the results of the election. The
party filing the objections shall serve a copy of the objections, including
the short statement of reasons therefor, but not the written offer of proof,
on each of the other parties to the case, and include a certificate of such
service with the objections. A person filing objections by facsimile pursuant
to §102.114(f) shall also file an original for the Agency's records, but failure
to do so shall not affect the validity of the filing if otherwise proper. In
addition, extra copies need not be filed if the filing is by facsimile or

electronically pursuant to §102.114(f) or (i). The regional director will transmit a copy of the objections to each of the other parties to the proceeding, but shall not transmit the offer of proof.

(b) *Certification in the absence of objections, determinative challenges and runoff elections.* If no objections are filed within the time set forth in paragraph (a) of this section, if the challenged ballots are insufficient in number to affect the results of the election, and if no runoff election is to be held pursuant to §102.70, the regional director shall forthwith issue to the parties a certification of the results of the election, including certification of representative where appropriate with the same force and effect as if issued by the Board.

(c)(1)(i) *Decisions resolving objections and challenges without a hearing.* If timely objections are filed to the conduct of an election or to conduct affecting the results of the election, and the regional director determines that the evidence described in the accompanying offer of proof would not constitute grounds for setting aside the election if introduced at a hearing, and the regional director determines that any determinative challenges do not raise substantial and material factual issues, the regional director shall issue a decision disposing of the objections and determinative challenges, and a certification of the results of the election, including certification of representative where appropriate.

(ii) *Notices of hearing on objections and challenges.* If timely objections are filed to the conduct of the election or to conduct affecting the results of the election, and the regional director determines that the evidence described in the accompanying offer of proof could be grounds for setting aside the election if introduced at a hearing, or if the challenged ballots are sufficient in number to affect the results of the election and raise substantial and material factual issues, the regional director shall transmit to the parties and their designated representatives by email, facsimile, or by overnight mail (if neither an email address nor facsimile number was provided) a notice of hearing before a hearing officer at a place and time fixed therein. The regional director shall set the hearing for a date 21 days after the preparation of the tally of ballots or as soon as practicable thereafter, unless the parties agree to an earlier date, except that the regional director may consolidate the hearing concerning objections and challenges with an unfair labor practice proceeding before an administrative law judge. In any proceeding wherein the election has been held pursuant to §102.62(a) or (c) and the representation case has been consolidated with an unfair labor practice proceeding for purposes of hearing, the administrative law judge shall, after issuing a decision, sever the representation case and transfer it to the regional director for further processing.

(iii) *Hearings; hearing officer reports; exceptions to regional director.* The hearing on objections and challenges shall continue from day to day until completed unless the regional director concludes that extraordinary circumstances warrant otherwise. Any hearing pursuant to this section shall be conducted in accordance with the provisions of §§102.64, 102.65, and 102.66, insofar as applicable. Any party shall have the right to appear at the hearing in person, by counsel, or by other representative, to call, examine, and cross-examine witnesses, and to introduce into the record evidence of the significant facts that support the party's contentions and are relevant to the objections and determinative challenges that are the subject of the hearing. The hearing officer may rule on offers of proof. Post-hearing briefs shall be filed only upon special permission of the hearing officer and within the time and addressing the subjects permitted by the hearing officer. Upon the close of such hearing, the hearing officer shall prepare and cause to be served on the parties a report resolving questions of credibility and containing findings of fact and recommendations as to the disposition of the issues. Any party may, within 14 days from the date of issuance of such report, file with the regional director an original and one copy of exceptions to such report, with supporting brief if desired. A copy of such exceptions, together with a copy of any brief filed, shall immediately be served on the other parties and a statement of service filed with the regional director. Within 7 days from the last date on which exceptions and any supporting brief may be filed, or such further time as the regional director may allow, a party opposing the exceptions may file an answering brief with the regional director. An original and one copy shall be submitted. A copy of such answering brief shall immediately be served on the other parties and a statement of service filed with the regional director. Extra copies of electronically-filed papers need not be filed. The regional director shall thereupon decide the matter upon the record or make other disposition of the case. If no exceptions are filed to such report, the regional director, upon the expiration of the period for filing such exceptions, may decide the matter forthwith upon the record or may make other disposition of the case.

(2) *Regional director decisions and Board review.* The decision of the regional director may include a certification of the results of the election, including certification of representative where appropriate, and shall be final unless a request for review is granted. If a consent

election has been held pursuant to §§102.62(a) or (c), the decision of the regional director is not subject to Board review. If the election has been conducted pursuant to §102.62(b), or by a direction of election issued following any proceeding under §102.67, the parties shall have the right to Board review set forth in §102.67, except that in any proceeding wherein a representation case has been consolidated with an unfair labor practice proceeding for purposes of hearing and the election was conducted pursuant to §§102.62(b) or 102.67, the provisions of §102.46 shall govern with respect to the filing of exceptions or an answering brief to the exceptions to the administrative law judge's decision, and a request for review of the regional director's decision and direction of election shall be due at the same time as the exceptions to the administrative law judge's decision are due.

(d)(1)(i) *Record in case with hearing.* In a proceeding pursuant to this section in which a hearing is held, the record in the case shall consist of the notice of hearing, motions, rulings, orders, stenographic report of the hearing, stipulations, exhibits, together with the objections to the conduct of the election or to conduct affecting the results of the election, offers of proof made at the post-election hearing, any briefs or other legal memoranda submitted by the parties, any report on such objections and/or on challenged ballots, exceptions, the decision of the regional director, any requests for review, and the record previously made as defined in §102.68. Materials other than those set out above shall not be a part of the record.

(ii) *Record in case with no hearing.* In a proceeding pursuant to this section in which no hearing is held, the record shall consist of the objections to the conduct of the election or to conduct affecting the results of the election, any decision on objections or on challenged ballots and any request for review of such a decision, any documentary evidence, excluding statements of witnesses, relied upon by the regional director in his decision, any briefs or other legal memoranda submitted by the parties, and any other motions, rulings or orders of the regional director. Materials other than those set out above shall not be a part of the record, except as provided in paragraph (d)(3) of this section.

(2) Immediately upon issuance of an order granting a request for review by the Board, the regional director shall transmit to the Board the record of the proceeding as defined in paragraph (d)(1) of this section.

(3) In a proceeding pursuant to this section in which no hearing is held, a party filing a request for review of a regional director's decision on challenged ballots or on objections or on both, or any opposition thereto, may support its submission to the Board by appending thereto copies of any offer of proof, including copies of any affidavits or other

documentary evidence, it has timely submitted to the regional director and which were not included in the decision. Documentary evidence so appended shall thereupon become part of the record in the proceeding. Failure to append that evidence to its submission to the Board in the representation proceeding as provided above, shall preclude a party from relying on such evidence in any subsequent unfair labor proceeding.

(e) *Revised tally of ballots.* In any case under this section in which the regional director or the Board, upon a ruling on challenged ballots, has directed that such ballots be opened and counted and a revised tally of ballots issued, and no objection to such revised tally is filed by any party within 7 days after the revised tally of ballots has been made available, the regional director shall forthwith issue to the parties certification of the results of the election, including certifications of representative where appropriate with the same force and effect as if issued by the Board.

(f) *Format of filings with regional director.* All documents filed with the regional director under the provisions of this section shall be filed double spaced, on 81/2- by 11-inch paper, and shall be printed or otherwise legibly duplicated. Extra copies of electronically-filed papers need not be filed. Briefs in support of exceptions or answering briefs shall not exceed 50 pages in length, exclusive of subject index and table of cases and other authorities cited, unless permission to exceed that limit is obtained from the regional director by motion, setting forth the reasons therefor, filed not less than 5 days, including Saturdays, Sundays, and holidays, prior to the date the brief is due. Where any brief filed pursuant to this section exceeds 20 pages, it shall contain a subject index with page references and an alphabetical table of cases and other authorities cited.

(g) *Extensions of time.* Requests for extensions of time to file exceptions, requests for review, supporting briefs, or answering briefs, as permitted by this section, shall be filed with the Board or the regional director, as the case may be. The party filing the request for an extension of time shall serve a copy thereof on the other parties and, if filed with the Board, on the regional director. A statement of such service shall be filed with the document.

§102.71 Dismissal of petition; refusal to proceed with petition; requests for review by the Board of action of the regional director.

***

(c) A request for review must be filed with the Board in Washington, DC, and a copy filed with the regional director and copies served on all the other parties within 14 days of service of the notice of dismissal or notification that the petition is to be held in abeyance. The request shall be submitted in eight copies and shall contain a complete statement setting forth facts and reasons upon which the request is based. The request shall be printed or otherwise legibly duplicated. Extra copies of electronically-filed papers need not be filed. Requests for an extension of time within which to file the request for review shall be filed with the Board in Washington, DC, and a certificate of service shall accompany the requests.

§102.76 Petition; who may file; where to file; contents.

When picketing of an employer has been conducted for an object proscribed by Section 8(b)(7) of the Act, a petition for the determination of a question concerning representation of the employees of such employer may be filed in accordance with the provisions of §§102.60 and 102.61, insofar as applicable, except that if a charge under §102.73 has been filed against the labor organization on whose behalf picketing has been conducted, the petition shall not be required to contain a statement that the employer declines to recognize the petitioner as the representative within the meaning of Section 9(a) of the Act; or that the union represents a substantial number of employees; or that the labor organization is currently recognized but desires certification under the Act; or that the individuals or labor organizations who have been certified or are currently recognized by the employer are no longer the representative; or, if the petitioner is an employer, that one or more individuals or labor organizations have presented to the petitioner a claim to be recognized as the exclusive representative of the employees in the unit claimed to be appropriate.

§102.77 Investigation of petition by regional director; directed election.

***

(b) If after the investigation of such petition or any petition filed under subpart C of this part, and after the investigation of the charge filed pursuant to §102.73, it appears to the regional director that an expedited election under section 8(b)(7)(C) of the Act is warranted, and that the policies of the Act would be effectuated thereby, the regional director shall forthwith proceed to conduct an election by secret ballot of the employees in an appropriate unit, or make other disposition of the matter, except that in any case in which it appears to the regional director that the proceeding raises questions which cannot be decided without a hearing, the director may issue and cause to be served on the parties, individuals, and labor organizations involved a notice of hearing before a hearing officer at a time and place fixed therein. In this event, the method of conducting the hearing and the procedure following shall be governed insofar as applicable by §§102.63 through 102.68 inclusive.

§102.83   Petition for referendum under section 9(e)(1) of the Act; who may file; where to file; withdrawal.

A petition to rescind the authority of a labor organization to make an agreement requiring as a condition of employment membership in such labor organization may be filed by an employee or group of employees on behalf of 30 percent or more of the employees in a bargaining unit covered by such an agreement. The petition shall be in writing and signed, and either shall be sworn to before a notary public, Board agent, or other person duly authorized by law to administer oaths and take acknowledgments or shall contain a declaration by the person signing it, under the penalties of the Criminal Code, that its contents are true and correct to the best of his knowledge and belief. One original of the petition shall be filed with the regional director wherein the bargaining unit exists or, if the unit exists in two or more Regions, with the regional director for any of such Regions. A person filing a petition by facsimile pursuant to §102.114(f) shall also file an original for the Agency's records, but failure to do so shall not affect the validity of the filing by facsimile, if otherwise proper. A person filing a petition electronically pursuant to §102.114(i) need not file an original. The petition may be withdrawn only with the approval of the regional director with whom such petition was filed. Upon approval of the withdrawal of any petition the case shall be closed.

§102.84   Contents of petition to rescind authority.

***

(i) The name and address of the petitioner, and the name, title, address, telephone number, facsimile number, and email address of the individual who will serve as the representative of the petitioner and accept service of all papers for purposes of the proceeding.

(j) A statement that 30 percent or more of the bargaining unit employees covered by an agreement between their employer and a labor organization made pursuant to Section 8(a)(3) of the Act, desire that the authority to make such an agreement be rescinded.

***

(*l*) Evidence supporting the statement that 30 percent or more of the bargaining unit employees desire to rescind the authority of their employer and labor organization to enter into an agreement made pursuant to Section 8(a)(3) of the Act. Such evidence shall be filed together with the petition, but shall not be served on any other party.

(m) Evidence filed pursuant to paragraph (*l*) of this section together with a petition that is filed by facsimile or electronically, which includes original signatures that cannot be transmitted in their original form by the method of filing of the petition, may be filed by facsimile or in electronic form provided that the original documents are received by the regional director no later than 2 days after the facsimile or electronic filing.

(n) The type, date(s), time(s) and location(s) of the election sought.

§102.85   Investigation of petition by regional director; consent referendum; directed referendum.

Where a petition has been filed pursuant to §102.83, and it appears to the regional director that the petitioner has made an appropriate showing, in such form as the regional director may determine, that 30 percent or more of the employees within a unit covered by an agreement between their employer and a labor organization requiring membership in such labor organization desire to rescind the authority of such labor organization to make such an agreement, the director shall proceed to conduct a secret ballot of the employees involved on the question whether they desire to rescind the authority of the labor organization to make such an agreement with their employer, except that in any case in which it appears to the regional director that the proceeding raises questions which cannot be decided without a hearing, the director may issue and cause to be served on the parties a notice of hearing before a hearing officer at a time and place fixed therein. The regional director shall fix the time and place of the election, eligibility requirements for voting, and other arrangements of the balloting, but the parties may enter into an agreement, subject to the approval of the regional director, fixing such arrangements. In any such consent agreements, provision may be made for final determination of all questions arising with respect to the balloting by the regional director or, upon grant of a request for review, by the Board.

§102.86   Hearing; posthearing procedure.

The method of conducting the hearing and the procedure following the hearing shall be governed, insofar as applicable, by §§102.63 to 102.69 inclusive of this part.

Subpart I — Service and Filing of Papers

§102.112   Date of service; date of filing.

The date of service shall be the day when the matter served is deposited in the United States mail, or is deposited with a private delivery service that will provide a record showing the date the document was tendered to the delivery service, or is delivered in person, as the case may be. Where service is made by electronic mail, the date of service shall be the date on which the message is sent. Where service is made by facsimile transmission, the date of service shall be the date on which transmission is received. The date of filing shall be the day when the matter is required to be received by the Board as provided by §102.111.

§102.113   Methods of service of process and papers by the Agency; proof of service.

***

(d) *Service of other documents.* Other documents may be served by the Agency by any of the foregoing methods as well as regular mail, electronic mail or private delivery service. Such other documents may be served by facsimile transmission with the permission of the person receiving the document.

***

§102.114   Filing and service of papers by parties; form of papers; manner and proof of filing or service; electronic filings.

(a) Service of documents by a party on other parties may be made personally, or by registered mail, certified mail, regular mail, electronic mail (if the document was filed electronically or if specifically provided for in these rules), or private delivery service. Service of documents by a party on other parties by any other means, including facsimile transmission, is permitted only with the consent of the party being served. Unless otherwise specified elsewhere in these rules, service on all parties shall be made in the same manner as that utilized in filing the document with the Board, or in a more expeditious manner; however, when filing with the Board is done by hand, the other parties shall be promptly notified of such action by telephone, followed by service of a copy in a manner designed to insure receipt by them by the close of the next business day. The provisions of this section apply to the General Counsel after a complaint has issued, just as they do to any other party, except to the extent that the provisions of §102.113(a) or (c) provide otherwise.

***

(d) Papers filed with the Board, General Counsel, Regional Director, Administrative Law Judge, or Hearing Officer shall be typewritten or otherwise legibly duplicated on 81/2- by 11-inch plain white paper, shall have margins no less than one inch on each side, shall be in a typeface no smaller than 12 characters-per-inch (elite or the equivalent), and shall be double spaced (except that quotations and footnotes may be single spaced). Nonconforming papers may, at the Agency's discretion, be rejected.

***

(g) Facsimile transmissions of the following documents will not be accepted for filing: Answers to Complaints; Exceptions or Cross-Exceptions; Briefs; Requests for Review of Regional Director Decisions; Administrative Appeals from Dismissal of Petitions or Unfair Labor Practice Charges; Objections to Settlements; EAJA Applications; Motions for Default Judgment; Motions for Summary Judgment; Motions to Dismiss; Motions for Reconsideration; Motions to Clarify; Motions to Reopen the Record; Motions to Intervene; Motions to Transfer, Consolidate or Sever; or Petitions for Advisory Opinions. Facsimile transmissions in contravention of this rule will not be filed.

***

§103.20   Election procedures and blocking charges; filing of blocking charges; simultaneous filing of offer of proof; prompt furnishing of witnesses.

Whenever any party to a representation proceeding files an unfair labor practice charge together with a request that it block the processing of the petition to the election, or whenever any party to a representation proceeding requests that its previously filed unfair labor practice charge block the further processing of a petition, the party shall simultaneously file, but not serve on any other party, a written offer of proof in support of the charge. The offer of proof shall provide the names of the witnesses who will testify in support of the charge and a summary of each witness's anticipated testimony. The party seeking to block the processing of a petition shall also promptly make available to the regional director the witnesses identified in its offer of proof. If the regional director determines that the party's offer of proof does not describe evidence that, if proven, would interfere with employee free choice in an election or would be inherently inconsistent with the petition itself, and thus would require that the processing of the petition be held in abeyance absent special circumstances, the regional director shall continue to process the petition and conduct the election where appropriate.

Selected Collective Bargaining Agreements

National Agreement Between General Electric and IUE-CWA (2011-2015)

ARTICLE I. UNION RECOGNITION

1. The Company agrees to recognize the Union on behalf of and in conjunction with its Locals for those bargaining units of Company employees for which the Union or any of its Locals, through National Labor Relations Board certifications, is designated as the exclusive collective bargaining representative of employees within such units for the purpose of collective bargaining in respect to rates of pay, wages, hours of employment and other conditions of employment.

2. Where the Union or any of its Locals through National Labor Relations Board certifications shall have been lawfully designated as the exclusive collective bargaining representative for any additional bargaining units of Company employees, such certified representative shall be recognized as provided above and become a party hereto, and the terms of this National Agreement shall thereupon be applicable to the employees within such unit.

ARTICLE II. UNION SECURITY

1. *Agency Shop*

(a) Subject to applicable law, all employees who, as of the date of this Agreement are members of the Union in good standing in accordance with the constitution and by-laws of the Union or who become members of the Union following the effective date of this Agreement, shall, as a condition of employment, remain members of the Union in good standing insofar as the payment of an amount equal to the periodic dues and initiation fees, uniformly required, is concerned.

(b) Subject to applicable law, all present employees who are not members of the Union and all individuals hired after the effective date of this agreement, shall, beginning on the thirtieth (30th) day following the effective date of this agreement or the thirtieth (30th) day following employment, whichever is later, as a condition of employment, either become and remain members of the Union in good standing insofar as the payment of an amount equal to the periodic dues and initiation fees, uniformly required, is concerned, or, in lieu of such Union membership, pay to the Union an equivalent service charge.

2.   *Union Dues or Service Charge Deduction Authorization*

(a) The Company, for each of its employees included within the bargaining units recognized by the Company pursuant to Article I hereof, who individually, in writing, duly authorizes his Company Paymaster to do so, will deduct from the earnings payable to such employee dues (including initiation fee, if any) for such employee's membership in the Local, or the equivalent service charge, and shall remit promptly to the **IUE-CWA International** all such deductions.

(b) Subject to applicable law, individual authorizations executed after the effective date of this Agreement shall be signed cards in the form agreed to by the Company and the Union.

3.   *Contributions to CWA COPE FUND*

(a) Employee Authorization

The Company agrees to deduct from the pay of each employee voluntary contributions to the CWA COPE Fund ("CWA-COPE-PCC"), provided that each such employee executes or has executed an "Authorization for Assignment and Check-Off of Contributions to CWA-COPE-PCC" form and provided further that such authorization has not been revoked.

Deductions shall be made only in accordance with the provisions of and in the amounts designated in said form, together with the provisions of this Section of the Agreement.

A properly executed copy of "Authorization for Assignment and Check-Off of Contributions to CWA-COPE-PCC" form for each employee for whom voluntary contributions to CWA-COPE PCC are to be deducted hereunder, shall be delivered to the Company before any such deductions are made. All deductions shall be made pursuant to such properly executed forms for so long as they remain in effect. Such deductions shall be made from the employee's regular pay each pay cycle that the authorization remains in effect.

(b) Termination of Company Obligations

The Company's obligation to make such deductions shall terminate automatically upon the termination of the employee who signs the authorization, upon written request, or upon his transfer to a job or location not covered by this Agreement.

(c) Remittance to the Union

The Company agrees to remit said deductions monthly to the Union as follows:

(1)   The total amount of CWA-COPE-PCC contributions deducted.

(2)   The names, social security number and amounts from whose wages such deductions have been made.

(3)   The Company shall, at the same time remit to the Union its check for the amount shown under item (a) above, care of IUE-CWA, The Industrial Division of the Communications Workers of America, AFL-CIO, CLC (IUE-CWA).

(d) Subject to applicable law, individual authorizations executed after the effective date of this Agreement shall be signed cards in the form agreed to by the Company and the Union.

ARTICLE III.   WORKING CONDITIONS

1. The Company will continue to provide systematic safety inspections, safety devices, guards, and medical service to minimize accidents and health hazards on its premises.

ARTICLE IV.   DISCRIMINATION AND COERCION

1. Neither the Company nor any of its Foremen, Superintendents, or other agents or representatives, shall discriminate against any employee because such employee is a member, Steward, Officer, or other agent or representative of the Union or of any Local.

2. Neither the Union nor any Local, nor any Steward, Officer, or other agent or representative of either, shall intimidate or coerce any employee, nor solicit members or funds in the plant during working hours.

3. (a) The Company, the Union and its IUE-CWA Locals shall not discriminate against any employee on account of race, color, sex, creed, marital status, age or national origin.

(b) The Company, the Union and its IUE-CWA Locals shall not discriminate against any employee because of physical or mental disability or because he or she is a disabled veteran or veteran of the Vietnam era in regard to any position for which the employee is qualified.

***

ARTICLE VI.   WAGE RATES

1. Any question which affects hourly rates, piecework rates or salary rates of individuals or groups shall be subject to negotiation between the Local and the local management.

2. The Company shall furnish the respective Locals concerned with information concerning all hourly and salaried job classifications, definitions, rates and progression schedules, including the anticipated earned rate, if any, for piecework jobs, and changes therein, for alljobs included within the bargaining units respectively represented by such Locals. Such Locals will also be informed of those piecework jobs within such bargaining units for which there is no anticipated earned rate. It is understood that the job classifications and definitions referred to above are merely for purposes of identification and general description and do not purport to be all-inclusive or exhaustive of the actual requirements of any job so classified or defined. In addition, upon request of any Local, the Company will furnish to such Local a copy of the currently applicable wage structure for the plant or location.

3. When an employee is hired or transferred through the Company Personnel Department, he will be given a card showing his job classification, starting rate, rate of progression or progression schedule, if any, job rate and anticipated earned rate and sharing rate, if any, applicable to the job for which he is hired or to which transferred.

***

ARTICLE XI.   REDUCTION OR INCREASE IN FORCES

1. Whenever there is a reduction in the working force or employees are laid off from their regular jobs, total length of seniority, applied on a plant, department, or other basis as negotiated locally, shall be the major factor determining the employees to be laid off or transferred (exclusive of upgrading or transfers to higher rated jobs). However, ability will be given consideration.

Similarly, in all cases of rehiring after layoff, total length of seniority, applied on a plant, department, or other basis as negotiated locally, shall be the major factor covering such rehiring if the employee is able to do the available work in a satisfactory manner after a minimum amount of training.

Where employees have accumulated six months or more of service credits, but have not established continuity of service, seniority will be considered in the above cases.

2. Since the number of employees in the individual bargaining units covered under this Agreement varies from less than 50 to more than 10,000, each Local shall negotiate with local management a written agreement covering the layoff and rehiring procedure for the employees represented by the Local.

3. Employees who have been or who may be transferred to jobs outside the bargaining units, may be returned to their former classification in the bargaining unit in accordance with their total length of continuous service.

Employees who, after October 3, 1966, are transferred to jobs outside the bargaining units may be returned to their former classification in the bargaining unit in accordance with their total length of continuous service at the time they left the unit plus the number of years outside the unit up to a maximum of five such years outside the unit.

Employees who, after June 30, 1985, are transferred to exempt management jobs outside the bargaining units may be returned to their former classification in the bargaining unit in accordance with their total length of continuous service during the period up to twenty-four (24) months following the first such transfer to a job outside the unit.

Employees who, after June 30, 1991, are transferred to jobs outside the bargaining units may be returned to their former classification in the bargaining unit in accordance with their total length of continuous service during the period up to six (6) months following the first such transfer to a job outside the unit.

4. An employee who retires at his or her option as provided in the Company Pension Plan shall cease to have any rights under the provisions of this Agreement. (However, this Agreement shall continue to be applicable to retired employees returned to active employment by the Company.)

5. Employees will be given at least one week's notice and one week's work at the prevailing schedule before layoffs are made due to decreasing forces.

6. An employee with continuity of service out due to illness for a period not exceeding one (1) year, or in the case of a work-related injury or illness, not exceeding eighteen (18) months, who returns to work shall be reemployed on his former job providing he is able to perform the job and normal seniority provisions permit.

ARTICLE **XII.**   UNION AND LOCAL REPRESENTATIVES AND STEWARDS

1. *Layoff Deferment*

(a) An employee who is an official of any Local, and who has accumulated six months or more of service credits shall, on written request of the Local, be deferred from layoff (except temporary layoffs) so long as work for which he is qualified is available and so long as the official's duties would permit such layoff deferment under applicable law. Such employee shall displace an employee with less actual seniority on work for which the employee who is a Local official is qualified or, in the event such employee does not have actual seniority to displace any employee, then the employee shall to the extent necessary to defer him from such layoff be deemed to have greater seniority than the shortest service employee in the bargaining unit on work for which the employee who is a Local official is qualified. If the foregoing provisions do not enable a Local official to be deferred from layoff, such official may displace to a higher rated position previously held by such official. Such deferral from layoff will continue only so long as the employee retains his position as an official of any Local. This provision shall apply to a minimum of four and a maximum of twelve such officials, dependent on the number of employees within such units as follows:

Employees	Union Officials
500 or less	4
501-2000	6
2001-5000	10
Over 5000	12

(b) An employee who is a Steward of such Local and who has accumulated six months or more of service credits shall, upon written request of the Local, and if a majority of the group of employees he represents assents as certified in writing by the Local, be deferred from layoff (except temporary layoffs) so long as work for which he is qualified is available among the group of employees he represents. In the event of a layoff affecting the group of employees represented by the employee who is a Steward, such employee shall, in accordance with the applicable local supplement or the local procedures on layoff and displacement, displace an employee within the group who has less actual seniority on work for which the Steward is qualified. In the event the Steward does not have sufficient actual seniority to displace any employee within the group, in accordance with the applicable local supplement or the local procedures on layoff, then such Steward shall be deemed to have sufficient seniority to retain his job classification and wage rate within the group. Such deferral from layoff will continue only so long as the employee retains his position as a Steward. This provision shall, in general, apply to a maximum of one Steward for each Company Foreman.

(c) Paragraph (a) and (b) hereof shall apply only to those officials whose names, titles and order of precedence, and to those Stewards whose names and sections, have been furnished in writing to the Company prior to the giving of notice of layoff by the Company and shall not apply to any such officials or Stewards who are on leave of absence pursuant to the provisions of Section 2 hereof.

2. *Leave of Absence*

Upon written request of the Union or any Local:

(a) Employees who are officials of the Union or officers of such a Local, who have at least one year of continuous service, and who represent the Union in its relations with the Company, shall be granted one year's leave of absence by the Company, without forfeiture of prior accumulated continuous service. This provision shall be limited at any one time to not more than 12 officials of the National Union and not more than 6 officers of any Local.

(b) If made at the end of such leave of absence

(1) such leave of absence may be extended yearly.

(2) such employees will be reemployed in work of the same or a similar character in the same or other divisions of the same plant, if qualified therefor, and if entitled thereto on the basis of their prior accumulated continuous service. In the case of employees who are officials of the Union or officers of a Local and who are granted a leave of absence after the effective date of this Agreement, such employees will be entitled (solely for determining their relative seniority for purposes of layoff and rehire under Article XI) to add to their prior accumulated continuous service the total period of any such leave of absence.

3. *Payment for Time on Local Union Activities*

(a) Unless otherwise provided by local written agreement, employees not on leave of absence pursuant to the provisions of Section 2 hereof will be paid by the Company at their respective rates then prevailing for absences from work while engaged in the following activities on Company premises:

(1) During each fiscal month, the number of weeks in such General Electric fiscal month multiplied by 1 1/2 hours per week for those Stewards whose names and sections have been furnished to the Company pursuant to the provisions of Section I (c) hereof, while engaged in processing grievances at Foreman level pursuant to the provisions of Article XIII, Section 2(a).

Where any plant is regularly scheduled on a forty-eight hour per week basis, the above allowances will be based on 2 hours per week.

Payment to Stewards will be made on a weekly basis within the above limits.

(2) Up to a total of eight hours per week (exclusive of time payable under Section 1 hereof) for members of Local Executive Board or for Negotiating Committee members while engaged in processing grievances with representatives of local management pursuant to the provisions of Article XIII, Section 2(b) and 2(c). Such Committee members or Executive Board representatives shall be limited at any one meeting as follows, unless the number is increased by mutual agreement of the Local and local management:

Bargaining Unit Size	*Maximum No. of Representatives*
0–1000	4
1001–2000	5
2001–3000	6
3001–5000	7

This does not limit the number of Executive Board members and does not prevent meeting of the full Executive Board with local management when such meetings are arranged in advance.

One of the Representatives in the Schedule above must be trained and dedicated to health care benefits and programs. This Representative will be compensated up to 8 hours per week for health care-related activities — irrespective of whether a grievance has been filed. The Company will determine the qualifications for this Representative and will participate with the Union in the selection of the most-qualified candidate.

(b) (1) Local management and the Local may negotiate a local agreement with respect to payment to local Stewards in excess of the limits provided in (a) (1) above.

(2) In those plant locations where the number of employees in the bargaining unit is 5000 employees or more or where more than one product department is located, local management and the Local may negotiate a local agreement with respect to payment to Local Executive Boards or Negotiating Committee members in excess of the limits provided in (a)(2) above.

(c) Employees requesting payment pursuant to the provisions of Paragraph (a) hereof, shall report all time spent on the handling of grievances to their respective Foremen or other immediate supervisors.

Chief Stewards or Executive Committee members in Works where they act as Chief Stewards, will be permitted to contact Stewards in their respective divisions when the officers of the Local deem such contact necessary. They will advise their own Foremen before leaving their departments and also contact the Foreman in the department which they are visiting before they contact the Steward.

The Company shall report their names, rates of pay and time absent from work to their respective Locals, and shall in no event be required to make any payments pursuant to Paragraph (a) hereof, except to the extent that such reports are approved by such Locals, and such Paragraph (a) is otherwise applicable.

(d) Whenever an OSHA inspection shall occur in a work area that includes employees represented by a Local Union listed in the Preamble, an employee designated by the Union who accompanies the OSHA inspector as the employees' representative will be paid for time lost from work during such inspection.

ARTICLE XIII.   GRIEVANCE PROCEDURE

1. Grievances may be filed by an employee or group of employees, a Steward or the Local. Grievances of a general nature filed by the Local shall be initiated at the second step of the grievance procedure.

2. *Steps.* Grievances other than those of a general nature may be processed only by recourse to the following successive steps:

(a) *Step One (Foreman Level)*

(1) Within a reasonable time after the occurrence or knowledge of the situation, condition or action of Management giving rise to the grievance, the employee affected thereby or his Steward may present the grievance to the employee's Foreman or other immediate supervisor. (If presented by the employee, he may also have his Steward present.)

(2) Within one working day after such presentation, such Foreman or other immediate supervisor shall give to such employee and Steward his decision with respect to such grievance, or shall advise them that additional time for such decision is needed, in which event he shall give them such decision within one week thereafter.

(3) A Steward who submits a written grievance to his Foreman shall receive, upon request, a written reply.

(4) If a settlement is not reached between the Steward and his immediate supervisor, the Local may refer the grievance to two representatives of the Local for discussion in the department with representatives of local management for settlement, if possible.

(b) *Step Two (Management Level)*

(1) If a settlement is not reached at Step One, the designated Local official may present to a representative designated by local management, a

written statement of such grievance within thirty (30) days of the Company answer at Step One of the grievance procedure giving all pertinent information relative to the grievance and indicating the relief requested, provided, however, that the designated Local official may advise local management that additional time is needed, in which case the Local shall have an additional one week to process the grievance to Step Two. The time limit between Step One and Step Two may be extended by mutual agreement.

(2) Meetings between representatives of the Local and local management shall be arranged at mutually agreeable times for the purpose of discussing such grievances. In those cases where it is mutually agreed by Management and Local representatives that an inspection of the job would be helpful in settling the case, a subcommittee of the Local with Management representatives shall be allowed to make an inspection of the job. Local representatives may include the Business Agent or his assistant or officers of the Local.

Grievances referred to Step Two will be scheduled and discussed as expeditiously as possible but not later than forty-five (45) days after the grievance has been presented to Step Two. Such time limits may be extended by mutual agreement.

(3) Upon request, local management will give the Local a written reply, such reply generally to be issued within two weeks following discussion of the grievance on the merits at the Second Step. Any extension necessary to issue a written reply shall be limited to two weeks.

(c) *Step Three (Headquarters Level)*

(1) Any grievance, having been processed through Step Two without satisfactory settlement, may be referred to the National Officers of the Union for submission to an Executive Officer of the Company or his designated representative, who shall arrange meetings for the purpose of discussing such grievances.

Such grievances shall be submitted to the Company not less than two weeks prior to the date of any discussion and not more than three months after the completion of discussions and the final decision of local management at Step Two.

When the Union requests an emergency meeting on a particular grievance or grievances, such a meeting shall take place within one week after the Company receives the request for such an emergency meeting.

The Company shall give its final decision to the Union in writing within a reasonable time after the completion of discussion on any grievance.

The discussions provided for above may, by mutual agreement, be held at the plant location of the Local submitting the grievance, if requested by the Union.

(2) A grievance filed on behalf of a candidate for preferential placement under Article XXII which arises solely due to the failure of Company

management at a designated location to select such candidate, where such designated location employs no employees represented by the Union, may be filed at the Headquarters level. A grievance filed on behalf of a candidate for preferential placement under Article XXII which arises solely due to the failure of Company management at a designated location to select such candidate, where the candidate's original location has closed, may also be filed at the Headquarters level, provided the grievance arises fallowing the original location's plant closing date. The Company shall give its final decision to the Union in writing within a reasonable time after discussions with the Union and an opportunity to investigate the facts.

3. *Discipline Based on Warning Notices*

Before imposing a disciplinary penalty or discharge which is based upon the cumulative effect of written warning notices; the Company will notify the employee concerned one week in advance. The matter may be made a subject for grievance discussions, but such discussions shall not prevent imposition of the penalty pending their final outcome, and in the event it is determined that an employee has been improperly penalized, he will be reimbursed for any loss of wages sustained as a result of the imposition of the penalty.

ARTICLE XIV.   STRIKES AND LOCKOUTS

1. There shall be no strike, sit-down, slowdown, employee demonstration or any other organized or concerted interference with work of any kind in connection with any matter subject to the grievance procedure, and no such interference with work shall be directly or indirectly authorized or sanctioned by a Local or the Union, or their respective Officers or Stewards, unless and until all of the respective provisions of the successive steps of the grievance procedure set forth in Article XIII shall have been complied with by the Local and the Union. The foregoing exception will not apply if (a) the matter is submitted to arbitration as provided in Article XV, or (b) 12 months shall have elapsed after receipt by the Union of the Company's final decision on the grievance at Step Three, or (c) the Company shall not have received written or telegraphic notice of such strike from the Local more than 24 hours prior to the commencement of such strike, which notice will specify the exhausted grievance over which the strike is being called. Upon receipt by the Company of such a strike notice, the Company and the Union will meet immediately to discuss the dispute and the contemplated action so that management may assess the situation.

2. The Company will not lock out any employee or transfer any job under dispute from the local Works, nor will the local management take similar

action while a disputed job is under discussion at any of the steps of the grievance procedure set forth in Article XIII, or if the matter is submitted to arbitration as provided in Article XV.

ARTICLE XV.   ARBITRATION

1. Any grievance which remains unsettled after having been fully processed pursuant to the provisions of Article XIII, and which involves either,

(a) the interpretation or application of a provision of the Agreement, or

(b) a disciplinary penalty (including discharge) imposed on or after the effective date of this Agreement, which is alleged to have been imposed without just cause, or

(c) nondisciplinary termination occurring after the effective date of this agreement, may be submitted to arbitration upon written request of either the Union or the Company, provided such request is made within 60 days after the final decision of the Company has been given to the Union pursuant to Article XIII, Section 2(c). For the purpose of proceedings within the scope of (b) above, the standard to be applied by an arbitrator to cases involving disciplinary penalties (including discharge) is that such penalties shall be imposed only for just cause.

2. (a) A request for arbitration shall state in reasonable detail the nature of the dispute and the remedy requested. A copy of the request shall be sent to the American Arbitration Association.

(b) Within 30 days after receipt of a request to arbitrate, the receiving party will give its response thereto in writing, with a copy to the Association, stating whether or not it believes the stated dispute to be arbitrable. If the receiving party believes the dispute not to be arbitrable, it will state its reasons in reasonable detail.

(c) If the response agrees to the arbitrability of the dispute, the Association will proceed to process the request in accordance with Section 3.

(d) If a response to a request for arbitration disagrees as to arbitrability of the dispute, either party may request a conference to discuss the arbitrability of the dispute, and to seek to resolve the differences between the parties.

3. (a) When a request for arbitration involves only relief from a disciplinary penalty or discharge alleged to have been imposed without just cause, or involves a dispute which the Company admits to be arbitrable, or when a final court judgment shall have ordered arbitration of a request, the Association shall submit the appropriate matter promptly to one of the Contract Arbitrators listed below for scheduling of a hearing thereon.

The Contract Arbitrators shall serve for the duration of this Agreement. The Association will assign each arbitration case in rotation, in the order of Contract Arbitrators listed below. If a Contract Arbitrator states that he is unable to accept a case, it will be referred to the next Contract Arbitrator in line.

Whenever the number of unresolved arbitration requests assigned to a Contract Arbitrator shall exceed three, any additional requests which would otherwise be assigned him in order of rotation shall be referred to the next Contract Arbitrator in line.

CONTRACT ARBITRATORS

Timothy L.Bornstein	Craig E. Overton
Leroy D. Clark	Jay Nadlebach
Larry Dias	Joan W. Parker
Phillip Dunn	Marsha Saylor
Lawrence T. Holden, Jr.	Joseph P. Sirefman
Charles F. Ipavec	Janet M. Spencer
Mark L. Irvings	Theodore St. Antoine
Michael Jedel	Jeffrey B. Tener
William Nowlin	Paul S. Zonderman

In all discharge and upgrading cases, the Association shall expedite the handling of such cases as follows:

(i) Request from the Contract Arbitrator, at the time of appointment, two or three proposed alternative hearing dates for hearing days within sixty (60) days of appointment.

(ii) Communicate proposed alternative hearing dates to designated representatives of the parties promptly and secure a firm commitment on a hearing date.

(iii) Schedule agreed upon hearing date in accordance with regular procedure.

(b) Only one request shall be scheduled for the same arbitration hearing, except by mutual agreement of the parties.

(c) In the conduct of an arbitration hearing, the applicable provisions of the Voluntary Labor Arbitration Rules of the Association shall control, except that either party may, if it desires, be represented by counsel.

(d) The dispute asstated in the request for arbitration shall constitute the sole and entire subject matter to be heard by the arbitrator, unless the parties agree to modify the scope of the hearing.

(e) In the event that a party initiating a request to cancel or postpone a hearing fails to provide notice to avoid incurring a cancellation fee, and no good cause can be shown for the untimely cancellation, such party shall be responsible for payment of the applicable fee:

(i) 1-2 weeks prior to hearing date 50% per diem rate

(ii) less than 1 week prior to hearing date 100% per diem rate

4. (a) In the event the receiving party has asserted that the dispute contained in a request for arbitration is not arbitrable, the Association shall have authority to process the request for arbitration and appoint an arbitrator in accordance with the procedure set forth in Section 3 above only after a final judgment of a court has determined that the grievance upon which arbitration has been requested raises arbitrable issues and has directed arbitration of such issues. The foregoing part of this section shall not be applicable if the request for arbitration involves only relief from a disciplinary penalty or discharge alleged to have been imposed without just cause.

(b) In the consideration and decision of any question involving arbitrability (including any application to a court for an order directing arbitration), it is the specific agreement of the parties that:

(i) Some types of grievance disputes which may arise during the term of this Agreement shall be subject to arbitration as a matter of right, enforceable in court, at the demand of either party. (See Section 6 below.)

(ii) Other types of disputes shall be subject only to voluntary arbitration, i.e., can be arbitrated only if both parties agree in writing, in the case of each dispute, to do so. (See Section 7 below.)

(iii) This Agreement sets out expressly all the restrictions and obligations assumed by the respective parties, and no implied restrictions or obligations inherent in this Agreement or were assumed by the parties in entering into this Agreement.

(iv) In the consideration of whether a matter is subject to arbitration as a matter of right, a fundamental principle shall be that the Company retains all its rights to manage the business, including (but not limited to) the right to determine the methods and means by which its operations are to be carried on, to direct the work force and to conduct its operations in a safe and effective manner, subject only to the express limitations set forth in this National Agreement, Local Seniority Supplements executed under the provisions of Article XI thereof, and Local Understandings executed in accordance with Section 3 of Article XXI thereof; and it is understood that the parties have not agreed to arbitrate demands which challenge action taken by the Company in the exercise of any such rights, except where such challenge is based upon a violation of any such express limitations (other than those set out in Section 7 below).

(v) No matter will be considered arbitrable unless it is found that the parties clearly agreed that the subject involved would be arbitrable in light of the principles of arbitrability set forth in this Article and no court or arbitrator shall or may proceed under any presumption that a request to arbitrate is arbitrable.

(b) If a final judgment of a court has determined that a request raises arbitrable issues, the court's decision shall specify in reasonable detail the issues as to which arbitration is directed. The arbitration shall thereafter proceed only upon the issues specified in such final court judgment and the arbitrator shall have no authority or jurisdiction to consider issues other than those specified.

5. The powers of an arbitrator shall include the authority to render a final and binding decision with respect to any dispute brought before him including the right to modify or reduce or rescind any disciplinary action taken by the Company but excluding the right to amend, modify or alter the terms of this Agreement, or any Local Understanding.

The expense of the arbitration will be borne equally by both parties.

Individuals who are covered by this Agreement do not have the right to invoke the arbitration procedure on their own initiative. The arbitration procedure can only be invoked by the Company on its behalf or the Union on behalf of its employees.

6. (a) Arbitration as a matter of right includes only requests to arbitrate which involve:

(i) Disciplinary action (including discharge) or nondisciplinary terminations but with certain exceptions spelled out in this article;

(ii) The claimed violation of a specific provision or provisions of the National Agreement (with the limitations and exceptions set out in this Article);

(iii) The claimed violation of a provision or provisions of a signed Local Seniority Supplement entered into in accordance with Article XI, Section 2 of this National Agreement or of a provision or provisions of a Local Understanding entered into in accordance with Article XXI, Section 3 of this National Agreement.

(b) A request for arbitration, in order to be subject to arbitration as a matter of right under the provisions of Subsections (a)(ii) and (a)(iii) above, must allege a direct violation of the express purpose of the contractual provision in question, rather than of an indirect or implied purpose. For example, a request which claims incorrect application of the method of computing overtime pay under the provisions of Section 2 of Article V would be arbitrable as a matter of right, whereas a request which questioned the right of the Company to require the performance of reasonable overtime work, on the claimed ground that Article V contains an implied limitation of that right, would be subject only to voluntary arbitration. A request that Article XI and the appropriate Local Seniority Supplement had been violated by the layoff of a senior employee in preference to a junior employee would be arbitrable as a matter of right but a request that subcontracting of work in the plant while bargaining unit employees are on layoff violated a claimed implied limitation of Article XI and the applicable Local Seniority Supplement would be subject only to voluntary arbitration.

7. All requests for arbitration which are not subject to arbitration as a matter of right under the provisions of Section 6 above, are subject only to voluntary arbitration. In particular, it is specifically agreed that arbitration requests shall be subject only to voluntary arbitration, by mutual agreement, if they

(a) Involve the existence or alleged violation of any agreement other than those described in 6(a) above.

(b) Involve issues which were discussed at national level negotiations, but which are not expressly covered in this National Agreement.

(c) Involve claims that an allegedly implied or assumed obligation of this National Agreement has been violated.

(d) Involve claims that Article I, or Section 3 of Article IV of this National Agreement has been violated; provided, however, that grievances which claim that a disciplinary action, discharge, upgrading action or transfer action violates Section 3 of Article IV will be subject to arbitration as a matter of right.

(e) Would require an arbitrator to consider, rule on or decide the appropriate hourly, salary or incentive rate at which an employee shall be paid, or the method (day, salary or incentive) by which his pay shall be determined. (See footnote)

(f) Would require an arbitrator to consider, rule on or decide any of the following:

(i) The elements of an employee's job assignment;

(ii) The level, title or other designation of an employee's job classification;

(iii) The right of management to assign or reassign work or elements of work. (See footnote)

(g) Would require an arbitrator to determine the method or data to be used by the Company in setting an incentive price or standard. (See footnote)

Footnote: Subsections e, f, and g reflect the fact that this National Agreement does not set out specific rates or classifications for jobs, and are designed to confirm the intent of Article VI, Section 1 and Article VI, Section 5 (first sentence) that disputes over individual job classifications, rates of pay, incentive standards, etc., are assigned by the parties to local negotiations, and not to arbitration.

(h) Involve claims of violation of Sections 1 and 2 of Article XI, in locations in which a Local Seniority Supplement has not been signed in accordance with Section 2 of Article XI.

(i) Pertain in any way to the establishment, administration, interpretation or application of Insurance, Pension or Savings Plans, or other Benefit plans in which employees covered by this Agreement are eligible to participate.

(j) Involve discipline or discharge imposed on employees having less than six months of service credits with the Company, provided that if by Local Understanding a period of less than six months has been agreed upon as the probationary period for new employees, and such Local Understanding is applicable to the particular employee involved, such agreed upon shorter period of time shall be substituted for "six months" in the foregoing; and provided further that nothing in this subsection shall limit the authority of an arbitrator with respect to disciplinary penalties or discharges imposed in violation of Section 1 of Article IV.

(k) Pertain in any way to Article XXII of this Agreement or its interpretation or application.

(*l*) Pertain in any way to the provisions of any local agreement covering a retraining program under the provisions of Article XXIV hereof, or the interpretation or application thereof.

8. (a) The parties shall refrain from requesting transcripts for those hearings where the submission to arbitration meets the fallowing criteria:

(i) The interpretation of one or more provisions of the collective bargaining agreement is not involved; and

(ii) There is no "procedural" question such as arbitrability or due process; and

(iii) There is no claim alleging discrimination in violation of Section 3 of Article IV of this Agreement; and

(iv) The only issue in a discharge or discipline case is whether the discharge or discipline was imposed for just cause.

(b) An arbitrator shall give his Award without an Opinion 1n certain arbitration cases in accordance with the following:

(i) An Award without an Opinion shall consist of a summary statement by an arbitrator of no more than two pages which briefly sets forth the basis of the Award.

(ii) An Award without an Opinion shall be given in all discipline or discharge cases meeting the criteria in Section 8(a), above, under the following procedure:

(1) If the party requesting arbitration believes the grievance meets the criteria, that party would so indicate in its written request for arbitration.

(2) If the party requesting arbitration does not indicate in its written request for arbitration that it believes the case meets the criteria, the other party may indicate that it believes the grievance meets the criteria in its written agreement to arbitrate.

(3) If the party requesting arbitration indicates that it believes the grievance meets the criteria in 8(a), above, in its request for arbitration, or if the other party so indicates in its written agreement to arbitrate, the Association will instruct the designated arbitrator to issue an Award without an Opinion subject to the discretion given the arbitrator in (4) below.

(4) If either party disagrees with the indication of the other party (provided for in (1) and (2), above) that the grievance meets the criteria set forth in 8(a), above, that party may request a written Opinion from the arbitrator so long as such request is made before the hearing is closed. When such a request is made by either party, the arbitrator shall rule whether a written Opinion is waived under the criteria set forth in 8(a) above.

(5) If evidence is adnlitted during the hearing at the instance of either party which, in the judgment of the other party, would change the case from one meeting the criteria in 8(a), above, to a case not meeting the criteria, the other party may then demand a written Opinion so long as such demand is made before the oral hearing is closed — notwithstanding prior agreement to waive the Opinion. This provision, however, should not be interpreted in any way to imply that either party would agree to the introduction of evidence at the hearing which would change the nature of the case.

9. Any arbitration case between the Company and the Union which is limited to a disciplinary penalty other than discharge is covered by the supplemental arbitration procedure set forth below:

(a) The following rules shall apply in cases covered by this section:

(i) The only issue before the arbitrator shall be whether the discipline was imposed for just cause.

(ii) There shall be no transcript of the hearing.

(iii) There shall be no post-hearing briefs or other written arguments by the parties.

(iv) If either party so requests, there shall be a thirty (30) minute recess before any closing oral argument by the parties.

(v) The arbitrator shall render an Award without an Opinion no more than twenty-four (24) hours after the closing of the oral hearing.

(b) The compensation for an arbitrator for hearing a case under this procedure shall be a fee of **$1,500.00** for each case. The arbitrator shall also be entitled to travel expenses in accordance with the regular procedures of the American Arbitration Association.

(c) A special panel of arbitrators shall be established to hear cases under this procedure by mutual agreement of the parties.

(d) Whenever a request for arbitration meets the criteria set forth above, the Association shall designate an arbitrator from the special panel of arbitrators, as provided for herein, to hear the case instead of a regular Contract Arbitrator, as provided for in Section 3 (a) of this Article, as follows:

(i) Assignments will be made by the American Arbitration Association based on the arbitrators' geographical proximity, the availability of the arbitrators, and the number of cases assigned particular arbitrators at given locations. No arbitrator will be assigned to more than 25% of the cases at a given location under this procedure without the mutual consent of the parties.

(ii) A date for a hearing shall be scheduled within sixty (60) days of the appointment of the arbitrator.

ARTICLE XVI.   POSTING

The Company will make bulletin boards available for the use of the Locals for the posting of notices. All notices shall be subject to the Manager's approval and he will also arrange for posting.

ARTICLE XVII.   NOTIFICATION AND PUBLICITY

1. The Company agrees to notify the Local and the National Officers of any matter affecting employees generally and concerning which the Union or the Local is the certified bargaining representative and not covered by this Agreement as soon as the Foremen are notified.

2. On any grievance or other matter which has been negotiated between the Company and the Union or the Local, the Company will notify the Union or Local of any decision or determination before it notifies the employees affected.

ARTICLE XVIII.   FINANCIAL SUPPORT

The Company shall not give financial aid to or otherwise support any labor organization. This, however, shall not prevent both parties to this contract from cooperating and exchanging such information essential for the furtherance of agreeable relations.

ARTICLE XIX.   INFORMATION

1. *New Employees — Reengaged Employees*

The Company will provide each Local, from information of record, with a monthly list of newly hired and reengaged employees; the information will consist of name, home address, seniority date, occupation, department, Foreman, and checkoff status.

2. *Laid Off Employees*

The Company will provide each Local, on a monthly basis, with information on employees laid off for lack of work after notification has been given to the employees; the information will consist of the name, home address of record, continuous service date, occupation, department, and Foreman. A list of employees on recall by work location shall also be provided quarterly (effective 1/1/01). The Foreman will give to the Steward information on extended layoffs, whenever possible one week before the employee is laid off.

3. *Transfers*

The Company will provide each Local with information on transfers which are made through the Personnel Office.

4. *Master List of Employees*

Semiannually, the Company, from information of record, will provide the Local with a complete list of all employees then in the bargaining unit and showing the name, home address, continuous service date, seniority date, occupation, department, job rate, paid rate/average earnings, clock card number, and checkoff status of each employee on such list.

***

ARTICLE XXII.   JOB AND INCOME SECURITY

1. *Definitions*

(a) The terms "plant closing" and "to close a plant" mean the announcement and carrying out of a plan to terminate and discontinue either all Company operations at any plant, service shop, or other facility, or those Company operations which would result in the termination of all employees represented by the Union at that location when those employees do not have displacement rights.

Such terms do not refer to the termination and discontinuance of only part of the Company's operations at any plant, service shop, or other facility (except as specifically provided in the paragraph above) nor to the termination or discontinuance of all of its former operations coupled with the announced intention to commence there either larger or smaller other operations. Any employees released by such latter changes will be considered as out for lack of work and will be subject to provisions applicable to those on layoff.

Also, such terms do not refer to the transfer or sale of such operations to a successor employer who offers continued employment to Company employees. Company employees who are not offered continued employment by the Company or by the successor employer will be considered as out for lack of work and will be subject to provisions applicable to those on layoff.

(b) The term "plant closing date" means the day when benefits for and terminations of represented employees begin because of a plant closing.

(c) The terms "transfer of work," "to transfer work," and "work transfer" mean the discontinuance of ongoing work at one location coupled with the assignment of the same work to a different location; including subcontracting the same work to another employer, if such assignment of work would directly cause a decrease in the number of represented employees performing such work at the first location.

(d) The term "robot" means a programmable, multi-function manipulator designed to move materials, parts, tools, or specialized devices through variable programmed motions for the performance of a variety of tasks.

(e) The term "automated manufacturing machine" means a device for doing work which has programmable controllers (PC), numerical controls (NC), computer numerical controls (CNC) or direct numerical controls (DNC).

(f) The term "automated office machine" means a device for doing office work which is computer-based and which includes word processing, data processing, image processing, electronic mail or business and engineering graphics devices.

(g) The term "week's pay" as used in this Article XXII, for a salaried employee shall be the higher of (a) the employee's normal straight-time weekly salary (including any night shift bonus) for the last full week worked by him or (b) the employee's normal straight-time weekly salary (including any night shift bonus) in effect during the last full calendar week worked by him during the calendar year preceding the year in which his current layoff began. A "week's pay" for an hourly employee on daywork shall be calculated by multiplying the higher of (a) his straight-time hourly rate (including any night shift bonus) which he was paid during the last week worked by him or (b) his straight-time hourly rate (including any night shift bonus) which he was paid during the last full calendar week worked by him during the calendar year preceding the year in which his current layoff began, times the number of hours in the employee's normal workweek, up to 40 hours. A "week's pay" for an hourly employee on incentive shall be calculated by multiplying the higher of (a) his average straight-time earning rate (including any night shift bonus) obtained from the last available periodic statistics applicable to time worked by him during his last week worked or (b) his average straight-time earning rate (including any night shift bonus) obtained from the last available periodic statistics applicable to time worked by him during the calendar year preceding the year in which his current layoff began, times the number of hours in the employee's normal work week, up to 40 hours.

(h) The term "Special Early Retirement Option Offset" shall have the meaning set forth in the GE Pension Plan.

2.   *Plant Closing*

(a) *General*

(1) Whenever the Company decides to close a plant, the Company shall give notice of its decision to the Union, the Local or Locals involved, and the employees concerned.

Thereafter, as the Company, in the course of such plant closing, no longer has need for the work then being done by an employee, his employment by the Company may be terminated, subject to compliance with the provisions of this Section 2.

(2) Each employee shall be given at least one week's advance notice of the specific date of his termination.

(b) *Severance Pay*

(1) An eligible employee whose employment is terminated because of plant closing shall be entitled to Severance Pay in a lump sum, for which he is eligible as described below and the full vacation allowance for which he might have qualified for the calendar year in which his employment is terminated and any other accumulated allowances due him, provided that after the announcement of intent to close a plant he:

(i) continues regularly at work at the closing location until the specific date of his termination, or

(ii) fails to continue regularly at work until the specific date of his termination due to verified personal illness, leave of absence, or layoff.

(2) An eligible employee will be similarly eligible for Severance Pay and his full vacation allowance if he was laid off or was placed on an approved

illness or injury absence prior to the Company's announcement of intent to close a plant and continues on layoff with protected service, or on illness or injury absence with protected service, until the location's plant closing date.

(3) Also eligible for Severance Pay under this Section 2 (b) are former employees of a closed location who in the period from 18 months to 12 months prior to the location's plant closing date were laid off and who broke service prior to such date. Except as provided in this paragraph, such former employees are ineligible for any other benefits payable to active employees affected by a plant closing. The payment of Severance Pay as described herein shall not serve to restore service or otherwise affect the benefit status of such former employees.

(4) Such employee may request that his date of termination be advanced so that he can accept other employment and the local management will give due regard to this request.

(5) Notwithstanding the provisions of this Section 2, an employee who is affected by plant closing may elect, prior to the specific date of his termination for plant closing, to be placed on lack of work status. In such event, the employee will be paid benefits under Section 4 below, in lieu of any and all of the benefits set forth in this Section 2.

(6) *Computation of Severance Pay*

(i) An employee with one or more but less than fifteen years of continuous service will, in accordance with the provisions set forth above, be eligible for Severance Pay computed on the basis of one and ½ week's pay for each of the employee's full years of continuous service plus ⅜ of a week's pay for each additional 3 months of continuous service at the time of termination; provided that the amount of the Severance Pay benefit as computed under this paragraph shall be subject to a minimum benefit equal to 4 weeks' pay.

(ii) An employee with fifteen or more years of continuous service will, in accordance with the provisions set forth above, be eligible for Severance Pay computed on the basis of two weeks' pay for each of the employee's full years of continuous service plus ½ of a week's pay for each additional 3 months of continuous service at the time of termination.

(7) *Deferral Election*

An employee who elects to receive Severance Pay in a lump sum may elect to defer payment of half or all of the lump sum until the first month of the year following his termination because of a plant closing. Once made, such election will be irrevocable. Payment shall be made to the estate of any employee electing to defer payment under this Section 2(b)(7) if such employee dies before payment has been made.

(c) *Employment Assistance Program*

To assist employees terminated because of a plant closing to find new jobs and to learn new skills, local management will establish an Employment Assistance Program following announcement of a decision to close a plant. The Employment Assistance Program will include job placement assistance and education and retraining assistance.

(1) *Job Placement Assistance*

(i) Job Placement Assistance will include job counseling as well as job information services. Examples of such services are counseling in job search and interviewing techniques, identification and assessment of skills, and employment application and resume preparation as well as providing employees information on placement opportunities.

(ii) Local Union involvement will be encouraged in these activities and local management may also use the expertise and resources of public and private agencies in providing these services.

(iii) Two (2) employee representatives designated by the Local (one such representative in a plant of less than 300 represented employees) will each be paid by the Company at their respective rate then prevailing, for approved absences from work up to a total of eight (8) hours per week to work with local management in the establishment and operation of the Employment Assistance Program.

(2) *Education and Retraining Assistance*

(i) An employee with one or more years of continuous service who is terminated as a result of a plant closing will be eligible to receive Education and Retraining Assistance for courses approved by the Company which contribute to or enhance the employee's ability to obtain other employment provided that the employee begins the approved course within one year following termination. Approved courses will normally be given at schools which are accredited by recognized regional or state accrediting agencies and may include:

- Occupational or vocational skill development;
- Fundamental reading or numerical skill improvement;
- High school diploma or equivalency achievement; and
- College level career oriented courses.

(ii) An employee will be reimbursed up to a maximum of twelve thousand five hundred dollars ($12,500) for authorized expenses which are incurred within three years following termination provided a passing grade is received in the course. Authorized expenses include verified tuition, registration and other compulsory fees, costs of necessary books, and other required supplies. However, if tuition or other authorized expenses are covered by government benefits, other employers, or scholarships, the Company reimbursement will not apply to that portion covered by such other plan.

(iii) An employee who elects to receive benefits under the Income Extension Aid layoff option in lieu of benefits under the Plant Closing section of this Article will not be eligible for Education and Retraining Assistance.

(b) *Optional Local Plant Closing Termination Agreement.*

Because the circumstances in a plant closing will vary in terms of employment, location and timing, as well as other local considerations, the Local Union and local management may negotiate a Special Local Agreement covering the plant closing termination procedure for employees represented by the Local. Any such agreement shall be in writing and approved in accordance with Article XXI, Section 2, of this National Agreement.

3. *Retraining and Readjustment Assistance*

(a) *Rate Guarantee*

An hourly rated or nonexempt salaried employee whose job is directly eliminated by a transfer of work, the discontinuance of a discrete, unreplaced product line, the introduction of a robot, or the introduction of an automated manufacturing or office machine shall be paid on any job to which transferred or recalled in the plant at a rate not less than the regular hourly daywork rate (average earnings exclusive of overtime premium in the case of incentive workers and actual straight time salary rate in the case of nonexempt salaried employees) of the job eliminated for up to seventy-eight (78) weeks immediately following the original transfer or layoff. In the event that an hourly rated or nonexempt salaried employee is displaced due to a reduction in force within six months of the Company's decision to subcontract work that would otherwise have been performed by the employee had it not been subcontracted, and where such decision did not reduce the number of represented employees performing ongoing work at that time, such. Subsequently displaced employee shall be eligible for rate guarantee under this Section 3(a), effective at the time of displacement.

(b) *Special Retirement Bonus*

(1) *Election*

An hourly rated or nonexempt salaried employee who is age sixty (60) or older with fifteen (15) or more years of continuous service and is assigned to a job classification which the Company has announced is expected to be directly adversely affected by a transfer of work, the discontinuance of a discrete, unreplaced product line, the introduction of a robot, or the introduction of an automated manufacturing or office machine may elect to be considered for termination with a Special Retirement Bonus. This election shall be made within fifteen (15) days following the Company announcement of its decision involving the transfer of work, the discontinuance of a discrete, unreplaced product line, introduction of a robot, or introduction of an automated manufacturing or office machine which is expected to result in the elimination of certain jobs.

(2) *Procedure*

Eligible employees electing this option will be designated by their seniority for a Special Retirement Bonus. A termination under this option will be effective and the Special Retirement Bonus will be paid when a job in the particular job classification to which the eligible employee is assigned is directly eliminated by the previously announced transfer of work, the discontinuance of a discrete, unreplaced product line, introduction of a robot, or introduction of an automated manufacturing or office machine, which directly results in a net reduction in the total number of employees working in that same job classification.

(3) *Special Payment*

This Special Retirement Bonus shall be $18,000.

(4) *Indirect Bonus Eligibility*

In the event that the number of eligible employees electing this option is less than the number of employees directly adversely affected by the Company's announced action, opportunities to elect Special Voluntary Layoff Bonus under Section 4(c) shall arise, up to the number of positions directly adversely affected by the transfer of work, the discontinuance of a discrete, unreplaced product line, or the introduction of an automated manufacturing or office machine. To be eligible an employee must be in a classification that is reduced due to displacement as a result of an announced Company action described above, and otherwise meets the criteria established in Section 4(c). Such displacement is hereby deemed to be a reduction of force of indefinite duration.

(c) *Special Placement Procedure*

(1) *Election.* An hourly rated or non-exempt salaried employee whose job is directly eliminated by a transfer of work, the discontinuance of a discrete, unreplaced product line, the introduction of a robot, or the introduction of an automated manufacturing machine or office machine may request a Special Placement from the eliminated job in lieu of placement, displacement or layoff under the regular local layoff and rehiring procedure. The Special Placement request must be made within two (2) working days

following notification to the employee of the regular placement, displacement or layoff

(2) *Placement*

(i) If a timely request is made, an eligible employee shall be placed, or displace with seniority, on an available equal or lower rated job classification if the employee has the necessary minimum qualifications for the job; provided the Special Placement would be on a higher rated job than that provided by the regular placement.

(ii) If an eligible hourly rated employee who has made a timely request is unable to be placed under Section 3(c)(2)(i) above, such employee shall be placed, or displace with seniority, on an equal or lower rated job up to the top of the one month progression schedule without regard to the regular minimum qualifications for the job; provided the Special Placement would be on a higher rated job than that provided by the regular placement.

(iii). An employee placed under this Section 3(c) is required to achieve normal performance within the time period of the regular progression schedule.

(d) *Optional Local Retraining and Placement Agreement*

Whenever the Company announces a transfer of work, the discontinuance of a discrete, unreplaced product line, the introduction of a robot, or the introduction of an automated manufacturing or office machine, the Local Union and local management may negotiate a Local Retraining and Placement Agreement.

(e) *Preferential Placement*

(1) *Eligibility*

An hourly rated or nonexempt salaried employee: (i) eligible for Severance Pay under Section 2 or (ii) eligible for Income Extension Aid ("IEA") resulting from being displaced and subject to layoff in the immediate chain of displacement resulting when a job is directly eliminated by a transfer of work, the discontinuation of a discrete, unreplaced product line, the introduction of a robot, or the introduction of an automated manufacturing or office machine, or (iii) who has spent six (6) months on protected service due to layoff may elect, prior to the employee's termination for plant closing or layoff per (i) and (ii) above, or after six (6) months on protected service due to layoff and up to thirty (30) days thereafter per (iii) above (except where the laid off employee has elected to receive his IEA in lump sum), to be placed in a Preferential Placement status.

(2) *Election Procedure*

To elect Preferential Placement the employee shall designate up to ten (10) domestic General Electric Company manufacturing plant, service shop or distribution center locations within the four-year eligibility period on forms provided exclusively by the Company. Effective January 1, 2004, the term "locations" used in the prior sentence shall be construed for the sole purpose of this paragraph to include like locations maintained by GE affiliates participating in the Job and Income Security Plan for Hourly Employees and the Job and Income Security Plan for Nonexempt Employees. This election will not affect an individual's continuity of service. Individuals otherwise eligible for Preferential Placement pursuant to Section (e)(l)(i) and Section (e)(l)(ii) above, and who have made this election, will be placed in Preferential Placement status either: (i) on their designated termination date for plant closing, or (ii) on their layoff date. Individuals eligible for Preferential Placement under Section 3 (e)(1)(iii) and who have made this election, will be placed on Preferential Placement after six(6) months on protected service due to layoff. Individuals otherwise eligible for Preferential Placement pursuant to Section 3(e)(l)(i) or Section 3(e) (1)(ii) above may request, following the conclusion of decision bargaining, that their plant closing or layoff date be advanced in order to assume Preferential Placement and accept placement prior to their anticipated plant closing or layoff date. Local management shall give due regard to such request. Locations can be added to the employee's list to reach the ten (10) limit, but no listed locations can be eliminated and replaced or substituted for (even if closed).

(3) *Placement Standard*

Individuals in Preferential Placement status will be given preference, to the extent practical, over new hires for job openings at the locations designated by them in order of their length of continuity of service when they possess the necessary job qualifications established by the hiring location. The term "necessary job qualifications" shall be applied based on the upgrade standard for jobs above entry level. For entry level jobs in the One Month Progression Schedule the term "necessary job qualifications" shall be the standard a current employee at the location must meet to be placed in the entry level job.

Notwithstanding the preceding paragraph, Preferential Placement candidates applying for entry level positions in the One Month Progression Schedule with 25 years or more of continuous service shall be provisionally placed in such positions for up to three months. Such candidate must either demonstrate satisfactory progress in performing the entry level duties or perform such duties at a fully satisfactory level by the end of this provisional placement period. Failure to so demonstrate or perform will result in the candidate's removal from provisional placement. The candidate will then continue in Preferential Placement status as if such provisional placement had not occurred. The administrative removal of provisionally placed Preferential Placement candidates shall not be subject to arbitration.

(4) *Benefits While in Preferential Placement Status*

While in Preferential Placement status, an eligible employee will be paid IEA or IEA-type layoff benefits under the procedures set forth in Section 4(b)(1)(i) of this Article up to the amount, as applicable, of either: (i) the employee's eligibility for Severance Pay under Section 2 (b)(6) of this Article or, (ii) the employee' s eligibility for IEA under Section 4 (a)(l) of this Article. For those employees affected by a Plant Closing, if at the end of the thirty (30) day period the employee does not elect to participate in Preferential Placement, the amount of Severance Pay available under Section 2, less any amount paid in IEA-type benefits, will be paid in lump sum and the employee will terminate service. Such payments shall be in lieu of any and all other benefits set forth in the applicable Section 2 or Section 3 of this Article; provided, however, that an eligible employee affected by a plant closing may receive reimbursement for authorized expenses incurred pursuant to Section 2 (c)(2) respecting courses registered for within one year, and completed within three years, of the employee's scheduled plant closing date, and an eligible employee electing Preferential Placement from layoff status is eligible to participate in the Individual Development Program.

(5) *Seniority*

Individuals placed or re-employed under this Section 3 (e) will have seniority for the purpose of subsequent layoff, recall, upgrading and other seniority purposes at their new location based upon the established seniority procedures and practices at their new location. Once placed through Preferential Placement, an employee will not be eligible for recall to his former location except in the event he is laid off or terminated by a plant closing at his new location. If laid off or terminated due to plant closing at the location at which he was placed, recall rights will be reinstated for the remainder of the original recall period.

(6) *Relocation Assistance*

If an individual who elected Preferential Placement is placed or re-employed under this Section 3 (e) within three (3) years from, as applicable, that individual's designated date of termination for plant closing, layoff date, or service break date for those breaking service after twelve (12) months on protected service due to layoff, that employee shall be eligible for reimbursement for substantiated reasonable and necessary relocation expenses to the new location up to a maximum of $4,000 for individual employees without dependents or $8,000 for employees with dependents living in the employee's home (as verified by federal income tax returns). An eligible individual who has elected Preferential Placement is eligible for reimbursement of documented expenses up to $275 per visit incurred for the purpose of attending approved selection procedures established by the designated locations.

(7) *Residual Benefits*

Except for employees electing Preferential Placement pursuant to Section 3(e)(1)(iii) above, if an employee who elected Preferential Placement is not placed or re-employed by the Company within one year from that individual 's designated date of, as applicable, (i) termination for plant closing or (ii) layoff, that individual will, as appropriate, be deemed either: to have been terminated as of that individual's respective date of termination for plant closing and paid the Severance Pay the individual would have received under Section 2 (b)(6) if the Preferential Placement status had not been elected, less any IEA-type benefits paid under paragraph 4 of this Section 3 (e), or break service and be paid any remaining IEA under Section 4 (a)(l), less any IEA benefits paid under paragraph 4 of this Section 3 (e). If placed or re-employed from Preferential Placement status, weekly EA-type or weekly IEA layoff benefits need not be repaid in order to restore eligibility for future layoff benefits based on prior service.

(8) *Termination of Preferential Placement Rights at a Selected Location*

An individual on Preferential Placement shall administratively forfeit placement opportunities at a selected location for repeated failure to make good faith efforts to respond to opportunities for placement consideration. Examples of such failure include:

— Rejecting an interview or offer of employment
— Failing to respond to a scheduled selection procedure without adequate notice

(9) *Termination of Preferential Placement Status*

Preferential Placement status will terminate upon the earlier of any of the following occurrences:

(i) recall at the work location that gave rise to the preferential placement status prior to placement,

(ii) placement at a designated preferential placement location,

(iii) acceptance of a job offer and failure to report as scheduled without satisfactory explanation,

(iv) refusal of three preferential placement job offers,

(v) the lapsing of four years since the election of this status.

Individuals placed under this Section 3(e) and thereafter laid off within eighteen months may, notwithstanding normal eligibility requirements, elect Preferential Placement.

4.   *Income Extension Aid*

(a) *Computation of Income Extension Aid*

(1) An employee with one or more years of continuous service will, in accordance with the provisions hereinafter set forth, have available Income

Extension Aid computed on the basis of one week's pay for each of the employee's full years of continuous service plus 1/4 of a week's pay for each additional 3 months of continuous service at the time of layoff. An employee with at least six months but less than one year of continuous service will, in accordance with the provisions hereinafter set forth, have available a total of two (2) weeks pay for Income Extension Aid.

(2) If the amount of Income Extension Aid available to any employee as computed in Subsection (a)(1) has been reduced by payments under any of the options below, then, providing he has returned to work from layoff, the total amount available as described in Subsection (a)(l) shall be automatically restored. This Subsection (2) shall not apply where payments have been made under Section 4(b)(1)(iii) or under Plant Closing Section 2 where the employee is rehired within 6 months of termination, except that when an employee makes repayment of benefits paid under such Section 4(b)(l)(iii) or Section 2, this Subsection (a)(2) shall apply when he returns to work with respect to a subsequent layoff.

(3) *Minimum Benefit*

The amount of the Income Extension Aid benefit as computed under Section 4(a)(1) shall be subject to a minimum benefit equal to 4 weeks' pay, except for employees with at least six months but less than one year continuous service, who shall have available a total of two (2) weeks pay. An employee laid off while in the process of service restoration under Article VIII, Section 2(e) shall qualify for the minimum benefit so long as his or her total service credits (including credits not yet restored) equal 12 months.

(b) *Benefits Available at Layoff*

(1) An eligible employee laid off for lack of work may elect from the following:

(i) The employee, while on layoff from the Company and so long as he is unemployed, may elect to receive a weekly payment from the Income Extension Aid payable to him, in such amounts and upon such conditions as set forth in this subsection.

Prior to the exhaustion of his entitlements to federal and state unemployment compensation benefits, the weekly payment shall be in that amount (if any) which, when added to the total federal and state unemployment compensation benefits received for that week, equals seventy-five percent of his weekly pay as defined in Section l(g), provided, however, that payment shall be made only if the employee has applied for and received unemployment compensation benefits for that week and only if he has provided the Company with satisfactory proof of the total of such benefits received for the week. In the event an employee seeking benefits under this Section 4 is denied unemployment compensation payment in whole or in part, solely because of a disability arising more than 31 days following layoff rendering the employee unable to work, or due to the receipt of public or private retirement income, because of insufficient earnings to establish unemployment compensation eligibility or because unemployment compensation benefits have been exhausted for the base year, that employee shall be entitled to weekly IEA payment as though there had been no such unemployment compensation disqualification.

After exhaustion of his entitlements to federal and state unemployment compensation benefits, the weekly payment shall be in that amount which equals seventy-five percent of his weekly pay as defined in Section l(g). Payments shall be made only if the employee certifies that he is still unemployed and they shall continue only until the full amount for which the employee qualifies under Section 4(a) is paid.

Payments (in such amount and upon such conditions as set forth above) may also be made to an employee on layoff while he is unemployed and attending a recognized trade or professional school or training course under the GE Individual Development Program, attendance at which makes him ineligible for state or federal unemployment compensation benefits. Percentage changes referenced in this Section 4(b)(l)(i) shall be effective 10/1/97.

(ii) In any event, at the end of one year on layoff, or upon termination of continuity of service due to voluntary retirement, any balance in the Income Extension Aid available to him not theretofore paid will be paid in a lump sum to the employee.

(iii) As a special option, an employee may, with the approval of local management, which approval shall not be unreasonably withheld, elect to receive the total amount of Income Extension Aid and any vacation or other accumulated allowances due, and at the time of such payment, terminate employment and thus forego recall rights.

(2) Income Extension payments made under Subsections (b)(1)(i) and (ii), above, shall not affect service credits previously accumulated, continuity of service, and recall rights. It will not be necessary for an employee to repay any Income Extension Aid payable under said Subsections (b)(1)(i) and (ii) above.

(3) In the event an employee elects, as provided for in Section 7(a) of Article IX of this Agreement with respect to a scheduled shutdown period, to take the time off without pay as though on a temporary layoff, the employee shall not be eligible for Income Extension Aid for that scheduled shutdown period.

(c) *Special Voluntary Layoff Bonus*

Whenever the Company announces an indefinite reduction in force, a Special Voluntary Layoff Bonus opportunity will exist. To be eligible an employee must be age sixty (60) or older, have fifteen (15) years of continuous service, be in a specific job classification directly adversely affected, and must have filed a request to be considered at least fifteen (15) days in advance of the announcement of the indefinite reduction in force. To the extent such requests exceed the number of affected jobs in each classification, selection will be on the basis of seniority. Alternatively, in the event that the number of eligible employees electing this option is less than the number of employees directly adversely affected, secondary opportunities, up to the total number of positions directly adversely affected, shall be available to eligible employees in classifications affected by displacements resulting from the indefinite reduction in force. Employees selected for a Special Voluntary Layoff Bonus must confirm their acceptance immediately following the Company's offer of the Special Voluntary Layoff Bonus. Employees accepting a Special Voluntary Layoff Bonus will receive a lump sum payment of $18,000 in lieu of any other payment under this Article and will terminate service with the Company.

5.   *Notice, Bargaining and Information Requirements*

This Section sets forth the full obligations of the Company with regard to notice, bargaining with and information to the Union concerning plant closing, work transfer, subcontracting and the installation of robots or automated manufacturing or office machines.

(a) *Plant Closing*

(1) *Notice.* The Company will give notice of its intent to close a manufacturing plant, service shop or distribution center a minimum of one year in advance of the plant closing date to the Union, the Local involved and to employees concerned. Such notice will include identification of the plant to be closed, the Local involved and the date when terminations of represented employees because of the plant closing are expected to begin.

(2) *Bargaining.* If the Local requests decision bargaining within ten (10) working days following a Company notice of intent to close a manufacturing plant, service shop, or distribution center, the Company will be available to meet with the Local within five (5) working days of such request and the bargaining period shall continue for up to sixty (60) calendar days from the date of the Company notice of intent to close the plant unless this period is extended by mutual agreement. The Company will make a decision whether or not to close the plant after this bargaining period.

(3) *Information.* If information is requested by the Local for bargaining provided for in Section 5(a)(2) of this Article, the Company will promptly

make the following information available to the Local for such bargaining. This information will specifically include the express reason(s) for intending to close the plant and, where employment cost is a significant factor, the related wages, payroll allowances and employee benefits expenses of represented employees at the plant intended to be closed. This information will be treated as confidential by the Local.

(b) *Transfer of Ongoing Production Work*

(1) *Notice.* The Company will give notice of its intent to transfer ongoing production work a minimum of six (6) months in advance of the effective date of the work transfer to the Local involved. Such notice will include identification of the work to be transferred, the expected decrease in the number of represented employees as a direct consequence of the transfer of work and the anticipated date of the transfer of work.

(2) *Bargaining.* If the Local requests decision bargaining within ten (10) working days following a Company notice of intent to transfer ongoing production work, the Company will be available to meet with the Local within five (5) working days of such request and the bargaining period shall continue for up to sixty (60) calendar days from the date of the Company notice of intent to transfer the work unless the period is extended by mutual agreement. The Company will make a decision whether or not to transfer such work after this bargaining period.

(3) *Information.* If information is requested by the Local for bargaining provided for in Section 5(b)(2) of this Article, the Company will promptly make the following information available to the Local for such bargaining. The information will specifically include the express reason(s) for intending to transfer the work. Where cost is a significant factor in the Company's intent to transfer the work, the Company will provide the Local with a cost comparison between the production cost of the work to be transferred and the projected cost to the Company of having the work performed elsewhere. Likewise, the Company will also provide the related wages, payroll allowances and employee benefits expenses of represented employees for the work intended to be transferred and of their counterparts who would be assigned the work. This information will be treated as confidential by the Local.

(c) *Transfer of Nonproduction Work*

(1) *Notice.* The Company will give notice of its intent to transfer nonproduction work, or subcontract nonproduction work at the same plant location or elsewhere if such subcontracting of work would directly cause a decrease in the number of represented employees performing such work, a minimum of sixty (60) calendar days in advance of the effective date of the work transfer or subcontracting to the Local involved. In the case of transfers of work or subcontracting that would directly cause a decrease of more

than 50 represented employees performing such work, the notice period will be six (6) months. Such notice will include identification of the work to be transferred or subcontracted, the expected decrease in the number of represented employees as a direct consequence of the transfer of work or subcontracting and the anticipated date of the transfer of work or subcontracting.

(2) *Bargaining*. If the Local requests decision bargaining within ten (10) working days following a Company notice of intent to subcontract or transfer nonproduction work, the Company will be available to meet with the Local within five (5) working days of such request and the bargaining period shall continue for up to forty-five (45) calendar days from the date of the Company notice of intent to subcontract or transfer the work unless this period is extended by mutual agreement. This bargaining period shall continue for up to sixty (60) days instead of forty-five (45) days in cases where the subcontract or transfer of nonproduction work would directly cause a decrease of more than fifty (50) represented employees performing such work. The Company will make a decision whether or not to subcontract or transfer such work after this bargaining period.

(3) *Information*. If information is requested by the Local for bargaining provided for in Section 5(c)(2) of this Article, the Company will promptly make the following information available to the Local for such bargaining. The information will specifically include the express reason(s) for intending to subcontract or transfer the work. Where cost is a significant factor in the Company's intent to transfer the work, the Company will provide the Local with a cost comparison between the cost of the nonproduction work to be transferred and the projected cost to the Company of having the work subcontracted or performed elsewhere. Likewise, the Company will also provide the related wages, payroll allowances and employee benefits expenses of represented employees for the work intended to be subcontracted or transferred and of their counterparts who would be assigned the work. This information will be treated as confidential by the Local.

(d) *Subcontracting of Trades Work at Plant Location*

(1) *Notice*. The Company will give notice to the Local of its intent to subcontract trades work, where the work will be done by a subcontractor at the same plant location or elsewhere and there is no decrease in the number of represented employees performing such trades work, before finalization of the proposed action provided that the work is of a nature that is normally performed by trades workers (maintenance, tool & die, and other similar classifications). Notice will not be required in emergency situations.

(2) *Bargaining*. If the Local requests bargaining concerning such subcontracting, the Company will promptly meet and discuss its plans with the

Local. However, in no event will the Company be obligated to withhold the effectuation of the proposed subcontracting for more than twenty-one (21) calendar days from the date of the notification to the Local.

(3) *Information.* If information is requested by the Local for bargaining provided for in Section 5(d)(2) of this Article, the Company will promptly make the following information available to the Local for such bargaining. This information will specifically include the express reason(s) for intending to subcontract the work and, where employment cost is a significant factor, comparative related wages, payroll allowances and employee benefits expenses of represented employees for the work intended to be subcontracted and of their counterparts who would be assigned the work. This bargaining information will be treated as confidential by the Local.

(e) *Installation of Robots or Automated Manufacturing or Office Machines*

With respect to the installation of robots or automated manufacturing or office machines, the Company will give a minimum of sixty (60) days' notice to the Local involved before the use of a robot or an automated manufacturing or office machine in a work area. Such notice will include a description of the function of the device, identification of the work involved, the expected decrease in the number of represented employees as a direct consequence of the use of the device and the anticipated date of the use of the device.

(f) The Company will notify the Local in writing of its decision to utilize a subcontractor to perform work of the type regularly performed by bargaining unit employees, where the work will be done by a subcontractor at another location and there is no decrease in the number of represented employees performing like work. The notice will give a general description of the work and state the express reasons for subcontracting the work.

6. *Job Preservation*

(a) *Decision Bargaining Guarantee*
In the event the Company announces its intention to close a plant under Section 5 (a), and following decision bargaining the Company retracts or modifies its announced intention based on a counter-proposal offered by the union to preserve jobs, such preserved jobs shall be excluded from further impact under Section 5 (a) for the earlier of three years or the duration of this Agreement and, in any case, for at least 12 months. In the event the Company announces its intention to transfer Ongoing Production Work under Section 5 (b), or transfer Nonproduction Work under Section 5 (c) and, following decision bargaining the Company retracts or modifies its announced intention

based on a counter-proposal offered by the union to preserve jobs, such preserved jobs shall be excluded from further impact under Section 5(b) and Section 5(c) for the earlier of three years or the duration of this Agreement and, in any case, for at least 18 months. Following the expiration of the Contract, such preserved jobs shall be subject to subsequent announcements of intent and decision bargaining in conformance with Section 5.

(b) *Job Competitiveness and Growth Committee*

The Company recognizes the importance of job growth and security to the Union and acknowledges that subcontracting work, the introduction of enhanced technology, and innovative manufacturing techniques, while enabling the Company to succeed in the many competitive environments in which it operates, may result in a decrease in General Electric Company jobs. In order to balance competitive realities with the Union's interest in protecting and growing jobs, the Company and Union will establish a joint Job Competitiveness and Growth Committee ("C&G Committee") at each Company location employing over 25 bargaining unit employees to meet and discuss issues such as:

- Opportunities for job creation
- Potential plant closing, outsourcing/subcontracting and work transfers, including situations where there is no direct decrease in the number of represented employees
- Training for anticipated technology changes
- Work practices and local agreements to increase efficiency and remove impediments to efficient operations
- Investment plans and potential impact on jobs
- Innovative manufacturing techniques
- Employee suggestions on process changes
- Marketplace and competitors
- Customer demands
- Labor costs

The C&G Committee will meet on a quarterly basis. Union representation on the C&G Committee will be determined solely by the Union and will be restricted to a maximum of 2 representatives for the first 25 to 500 bargaining unit employees, and 1 for each additional 500 unit employees up to a maximum of 6 representatives in total. Such representatives will be compensated at their regular rate for up to four hours for time spent participating in the quarterly C&G Committee meetings. This C&G Committee structure is not intended to displace the workings of other ongoing union management activities, including the grievance procedure and the decision bargaining provisions of Article XXII, which exist at each plant location.

The Company and the Union mutually agree to require Local management and Local unions at every covered location to fully participate in C&G Committee discussions in order to preserve and create jobs. Recognizing that there may be some issues that would benefit from the presence of other representatives from the Company and the Union, the Company agrees to consider requests for participation by the Company and Union representatives at specific local C&G Committee meetings on key job creation and competitive issues identified by the Union.

It is recognized by the Company and the Union that locations not meeting the 25 employee threshold may have job preservation issues that would justify conducting job preservation meetings on a periodic basis. Local management and the Local union are authorized and encouraged to hold such meetings where a need exists.

The Company and the Union recognize the value of holding periodic meetings at the business level to discuss the state of the business and future plans that may impact employees represented by the Union. To that end, the Company and the Union will develop a process to conduct semi-annual meetings at the business level for this purpose.

(c) *Job Preservation Guarantee*

In the event that the Company decides not to pursue potential outsourcing and work transfer opportunities reviewed in a Job Competitiveness and Growth Committee as a result of proposals made by the union, the jobs that would have been directly impacted by the potential outsourcing or work transfer shall be excluded from further impact under Section 5 for the earlier of three years or the duration of this Agreement but, in any case, for at least 12 months provided the Company and the Local agree in writing on the specific jobs that were preserved by the union's proposals.

7.   *Vested Rights Under Pension Plan*

The receipt of Income Extension Aid, Severance Pay, or a rate guarantee will not affect any rights the employee may have under the Vesting Provision of the Pension Plan.

8.   *Lump Sum Payments*

Service credits previously accumulated, continuity of service, and recall rights will be lost upon receipt by the employee of an Income Extension Aid payment in lump sum under Section 4(b)(1)(iii), special termination payments under this Article, or payment of Severance Pay under the Plant Closing Section 2. However, an employee eligible for such a payment, who is within one year of reaching optional retirement at age 60 under the GE Pension Plan, shall retain such previously accumulated service credits and continuity of service until such employee reaches optional retirement age notwithstanding the receipt of such a payment unless the employee retires before electing optional retirement at age 60.

In the event of a subsequent rehire as a "new" employee within a period of time which does not exceed the length of prior service, service credits, and recall rights previously lost shall be automatically restored provided repayment of the Income Extension Aid is made by the employee within a reasonable time after rehire. No such repayment, however, shall be required if the rehire date is more than one year from the date of termination which resulted from the election of a lump sum payment under Section 4(b)(1)(iii) or the special termination payments under Section 3(b) or Section 4(c).

Service credits, continuity of service, and recall rights lost at termination upon receipt of payments under Plant Closing Section 2, shall be restored automatically without repayment in the event of subsequent rehire more than 6 months after such termination. An employee who having received payments under Plant Closing Section 2, is rehired 6 months or less after his termination and who has made arrangements satisfactory to the Company providing for repayment shall, during such time as he is not in default of such arrangements and for the purpose only of layoff and recall, be deemed to possess the service credits, continuity of service, and recall rights to be restored to him upon full repayment.

9. *Non-Duplication*

If any part of an employee's continuous service is used as the basis for an actual payment under any of the options of the Income Extension Aid or Severance Pay arrangement, that part of his continuous service may not be used again for such purpose, either during that period of layoff or any subsequent period of layoff or plant closing, unless repayment has been made as provided in Section 8, above.

Where an indefinite reduction in force triggers eligibility for benefits under this Article, the designation of individuals who may exercise the benefits under this Article will be based on the integrated order of their seniority so that the number of employees electing benefits does not exceed the net number of positions eliminated.

Employees, eligible for a benefit under this Article either by designation or by election, may exercise only one severance or layoff benefit. Employees who have exercised the Special Early Retirement Option or Plant Closing

Pension Option under the Pension Plan shall have the Special Early Retirement Option Offset deducted from any severance or layoff benefit otherwise due under this Article.

10. *Other*

The provisions of this article shall not be applicable where the Company decides to close a plant or lay off an employee because of the Company's inability to secure production, or carry on its operations, as a consequence of a strike, slowdown, or other interference with or interruption with work participated in by employees in a Company plant, service shop, or other facility. However, the operation of this section shall not affect the rights or benefits already provided hereunder to an employee laid off for lack of work prior to the commencement of any such strike, interference, or interruption.

11. A grievance arising under this article may be processed in accordance with the grievance procedure set forth in Article XIII. However, no matter or controversy concerning the provisions of this article or the interpretation or application thereof shall be subject to arbitration under the provisions of Article XV hereof, except by mutual agreement.

***

Article XXVIII.   Upgrading and Job Posting

1. *Standard for Filling Open Jobs and Upgrading*

The Company will, to the extent practical, give first consideration for job openings and upgrading to present employees, when employees with the necessary qualifications are available. In upgrading employees to higher rated jobs, the Company will take into consideration as an important factor, the relative length of seniority of the employees who it finds are qualified for such upgrading; provided, however, that in upgrading employees to job openings with job rates within the one-month progression schedule, as provided for in Article VI, Section 5(a)(4)(a) of this Agreement, the relative seniority of those employees found qualified for such upgrading shall be the controlling factor.

When filling a job opening by upgrading, a request for the open job by an employee in a different, equal rated job classification or a higher rated job classification shall be treated as though it were a request to be considered for a higher rated job classification if the job opening affords the employee with an immediate or future higher earnings opportunity; provided that the employee has not previously so transferred during the same calendar year.

2. *Local Negotiations*

Because the product mix, organization complexity, and other circumstances vary in the plant locations covered by this agreement and to improve the opportunity for upward mobility of all employees represented by the Union and to continue to assure an equal opportunity for such employees to express their interests in and be considered for upgrading to job openings without regard to race, color, sex, creed, marital status, age, or national origin, local management and the Local Union shall negotiate a written upgrading agreement for each of the locations listed in the Preamble. In order to implement the provisions of Section 1, above, it is the intent of the parties that such agreement would provide for advance notice of job openings which are to be filled by upgrading where practical. Such agreement shall be approved in accordance with Article XXI, Section 2, of this National Agreement and shall not alter any obligation or right not to fill an opening by upgrading nor shall it limit any right an employee or the Union may have under Article XIII, XIV, and XV of this National Agreement to protest a selection.

ARTICLE XXIX. RESPONSIBILITY OF THE PARTIES

The parties recognize that, under this Agreement, each of them has responsibilities for the welfare and security of the employees:

(a) The Company recognizes that it is the responsibility of the Union to represent the employees effectively and fairly;

(b) Subject only to any limitations stated in this Agreement, or in any other agreement between the Company and the Union or a Local, the Union and the Locals recognize that the Company retains the exclusive right to manage its business, including (but not limited to) the right to determine the methods and means by which its operations are to be carried on, to direct the work force, and to conduct its operations in a safe and effective manner.

This article does not modify or limit the rights of the parties, or of the employees, under any other provisions of this Agreement or under any other agreement between the Company and the Union or the Locals, nor will it operate to deprive employees of any wage or other benefits to which they have been or will become entitled by virtue of an existing or future agreement between the Company and the Union or a Local.

ARTICLE XXX.   ISSUES OF GENERAL APPLICATION

This Agreement, the 2011-2015 Settlement Agreement, the 2011-2015 Wage Agreement, and the 2011-2015 Pension and Insurance Agreement between the parties are intended to be and shall be in full settlement of all issues which were the subject of collective bargaining between the parties in national level collective bargaining negotiations in 2011. Consequently, it is agreed that none of such issues shall be subject to collective bargaining during the term of this Agreement and there shall be no strike or lockout in connection with any such issue or issues; provided, however, that this provision shall not be construed to limit or modify the rights of the parties hereto under Article VI, Section 1, and Article XIV of this Agreement.

ARTICLE XXXI.   DURATION OF AGREEMENT

This National Agreement shall be effective as of June 20, 2011, between the Company, the Union, and each of the IUE-CWA, AFL-CIO, CLC Locals now certified as the representative of Company employees, as set forth in the Preamble to this Agreement, and shall continue in full force and effect to and including the 21st day of June, 2015, and from year to year thereafter unless modified or terminated as hereinafter provided.

ARTICLE XXXII.   MODIFICATION AND TERMINATION

(a) Either the Company or the Union may terminate this National Agreement by written notice to the other not more than ninety days and not less than sixty days prior to June 21, 2015, or prior to June 21 of any subsequent year. Not more than 15 days following receipt of such notice, collective bargaining negotiations shall commence between the parties for the purpose of considering the terms of a new agreement, and a proposal for a revision of wages which may be submitted by either the Company or the Union.

(b) If either the Company or the Union desires to modify this National Agreement, it shall, not more than ninety days and not less than sixty days prior to June 21, 2015, or prior to June 21 of any subsequent year, so notify the other in writing. Not more than 15 days following receipt of such notice, collective bargaining negotiations shall commence between the parties for the purpose of considering changes in this National Agreement, and a proposal for revision of wages which may be submitted by either the Company or the Union.

If settlement is not reached by June 21, 2015, or prior to June 21 of any subsequent year, this National Agreement shall continue in full force and effect until the tenth day following written notice given by either the Company or the Union of its intention to terminate such Agreement, during which time there shall be no strike or lockout.

ARTICLE XXXIII. NOTICES

All notices given under the provisions of this Agreement shall be in writing and shall be sufficient if sent by mail addressed, if to the Union, to IUE-CWA, The Industrial Division of the Communications Workers of America, AFL-CIO, CLC, 1275 K Street, N.W., Washington, D.C. 20005, or to such other address the Union shall furnish the Company in writing; and if to the Company, to General Electric Company, Fairfield, Connecticut 06828, or to such other address the Company shall furnish the Union in writing.

Dated: August 1, 2011

Selected Worker Center Materials

Summary of New York Greengrocer Code of Conduct (2002)
available at: *http://ag.ny.gov/sites/default/files/pdfs/bureaus/labor/ final_ggcode_english_short.pdf*

1. *Minimum Wage & Overtime.* Pay all employees at least minimum wage, now $5.15 per hour. Pay all employees "overtime" — 1 ½ an employee's regular hourly rate for all hours worked past forty per week.

2. *Timely Pay.* Pay employees in a timely manner.

3. *Records & Pay stubs.* Keep all payroll & time records required by state and federal law. Give each employee a weekly pay stub of hours and wages (gross & net)

4. *Rest.* for meal break and others as required by law.

5. *Rights Poster.* Post this Code on a wall in an easy-to-see location. Post a notice on a wall about basic wage and hour Give each employee one full unpaid day of rest per week. Give each employee at least ½ hour uninterrupted rights. The Code and notice will be in at least English, Spanish, and Korean.

6. *Days off.* For employees who have worked at the store for at least one year: provide 2 paid sick days and one workweek of paid vacation days per year. For employees who have worked at the store for at least two years: provide 3 paid sick days and one workweek of paid vacation days per year.

7. *Seminars.* Attend at least one labor law seminar by Attorney General's Office

8. *Not Retaliate.* The Code employer will not discharge or retaliate against any employee for making a complaint to the employer, the government, or the Monitor about violations of the Labor Law or this Code.

9. *Organizing.* The Code employer recognizes employees have legal right to organize and to join labor unions of their own choosing, and that the law prohibits retaliation against employees for organizing or joining a labor union.

10. *Monitoring.* The Code employer agrees to submit to unannounced monitoring of compliance with the Code at least two to three times per year. When monitoring occurs, the Code employer will show all payroll and time records, and make employees available for private, confidential interviews.

11. *Consumers.* A Code of Conduct Seal will be displayed in the store window as long as the Code Employer is in good standing. A list of Code members in good standing is available at the New York State Attorney General's website: www.oag.ny.gov. Code members no longer in good standing must post a notice stating as such, and will also be listed on the website.

12. *Hotline.* Call 1-800-729-1180 with complaints of violations.

Selected Cross-Border Labor Law Instruments

U.S. Generalized System of Preferences (GSP)
19 U.S.C. §§2461 et seq.

§2461. Authority to extend preferences

The President may provide duty-free treatment for any eligible article from any beneficiary developing country in accordance with the provisions of this title. . . .

§2462. Designation of beneficiary developing countries . . .

(b)(2) Other bases for ineligibility. The President shall not designate any country a beneficiary developing country under this title if any of the following applies: . . .

> (G) Such country has not taken or is not taking steps to afford internationally recognized worker rights to workers in the country (including any designated zone in that country).

> (H) Such country has not implemented its commitments to eliminate the worst forms of child labor.

Subparagraphs . . . (G) and (H) . . . shall not prevent the designation of any country as a beneficiary developing country under this title if the President determines that such designation will be in the national economic interest of the United States and reports such determination to the Congress with the reasons therefor.

(c) Factors affecting country designation. In determining whether to designate any country as a beneficiary developing country under this title, the President shall take into account . . .

> (7) whether or not such country has taken or is taking steps to afford to workers in that country (including any designated zone in that country) internationally recognized worker rights.

(d) Withdrawal, suspension, or limitation of country designation.

> (1) In general. The President may withdraw, suspend, or limit the application of the duty-free treatment accorded under this title with

respect to any country. In taking any action under this subsection, the President shall consider the factors set forth in ... subsection (c) of this section. ...

§2464. Review and Report to Congress

The President shall submit an annual report to the Congress on the status of internationally recognized worker rights within each beneficiary developing country ...

§2467. Definitions

For purposes of this title: ...

(4) *Internationally recognized worker rights.* The term "internationally recognized worker rights" includes —

(A) the right of association;

(B) the right to organize and bargain collectively;

(C) a prohibition on the use of any form of forced or compulsory labor;

(D) a minimum age for the employment of children, and a prohibition on the worst forms of child labor ... and

(E) acceptable conditions of work with respect to minimum wages, hours of work, and occupational safety and health. ...

North American Agreement on Labor Cooperation (1994)
(As implemented by Pub. Law. No. 103-182)

Article 2:   General Commitment

Affirming full respect for each Party's constitution, and recognizing the right of each Party to establish its own domestic labor standards, and to adopt or modify accordingly its labor laws and regulations, each Party shall ensure that its labor laws and regulations provide for high labor standards, consistent with high quality and productivity workplaces, and shall continue to strive to improve those standards in that light.

Article 3:   Government Enforcement Action

1. Each Party shall promote compliance with and effectively enforce its labor law through appropriate government action, subject to Article 42 [which states that the agreement does not "empower a Party's authorities to undertake labor law enforcement activities in the territory of another Party"], such as:

   (a) appointing and training inspectors;

   (b) monitoring compliance and investigating suspected violations, including through on-site inspections;

   (c) seeking assurances of voluntary compliance;

   (d) requiring recordkeeping and reporting;

   (e) encouraging the establishment of worker-management committees to address labor regulation of the workplace;

   (f) providing or encouraging mediation, conciliation and arbitration services; or

   (g) initiating in a timely manner, proceedings to seek appropriate sanctions or remedies for violations of its labor law

2. Each Party shall ensure that its competent authorities give due consideration in accordance with its law to any request by an employer, employee or their representatives, or other interested person, for an investigation of an alleged violation of the Party's labor law . . .

Annex 1 — Labor Principles

The following are guiding principles that the Parties are committed to promote, subject to each Party's domestic law, but do not establish common minimum standards for their domestic law. They indicate broad areas of concern where the Parties have developed, each in its own way, laws, regulations, procedures and practices that protect the rights and interests of their respective workforces.

1. *Freedom of association and protection of the right to organize.* The right of workers exercised freely and without impediment to establish and join organizations of their own choosing to further and defend their interests.

2. *The right to bargain collectively.* The protection of the right of organized workers to freely engage in collective bargaining on matters concerning the terms and conditions of employment.

3. *The right to strike.* The protection of the right of workers to strike in order to defend their collective interests. . . .

Dominican Republic-Central America Free Trade Agreement (2005)
(As implemented by Pub. Law. No. 109-53)

CH. SIXTEEN: LABOR

Article 16.1:   Statement of Shared Commitment

1. The Parties reaffirm their obligations as members of the International Labor Organization (ILO) and their commitments under the *ILO Declaration on Fundamental Principles and Rights at Work and its Follow-Up (1998)* (ILO Declaration). Each Party shall strive to ensure that such labor principles and the internationally recognized labor rights set forth in Article 16.8 are recognized and protected by its law.

2. The Parties affirm their full respect for their Constitutions. Recognizing the right of each Party to establish its own domestic labor standards, and to adopt or modify accordingly its labor laws, each Party shall strive to ensure that its laws provide for labor standards consistent with the internationally recognized labor rights set forth in Article 16.8 and shall strive to improve those standards in that light.

Article 16.2:   Enforcement of Labor Laws

1. (a) A Party shall not fail to effectively enforce its labor laws, through a sustained or recurring course of action or inaction, in a manner affecting trade between the Parties, after the date of entry into force of this Agreement.

   (b) Each Party retains the right to exercise discretion with respect to investigatory, prosecutorial, regulatory, and compliance matters and to make decisions regarding the allocation of resources to enforcement with respect to other labor matters determined to have higher priorities. Accordingly, the Parties understand that a Party is in compliance with subparagraph (a) where a course of action or inaction reflects a reasonable exercise of such discretion, or results from a *bona fide* decision regarding the allocation of resources.

2. The Parties recognize that it is inappropriate to encourage trade or investment by weakening or reducing the protections afforded in domestic labor laws. Accordingly, each Party shall strive to ensure that it does not waive or otherwise derogate from, or offer to waive or otherwise derogate from, such laws in a manner that weakens or reduces adherence to the internationally recognized labor rights referred to in Article 16.8 as an encouragement for trade with another Party, or as an encouragement for the

establishment, acquisition, expansion, or retention of an investment in its territory.

3. Nothing in this Chapter shall be construed to empower a Party's authority to undertake labor law enforcement activities in the territory of another Party.

Article 16.3: Procedural Guarantees and Public Awareness

1. Each Party shall ensure that persons with a legally recognized interest under its law in a particular matter have appropriate access to tribunals for the enforcement of the Party's labor laws. Such tribunals may include administrative, quasi-judicial, judicial, or labor tribunals, as provided in the Party's domestic law.

2. Each Party shall ensure that proceedings before such tribunals for the enforcement of its labor laws are fair, equitable, and transparent . . .

Article 16.4: Institutional Arrangements

1. The Parties hereby establish a Labor Affairs Council, comprising cabinet-level or equivalent representatives of the Parties, or their designees.

2. The Council shall meet within the first year after the date of entry into force of this Agreement and thereafter as often as it considers necessary to oversee the implementation of and review progress under this Chapter, including the activities of the Labor Cooperation and Capacity Building Mechanism established under Article 16.5, and to pursue the labor objectives of this Agreement. Unless the Parties otherwise agree, each meeting of the Council shall include a session at which members of the Council have an opportunity to meet with the public to discuss matters relating to the implementation of this Chapter.

3. Each Party shall designate an office within its labor ministry that shall serve as a contact point with the other Parties, and with the public, for purposes of carrying out the work of the Council, including coordination of the Labor Cooperation and Capacity Building Mechanism. Each Party's contact point shall provide for the submission, receipt, and consideration of communications from persons of a Party on matters related to the provisions of this Chapter, and shall make such communications available to the other Parties and, as appropriate, to the public. Each Party shall review such communications, as appropriate, in accordance with domestic procedures. The Council shall develop general guidelines for considering such communications.

4. Each Party may convene a new, or consult an existing, national labor advisory or consultative committee, comprising members of its public, including representatives of its labor and business organizations, to provide views on any issues related to this Chapter.

5. All decisions of the Council shall be taken by consensus. All decisions of the Council shall be made public, unless otherwise provided in this Agreement, or unless the Council otherwise decides.

6. The Council may prepare reports on matters related to the implementation of this Chapter, and shall make such reports public. . . .

Article 16.6:   Cooperative Labor Consultations

1. A Party may request consultations with another Party regarding any matter arising under this Chapter by delivering a written request to the contact point that the other Party has designated under Article 16.4.3.

2. The consultations shall begin promptly after delivery of the request. The request shall contain information that is specific and sufficient to enable the Party receiving the request to respond.

3. The consulting Parties shall make every attempt to arrive at a mutually satisfactory resolution of the matter, taking into account opportunities for cooperation relating to the matter, and may seek advice or assistance from any person or body they deem appropriate in order to fully examine the matter at issue.

4. If the consulting Parties fail to resolve the matter pursuant to paragraph 3, a consulting Party may request that the Council be convened to consider the matter by delivering a written request to the contact point of each of the other Parties.

5. The Council shall promptly convene and shall endeavor to resolve the matter, including, where appropriate, by consulting outside experts and having recourse to such procedures as good offices, conciliation, or mediation.

6. If the matter concerns whether a Party is conforming to its obligations under Article 16.2.1(a), and the consulting Parties have failed to resolve the matter within 60 days of a request under paragraph 1, the complaining Party may request consultations under Article 20.4 (Consultations) or a meeting of the Commission under Article 20.5 (Commission — Good Offices, Conciliation, and Mediation) and, as provided in Chapter Twenty (Dispute Settlement), thereafter have recourse to the other provisions of that Chapter. The Council may, as appropriate, provide information to the Commission on consultations held on the matter.

7. No Party may have recourse to dispute settlement under this Agreement for any matter arising under any provision of this Chapter other than Article 16.2.1(a).

8. No Party may have recourse to dispute settlement under this Agreement for a matter arising under Article 16.2.1(a) without first pursuing resolution of the matter in accordance with this Article.

9. In cases where the consulting Parties agree that a matter arising under this Chapter would be more appropriately addressed under another agreement to which the consulting Parties are party, they shall refer the matter for appropriate action in accordance with that agreement.

Article 16.7: Labor Roster

1. The Parties shall establish within six months after the date of entry into force of this Agreement and maintain a roster of up to 28 individuals who are willing and able to serve as panelists in disputes arising under Article 16.2.1(a). Unless the Parties otherwise agree, up to three members of the roster shall be nationals of each Party, and up to seven members of the roster shall be selected from among individuals who are not nationals of any Party. Labor roster members shall be appointed by consensus, and may be reappointed. Once established, a roster shall remain in effect for a minimum of three years, and shall remain in effect thereafter until the Parties constitute a new roster. The Parties may appoint a replacement where a roster member is no longer available to serve.

2. Labor roster members shall:

(a) have expertise or experience in labor law or its enforcement, international trade, or the resolution of disputes arising under international agreements;

(b) be chosen strictly on the basis of objectivity, reliability, and sound judgment;

(c) be independent of, and not affiliated with or take instructions from, any Party; and

(d) comply with a code of conduct to be established by the Commission.

3. Where a Party claims that a dispute arises under Article 16.2.1(a), Article 20.9 (Panel Selection) shall apply, except that the panel shall be composed entirely of panelists meeting the qualifications in paragraph 2.

Article 16.8:   Definitions

For purposes of this Chapter:
labor laws means a Party's statutes or regulations, or provisions thereof, that are directly related to the following internationally recognized labor rights:

(a) the right of association;

(b) the right to organize and bargain collectively . . .

CH. 20: DISPUTE SETTLEMENT

Section A: Dispute Settlement

Article 20.1:   Cooperation

The Parties shall at all times endeavor to agree on the interpretation and application of this Agreement, and shall make every attempt through cooperation and consultations to arrive at a mutually satisfactory resolution of any matter that might affect its operation.

Article 20.2:   Scope of Application

Except as otherwise provided in this Agreement, the dispute settlement provisions of this Chapter shall apply:

(a) with respect to the avoidance or settlement of all disputes between the Parties regarding the interpretation or application of this agreement;

(b) wherever a Party considers that an actual or proposed measure of another Party is or would be inconsistent with the obligations of this Agreement or that another Party has otherwise failed to carry out its obligations under this Agreement; and

(c) wherever a Party considers that an actual or proposed measure of another Party causes or would cause nullification or impairment in the sense of Annex 20.2.

Article 20.3:   Choice of Forum

1. Where a dispute regarding any matter arises under this Agreement and under another free trade agreement to which the disputing Parties are party or the WTO Agreement, the complaining Party may select the forum in which to settle the dispute.

2. Once the complaining Party has requested a panel under an agreement referred to in paragraph 1, the forum selected shall be used to the exclusion of the others.

Article 20.4:   Consultations

1. Any Party may request in writing consultations with any other Party with respect to any actual or proposed measure or any other matter that it considers might affect the operation of this Agreement.

2. The requesting Party shall deliver the request to the other Parties, and shall set out the reasons for the request, including identification of the actual or proposed measure or other matter at issue and an indication of the legal basis for the complaint.

3. A Party that considers it has a substantial trade interest in the matter may participate in the consultations on delivery of written notice to the other Parties within seven days of the date of delivery of the request for consultations. The Party shall include in its notice an explanation of its substantial trade interest in the matter.

4. Consultations on matters regarding perishable goods shall commence within 15 days of the date of delivery of the request.

5. The consulting Parties shall make every attempt to arrive at a mutually satisfactory resolution of any matter through consultations under this Article or other consultative provisions of this Agreement. To this end, the consulting Parties shall:

（a) provide sufficient information to enable a full examination of how the actual or proposed measure or other matter might affect the operation and application of this Agreement; and

（b) treat any confidential information exchanged in the course of consultations on the same basis as the Party providing the information.

6. In consultations under this Article, a consulting Party may request another consulting Party to make available personnel of its government agencies or other regulatory bodies who have expertise in the matter subject to consultations.

Article 20.5:   Commission — Good Offices, Conciliation, and Mediation

1. If the consulting Parties fail to resolve a matter pursuant to Article 20.4 within:

（a) 60 days of delivery of a request for consultations;

（b) 15 days of delivery of a request for consultations in matters regarding perishable goods; or

（c) such other period as they may agree,

any such Party may request in writing a meeting of the Commission.

2. A consulting Party may also request in writing a meeting of the Commission where consultations have been held pursuant to Article 16.6 (Cooperative Labor Consultations), Article 17.10 (Collaborative Environmental Consultations), or Article 7.8 (Committee on Technical Barriers to Trade).

3. The requesting Party shall deliver the request to the other Parties, and shall set out the reasons for the request, including identification of the actual or proposed measure or other matter at issue and an indication of the legal basis for the complaint.

4. Unless it decides otherwise, the Commission shall convene within ten days of delivery of the request and shall endeavor to resolve the dispute promptly. The Commission may:

    (a) call on such technical advisers or create such working groups or expert groups as it deems necessary;

    (b) have recourse to good offices, conciliation, mediation, or such other dispute resolution procedures; or

    (c) make recommendations, as may assist the consulting Parties to reach a mutually satisfactory resolution of the dispute.

5. Unless it decides otherwise, the Commission shall consolidate two or more proceedings before it pursuant to this Article regarding the same measure or matter. The Commission may consolidate two or more proceedings regarding other matters before it pursuant to this Article that it determines are appropriate to be considered jointly.

Article 20.6:   Request for an Arbitral Panel

1. If the consulting Parties fail to resolve a matter within:

    (a) 30 days after the Commission has convened pursuant to Article 20.5;

    (b) 30 days after the Commission has convened in respect of the matter most recently referred to it, where proceedings have been consolidated pursuant to Article 20.5.5;

    (c) 30 days after a Party has delivered a request for consultations under Article 20.4 in a matter regarding perishable goods, if the Commission has not convened pursuant to Article 20.5.4;

    (d) 75 days after a Party has delivered a request for consultations under Article 20.4, if the Commission has not convened pursuant to Article 20.5.4; or

    (e) such other period as the consulting Parties may agree,

any consulting Party that requested a meeting of the Commission with regard to the measure or other matter in accordance with Article 20.5 may request in writing the establishment of an arbitral panel to consider the matter. The requesting Party shall deliver the request to the other Parties, and shall set out the reasons for the request, including identification of the measure or other matter at issue and an indication of the legal basis for the complaint.

2. An arbitral panel shall be established upon delivery of a request.

3. A Party that is eligible under paragraph 1 to request the establishment of a panel and considers it has a substantial interest in the matter may join the arbitral panel proceedings as a complaining Party on delivery of written notice to the other Parties. The notice shall be delivered at the earliest possible time, and in any event no later than seven days after the date of delivery of the request by the Party for the establishment of a panel.

4. If a Party does not join as a complaining Party in accordance with paragraph 3, it normally shall refrain thereafter from initiating or continuing:

(a) a dispute settlement procedure under this Agreement; or

(b) a dispute settlement proceeding under the WTO Agreement or under another free trade agreement to which it and the Party complained against are party, on grounds that are substantially equivalent to those available to it under this Agreement,

regarding the same matter in the absence of a significant change in economic or commercial circumstances.

5. Unless otherwise agreed by the disputing Parties, the panel shall be established and perform its functions in a manner consistent with the provisions of this Chapter.

6. An arbitral panel may not be established to review a proposed measure.

Article 20.7:   Roster

1. The Parties shall establish within six months of the date of entry into force of this Agreement and maintain a roster of up to 70 individuals who are willing and able to serve as panelists. Unless the Parties otherwise agree, up to eight members of the roster shall be nationals of each Party, and up to 14 members of the roster shall be selected from among individuals who are not nationals of any Party. The roster members shall be appointed by consensus, and may be reappointed. Once established, a roster shall remain in effect for a minimum of three years, and shall remain in effect thereafter until the Parties constitute a new roster. The Parties may appoint a replacement where a roster member is no longer available to serve.

2. Roster members shall:

(a) have expertise or experience in law, international trade, other matters covered by this Agreement, or the resolution of disputes arising under international trade agreements;

(b) be chosen strictly on the basis of objectivity, reliability, and sound judgment;

(c) be independent of, and not be affiliated with or take instructions from, any Party; and

(d) comply with a code of conduct to be established by the Commission.

Article 20.8:   Qualifications of Panelists

All panelists shall meet the qualifications set out in Article 20.7.2. Individuals may not serve as panelists for a dispute in which they have participated pursuant to Article 20.5.4.

Article 20.9:   Panel Selection

1. The Parties shall apply the following procedures in selecting a panel:

(a) the panel shall comprise three members;

(b) the disputing Parties shall endeavor to agree on the chair of the panel within 15 days of the delivery of the request for the establishment of the panel. If the disputing Parties are unable to agree on the chair within this period, the chair shall be selected by lot within three days from among the roster members who are not nationals of a disputing Party;

(c) within 15 days of selection of the chair, the complaining Party or Parties shall select one panelist and the Party complained against shall select one panelist;

(d) if the complaining Party or Parties or the Party complained against fail to select a panelist within this period, the panelist shall be selected by lot within three days from among the roster members who are nationals of such Party or Parties, as the case may be; and

(e) each disputing Party shall endeavor to select panelists who have expertise or experience relevant to the subject matter of the dispute, as appropriate.

2. Panelists shall normally be selected from the roster. Any disputing Party may exercise a peremptory challenge against any individual not on the roster who is proposed as a panelist by a disputing Party within 15 days after the individual has been proposed.

3. If a disputing Party believes that a panelist is in violation of the code of conduct, the disputing Parties shall consult and if they agree, the panelist shall be removed and a new panelist shall be selected in accordance with this Article.

Article 20.10:   Rules of Procedure

1. The Commission shall establish by the date of entry into force of this Agreement Model Rules of Procedure, which shall ensure:

(a) a right to at least one hearing before the panel, which, subject to subparagraph (e), shall be open to the public;

(b) an opportunity for each disputing Party to provide initial and rebuttal written submissions;

(c) that each participating Party's written submissions, written versions of its oral statement, and written responses to a request or questions from the panel shall be public, subject to subparagraph (e);

(d) that the panel will consider requests from non-governmental entities in the disputing Parties' territories to provide written views regarding the dispute that may assist the panel in evaluating the submissions and arguments of the disputing Parties; and

(e) the protection of confidential information.

2. Unless the disputing Parties otherwise agree, the panel shall conduct its proceedings in accordance with the Model Rules of Procedure.

3. The Commission may modify the Model Rules of Procedure.

4. Unless the disputing Parties otherwise agree within 20 days from the date of the delivery of the request for the establishment of the panel, the terms of reference shall be:

> "To examine, in the light of the relevant provisions of this Agreement, the matter referenced in the panel request and to make findings, determinations, and recommendations as provided in Articles 20.10.6 and 20.13.3 and to deliver the written reports referred to in Articles 20.13 and 20.14."

5. If a complaining Party in its panel request has identified that a measure has nullified or impaired benefits, in the sense of Annex 20.2, the terms of reference shall so indicate.

6. If a disputing Party wishes the panel to make findings as to the degree of adverse trade effects on any Party of a Party's failure to conform with the obligations of this Agreement or of a Party's measure found to have caused nullification or impairment in the sense of Annex 20.2, the terms of reference shall so indicate. . . .

Article 20.13:   Initial Report

1. Unless the disputing Parties otherwise agree, the panel shall base its report on the relevant provisions of this Agreement, the submissions and

arguments of the disputing Parties, and on any information before it pursuant to Article 20.12.

2. If the disputing Parties request, the panel may make recommendations for resolution of the dispute.

3. Unless the disputing Parties otherwise agree, the panel shall, within 120 days after the last panelist is selected or such other period as the Model Rules of Procedure established pursuant to Article 20.10 may provide, present to the disputing Parties an initial report containing:

(a) findings of fact, including any findings pursuant to a request under Article 20.10.6;

(b) its determination as to whether a disputing Party has not conformed with its obligations under this Agreement or that a Party's measure is causing nullification or impairment in the sense of Annex 20.2, or any other determination requested in the terms of reference; and

(c) its recommendations, if the disputing Parties have requested them, for resolution of the dispute.

4. When the panel considers that it cannot provide its report within 120 days, it shall inform the disputing Parties in writing of the reasons for the delay together with an estimate of the period within which it will provide its report. In no case should the period to provide the report exceed 180 days. The panel shall inform the disputing Parties of any determination under this paragraph no later than seven days after the initial written submission of the complaining Party or Parties and shall adjust the remainder of the schedule accordingly.

5. Panelists may furnish separate opinions on matters not unanimously agreed.

6. A disputing Party may submit written comments to the panel on its initial report within 14 days of presentation of the report or within such other period as the disputing Parties may agree.

7. After considering any written comments on the initial report, the panel may reconsider its report and make any further examination it considers appropriate.

Article 20.14:   Final Report

1. The panel shall present a final report to the disputing Parties, including any separate opinions on matters not unanimously agreed, within 30 days of presentation of the initial report, unless the disputing Parties otherwise agree. The disputing Parties shall release the final report to the public within 15 days thereafter, subject to the protection of confidential information.

2. No panel may, either in its initial report or its final report, disclose which panelists are associated with majority or minority opinions.

Article 20.15:   Implementation of Final Report

1. On receipt of the final report of a panel, the disputing Parties shall agree on the resolution of the dispute, which normally shall conform with the determinations and recommendations, if any, of the panel.

2. If, in its final report, the panel determines that a disputing Party has not conformed with its obligations under this Agreement or that a disputing Party's measure is causing nullification or impairment in the sense of Annex 20.2, the resolution, whenever possible, shall be to eliminate the non-conformity or the nullification or impartment.

3. Where appropriate, the disputing Parties may agree on a mutually satisfactory action plan to resolve the dispute, which normally shall conform with the determinations and recommendations, if any, of the panel. If the disputing Parties agree on such an action plan, a complaining Party may have recourse to Article 20.16.2 or Article 20.17.1, as the case may be, only if it considers that the Party complained against has failed to carry out the action plan.

Article 20.16:   Non-Implementation — Suspension of Benefits

1. If a panel has made a determination of the type described in Article 20.15.2, and the disputing Parties are unable to reach agreement on a resolution pursuant to Article 20.15 within 45 days of receiving the final report, or such other period as the disputing Parties agree, the Party complained against shall enter into negotiations with the complaining Party or Parties with a view to developing mutually acceptable compensation.

2. If the disputing Parties:

(a) are unable to agree on compensation within 30 days after the period for developing such compensation has begun; or

(b) have agreed on compensation or on a resolution pursuant to Article 20.15 and a complaining Party considers that the Party complained against has failed to observe the terms of the agreement,

any such complaining Party may at any time thereafter provide written notice to the Party complained against that it intends to suspend the application to the Party complained against of benefits of equivalent effect. The notice shall specify the level of benefits that the Party proposes to suspend. Subject to paragraph 6, the complaining Party may begin suspending benefits 30 days after the later of the date on which it provides notice under this paragraph or the panel issues its determination under paragraph 3, as the case may be.

3. If the Party complained against considers that:

(a) the level of benefits proposed to be suspended is manifestly excessive; or

(b) it has eliminated the non-conformity or the nullification or impairment that the panel has found, it may, within 30 days after the complaining Party provides notice under paragraph 2, request that the panel be reconvened to consider the matter. The Party complained against shall deliver its request in writing to the complaining Party. The panel shall reconvene as soon as possible after delivery of the request and shall present its determination to the disputing Parties within 90 days after it reconvenes to review a request under subparagraph (a) or (b), or within 120 days for a request under subparagraphs (a) and (b). If the panel determines that the level of benefits proposed to be suspended is manifestly excessive, it shall determine the level of benefits it considers to be of equivalent effect.

4. The complaining Party may suspend benefits up to the level the panel has determined under paragraph 3 or, if the panel has not determined the level, the level the complaining Party has proposed to suspend under paragraph 2, unless the panel has determined that the Party complained against has eliminated the non-conformity or the nullification or impairment.

5. In considering what benefits to suspend pursuant to paragraph 2:

(a) the complaining Party should first seek to suspend benefits in the same sector or sectors as that affected by the measure or other matter that the panel has found to be inconsistent with the obligations of this Agreement or to have caused nullification or impairment in the sense of Annex 20.2; and

(b) if the complaining Party considers that it is not practicable or effective to suspend benefits in the same sector or sectors, it may suspend benefits in other sectors.

6. The complaining Party may not suspend benefits if, within 30 days after it provides written notice of intent to suspend benefits or, if the panel is reconvened under paragraph 3, within 20 days after the panel provides its determination, the Party complained against provides written notice to the complaining Party that it will pay an annual monetary assessment. The disputing Parties shall consult, beginning no later than ten days after the Party complained against provides notice, with a view to reaching agreement on the amount of the assessment. If the disputing Parties are unable to reach an agreement within 30 days after consultations begin, the amount of the assessment shall be set at a level, in U.S. dollars, equal to 50 percent of the level of the benefits the panel has determined under paragraph 3 to be of equivalent effect or, if the panel has not determined the level, 50 percent of the level that the complaining Party has proposed to suspend under paragraph 2.

7. Unless the Commission otherwise decides, a monetary assessment shall be paid to the complaining Party in U.S. dollars, or in an equivalent amount of the currency of the Party complained against, in equal, quarterly installments beginning 60 days after the Party complained against gives notice that it intends to pay an assessment. Where the circumstances warrant, the Commission may decide that an assessment shall be paid into a fund established by the Commission and expended at the direction of the Commission for appropriate initiatives to facilitate trade between the disputing Parties, including by further reducing unreasonable trade barriers or by assisting a disputing Party in carrying out its obligations under this Agreement.

8. If the Party complained against fails to pay a monetary assessment, the complaining Party may suspend the application to the Party complained against of benefits in accordance with paragraph 4.

9. This Article shall not apply with respect to a matter described in Article 20.17.1.

Article 20.17:   Non-Implementation in Certain Disputes

1. If, in its final report, a panel determines that a Party has not conformed with its obligations under Article 16.2.1(a) (Enforcement of Labor Laws) or Article 17.2.1(a) (Enforcement of Environmental Laws), and the disputing Parties:

    (a) are unable to reach agreement on a resolution pursuant to Article 20.15 within 45 days of receiving the final report; or

    (b) have agreed on a resolution pursuant to Article 20.15 and a complaining Party considers that the Party complained against has failed to observe the terms of the agreement,

any such complaining Party may at any time thereafter request that the panel be reconvened to impose an annual monetary assessment on the Party complained against. The complaining Party shall deliver its request in writing to the Party complained against. The panel shall reconvene as soon as possible after delivery of the request.

2. The panel shall determine the amount of the monetary assessment in U.S. dollars within 90 days after it reconvenes under paragraph 1. In determining the amount of the assessment, the panel shall take into account:

    (a) the bilateral trade effects of the Party's failure to effectively enforce the relevant law;

    (b) the pervasiveness and duration of the Party's failure to effectively enforce the relevant law;

    (c) the reasons for the Party's failure to effectively enforce the relevant law, including, where relevant, its failure to observe the terms of an action plan;

(d) the level of enforcement that could reasonably be expected of the Party given its resource constraints;

(e) the efforts made by the Party to begin remedying the non-enforcement after the final report of the panel, including through the implementation of any mutually agreed action plan; and

(f) any other relevant factors.

The amount of the assessment shall not exceed 15 million U.S. dollars annually, adjusted for inflation as specified in Annex 20.17.

3. On the date on which the panel determines the amount of the monetary assessment under paragraph 2, or at any time thereafter, the complaining Party may provide notice in writing to the Party complained against demanding payment of the monetary assessment. The monetary assessment shall be payable in U.S. dollars, or in an equivalent amount of the currency of the Party complained against, in equal, quarterly installments beginning 60 days after the complaining Party provides such notice.

4. Assessments shall be paid into a fund established by the Commission and shall be expended at the direction of the Commission for appropriate labor or environmental initiatives, including efforts to improve or enhance labor or environmental law enforcement, as the case may be, in the territory of the Party complained against, consistent with its law. In deciding how to expend monies paid into the fund, the Commission shall consider the views of interested persons in the disputing Parties' territories.

5. If the Party complained against fails to pay a monetary assessment, the complaining Party may take other appropriate steps to collect the assessment or otherwise secure compliance.

These steps may include suspending tariff benefits under the Agreement as necessary to collect the assessment, while bearing in mind the Agreement's objective of eliminating barriers to trade and while seeking to avoid unduly affecting parties or interests not party to the dispute.

Article 20.18:   Compliance Review

1. Without prejudice to the procedures set out in Article 20.16.3, if the Party complained against considers that it has eliminated the non-conformity or the nullification or impairment that the panel has found, it may refer the matter to the panel by providing written notice to the complaining Party or Parties. The panel shall issue its report on the matter within 90 days after the Party complained against provides notice.

2. If the panel decides that the Party complained against has eliminated the non-conformity or the nullification or impairment, the complaining Party or Parties shall promptly reinstate any benefits that Party has or those Parties

have suspended under Article 20.16 or Article 20.17 and the Party complained against shall no longer be required to pay any monetary assessment it has agreed to pay under Article 20.16.6 or that has been imposed on it under Article 20.17.1.

Article 20.19:   Five-Year Review

The Commission shall review the operation and effectiveness of Articles 20.16 and 20.17 not later than five years after the Agreement enters into force, or within six months after benefits have been suspended or monetary assessments have been imposed in five proceedings initiated under this Chapter, whichever occurs first.

Section B: Domestic Proceedings and Private Commercial Dispute Settlement

Article 20.20:   Referral of Matters from Judicial or Administrative Proceedings

1. If an issue of interpretation or application of this Agreement arises in any domestic judicial or administrative proceeding of a Party that any Party considers would merit its intervention, or if a court or administrative body solicits the views of a Party, that Party shall notify the other Parties. The Commission shall endeavor to agree on an appropriate response as expeditiously as possible.
2. The Party in whose territory the court or administrative body is located shall submit any agreed interpretation of the Commission to the court or administrative body in accordance with the rules of that forum.
3. If the Commission is unable to agree, any Party may submit its own views to the court or administrative body in accordance with the rules of that forum.

Article 20.21:   Private Rights

No Party may provide for a right of action under its law against any other Party on the ground that the other Party has failed to conform with its obligations under this Agreement.

Article 20.22:   Alternative Dispute Resolution

1. Each Party shall, to the maximum extent possible, encourage and facilitate the use of arbitration and other means of alternative dispute

resolution for the settlement of international commercial disputes between private parties in the free trade area.

2. To this end, each Party shall provide appropriate procedures to ensure observance of agreements to arbitrate and for the recognition and enforcement of arbitral awards in such disputes.

3. A Party shall be deemed to be in compliance with paragraph 2 if it is a party to and is in compliance with the 1958 *United Nations Convention on the Recognition and Enforcement of Foreign Arbitral Awards* or the 1975 *Inter-American Convention on International Commercial Arbitration*.

4. The Commission may establish an Advisory Committee on Private Commercial Disputes comprising persons with expertise or experience in the resolution of private international commercial disputes.

5. This committee shall:

(a) report and provide recommendations to the Commission on general issues referred to it by the Commission respecting the availability, use, and effectiveness of arbitration and other procedures for the resolution of such disputes in the free trade area; and

(b) when the committee considers appropriate, promote technical cooperation between the Parties, in furtherance of the objectives identified in paragraph 1.

Annex 20.2 Nullification or Impairment

1. If any Party considers that any benefit it could reasonably have expected to accrue to it under any provision of:

(a) Chapters Three through Five (National Treatment and Market Access for Goods, Rules of Origin and Origin Procedures, and Customs Administration and Trade Facilitation);

(b) Chapter Seven (Technical Barriers to Trade);

(c) Chapter Nine (Government Procurement);

(d) Chapter Eleven (Cross-Border Trade in Services); or

(e) Chapter Fifteen (Intellectual Property Rights),

is being nullified or impaired as a result of the application of any measure that is not inconsistent with this Agreement, the Party may have recourse to dispute settlement under this Chapter.

2. A Party may not invoke paragraph 1(d) or (e) with respect to any measure subject to an exception under Article 21.1 (General Exceptions). . . .

International Labour Organization (ILO), Constitution of the International Labor Organization (ILO) (1 Apr. 1919, as amended)

Preamble

Whereas universal and lasting peace can be established only if it is based upon social justice;

And whereas conditions of labour exist involving such injustice, hardship and privation to large numbers of people as to produce unrest so great that the peace and harmony of the world are imperiled; and an improvement of those conditions is urgently required; as, for example, by the regulation of the hours of work, including the establishment of a maximum working day and week, the regulation of the labour supply, the prevention of unemployment, the provision of an adequate living wage, the protection of the worker against sickness, disease and injury arising out of his employment, the protection of children, young persons and women, provision for old age and injury, protection of the interests of workers when employed in countries other than their own, recognition of the principle of equal remuneration for work of equal value, recognition of the principle of freedom of association, the organization of vocational and technical education and other measures;

Whereas also the failure of any nation to adopt humane conditions of labour is an obstacle in the way of other nations which desire to improve the conditions in their own countries;

The High Contracting Parties, moved by sentiments of justice and humanity as well as by the desire to secure the permanent peace of the world, and with a view to attaining the objectives set forth in this Preamble, agree to the following Constitution of the International Labour Organization. . . .

[The 1944 Declaration of Philadelphia, which is annexed to the International Labour Organization's Constitution, states:]

The Conference reaffirms the fundamental principles on which the Organization is based and, in particular, that —

(a) labour is not a commodity

(b) freedom of expression and of association are essential to sustained progress;

(c) poverty anywhere constitutes a danger to prosperity everywhere;

(d) the war against want requires to be carried on with unrelenting vigour within each nation, and by continuous and concerted international effort in which the representatives of workers and employers, enjoying equal status with those of governments, join with them in free discussion and democratic decision with a view to the promotion of the common welfare . . .

The Conference recognizes the solemn obligation of the International Labour Organization to further among the nations of the world programmes which will achieve . . . the effective recognition of the right of collective bargaining, the cooperation of management and labour in the continuous improvement of productive efficiency, and the collaboration of workers and employers in the preparation and application of social and economic measures. . . .

ILO Convention No. 87 Freedom of Association and Protection of the Right to Organize (1948)

available at: *www.ilo.org/dyn/normlex/en/f?p=NORMLEXPUB:12100:0: NO:12100:P12100_INSTRUMENT_ID:312232:NO*

Article 2. Workers and employers, without distinction whatsoever, shall have the right to establish and, subject only to the rules of the organization concerned, to join organizations of their own choosing without previous authorization.

Article 3.

(1.) Workers' and employers' organizations shall have the right to draw up their constitutions and rules, to elect their representatives in full freedom, to organize their administration and activities and to formulate their programs.

(2.) The public authorities shall refrain from any interference which would restrict this right or impede the lawful exercise thereof.

***

Article 11. Each Member of the International Labor Organization for which this Convention is in force undertakes to take all necessary and appropriate measures to ensure that workers and employers may exercise freely the right to organize . . .

Article 15.

(1.) This Convention shall be binding only upon those Members of the International Labor Organization whose ratifications have been registered with the Director-General.

ILO Convention No. 98 on the Right to Organize and Collective Bargaining (1949)
available at: *www.ilo.org/dyn/normlex/en/f?p=NORMLEXPUB:*
12100:0::NO::P12100_INSTRUMENT_ID:312243

Article 1: Workers shall enjoy adequate protection against acts of anti-union discrimination in respect of their employment. . . . Such protection shall apply more particularly in respect of acts calculated to — a) make the employment of a worker subject to the condition that he shall not join a union or shall relinquish trade union membership; b) cause the dismissal of or otherwise prejudice a worker by reason of union membership or because of participation in union activities outside working hours, or with the consent of the employer, within working hours.

Article 2: Workers' and employers' organizations shall enjoy adequate protection against any acts of interference by each other or each other's agents or members in their establishment, functioning or administration . . .

Article 4: Measures appropriate to national conditions shall be taken . . . to encourage and promote the full development and utilization of machinery for voluntary negotiation between employers or employers' organizations and workers' organizations, with a view to the regulation of terms and conditions of employment by means of collective agreements . . .

ILO Declaration on Fundamental Principles and Rights at Work (1998)
available at: *www.ilo.org/declaration/lang — en/index.htm*

The International Labor Conference

***

1. Declares that all Members, even if they have not ratified the Conventions in question, have an obligation arising from the very fact of membership in the Organization to respect, to promote and to realize, in good faith and in accordance with the Constitution, the principles concerning the fundamental rights which are the subject of those Conventions, namely:

(a.) Freedom of association and the effective recognition of the right to collective bargaining;

(b.) The elimination of all forms of forced or compulsory labor;

(c.) The effective abolition of child labor; and

(d.) The elimination of discrimination in respect of employment and occupation.

2. Recognizes the obligation on the Organization to assist its Members, in response to their established and expressed needs, in order to attain these objectives by making full use of its constitutional, operational and budgetary resources, including, by the mobilization of external resources and support, as well as by encouraging other international organizations with which the ILO has established relations, pursuant to article 12 of its Constitution, to support these efforts:

(a.) by offering technical cooperation and advisory services to promote the ratification and implementation of the fundamental Conventions;

(b.) by assisting those Members not yet in a position to ratify some or all of these Conventions in their efforts to respect, to promote and to realize the principles concerning fundamental rights which are the subject of these Conventions; and

(c.) by helping the Members in their efforts to create a climate for economic and social development.

***

5. Stresses that labor standards should not be used for protectionist trade purposes, and that nothing in this Declaration and its follow-up shall be invoked or otherwise used for such purposes; in addition, the comparative advantage of any country should in no way be called into question by this Declaration and its follow-up.

Organization for Economic Cooperation and Development (OECD), OECD Guidelines for Multinational Enterprises, 2011
available at: *www.oecd.org/investment/mne/48004323.pdf*

II. GENERAL POLICIES

A. Enterprises should . . .

11. Avoid causing or contributing to adverse impacts on matters covered by the Guidelines, through their own activities, and address such impacts when they occur.

12. Seek to prevent or mitigate an adverse impact where they have not contributed to that impact, when the impact is nevertheless directly linked to their operations, products or services by a business relationship. This is not intended to shift responsibility from the entity causing an adverse impact to the enterprise with which it has a business relationship.

13. In addition to addressing adverse impacts in relation to matters covered by the Guidelines, encourage, where practicable, business partners, including suppliers and sub-contractors, to apply principles of responsible business conduct compatible with the *Guidelines*.

B. Enterprises are encouraged to . . .

2. Engage in or support, where appropriate, private or multi-stakeholder initiatives and social dialogue on responsible supply chain management while ensuring that these initiatives take due account of their social and economic effects on developing countries and of existing internationally recognized standards. . . .

V. EMPLOYMENT AND INDUSTRIAL RELATIONS

Enterprises should, within the framework of applicable law, regulations and prevailing labor relations and employment practices and applicable international labor standards:

1. (a) Respect the right of workers employed by the multinational enterprise to establish or join trade unions and representative organizations of their own choosing.

(b) Respect the right of workers employed by the multinational enterprise to have trade unions and representative organizations of their own choosing recognized for the purpose of collective bargaining, and engage in constructive negotiations, either individually or through employers' associations, with such representatives with a view to reaching agreements on terms and conditions of employment. . . .

2. (a) Provide such facilities to workers' representatives as may be necessary to assist in the development of effective collective agreements.

(b) Provide information to workers' representatives which is needed for meaningful negotiations on conditions of employment.

(c) Provide information to workers and their representatives which enables them to obtain a true and fair view of the performance of the entity or, where appropriate, the enterprise as a whole.

3. Promote consultation and co-operation between employers and workers and their representatives on matters of mutual concern.

4. (a) Observe standards of employment and industrial relations not less favorable than those observed by comparable employers in the host country.

(b) When multinational enterprises operate in developing countries, where comparable employers may not exist, provide the best possible wages, benefits and conditions of work, within the framework of government policies. These should be related to the economic position of the enterprise, but should be at least adequate to satisfy the basic needs of the workers and their families. . . .

6. In considering changes in their operations which would have major employment effects, in particular in the case of the closure of an entity involving collective lay-offs or dismissals, provide reasonable notice of such changes to representatives of the workers in their employment and their organizations, and, where appropriate, to the relevant governmental authorities, and co-operate with the worker representatives and appropriate governmental authorities so as to mitigate to the maximum extent practicable adverse effects. In light of the specific circumstances of each case, it would be appropriate if management were able to give such notice prior to the final decision being taken. Other means may also be employed to provide meaningful co-operation to mitigate the effects of such decisions.

7. In the context of bona fide negotiations with workers' representatives on conditions of employment, or while workers are exercising a right to organize, not threaten to transfer the whole or part of an operating unit from the country concerned nor transfer workers from the enterprises' component entities in other countries in order to influence unfairly those negotiations or to hinder the exercise of a right to organize. . . .

Chiquita-IUF-COLSIBA Agreement on Freedom of Association, Minimum Labor Standards and Employment in Latin American Banana Operations (2001)
available at: *www.iufdocuments.org/www/documents/Chiquita-e.pdf*

PART I: MINIMUM LABOR STANDARDS

IUF/COLSIBA and Chiquita:

Acknowledge the fundamental right of each employee to choose to belong to and be represented by an independent and democratic trade union of his or her choice, and to bargain collectively;

Are convinced that reinforcing democratic forms of co-operation in the company is the responsibility of both management and trade unions;

Seek to identify practical opportunities for continuous improvement in the employment conditions of CHIQUITA employees recognizing this as a necessary condition to advance the common interests of CHIQUITA and its employees;

Respect the responsibilities of local Chiquita managers and unions to address local issues of concern through collective bargaining and to put into practice the following general principles;

In this spirit, IUF/COLSIBA and CHIQUITA agree on the following:

On Minimum Labor Standards: ... Chiquita reaffirms its commitment to respect the following core ILO Conventions [freedom of association; the right to collective bargaining; and the protection and facilities to be afforded to workers' representatives]. ...

... Chiquita will ensure that representatives of trade unions are not the subject of discrimination and that such representatives have access to employees in the workplace. The practical details of such access will be determined through national discussions and agreement. Chiquita guarantees that employees will suffer no discrimination, threats or sanctions as a result of any such visit by a union representative ...

... Where Chiquita is engaged in collective bargaining with unions, Chiquita will continue sharing with union representatives the information about the corporation as a whole and its local operations that they reasonably require to bargain effectively ...

... CHIQUITA and the IUF/COLSIBA will publicize this agreement in all the Company's banana operations in Latin America ...

PART II: EMPLOYMENT

In the event of any situation that would seriously affect the volume of employment, working conditions or the type of contracts of work, such as changes or transfers in production or the closure of all or part of a facility, CHIQUITA commits to:

... Consult those local trade unions that have been duly appointed as the representatives of the affected workers, which discussions should occur as soon as possible, especially when the change affects a significant number of employees such as in a partial or total closure. ...

... Chiquita will seriously consider alternative proposals presented by unions representing Chiquita workers. Chiquita will provide a response to those proposals within a time frame agreed on a case-by-case basis ...

ON SUPPLIERS

Chiquita will require its suppliers, contract growers and joint venture partners to provide reasonable evidence that they respect national legislation and the Minimum Labor Standards outlined in Part I of this agreement. The parties agree that the effective implementation of this provision is dependent on a number of factors such as Chiquita's relative degree of influence over its suppliers and the availability of appropriate and commercially viable supply alternatives. Implementation of this part of the agreement shall therefore be jointly assessed by the Review Committee taking into account these factors.

PART III: OVERSIGHT OF THIS AGREEMENT

CHIQUITA and IUF/COLSIBA will each appoint up to four members to a Review Committee that will meet periodically to oversee the application of this agreement and to discuss other areas of mutual concern. In case of a major conflict, CHIQUITA and IUF/COLSIBA may, in addition, include in the meeting a representative of the local union and a representative of local management.

CHIQUITA and IUF/COLSIBA recognize that this Agreement is not a substitute for, and that they should do everything reasonable to encourage, effective local bargaining processes. The parties agree that local parties should exhaust every effort to resolve local issues, and that the work of the Review Committee, as well as any intervention required between meetings of this Committee, will relate only to alleged serious and/or systematic violations of the rights outlined in this agreement.

The agendas for these meetings will be agreed in advance and both parties shall provide the relevant information necessary to carry out the intent of the meetings.

The Review Committee meetings will take place twice a year. An extraordinary meeting may be convened at the request of either party, in case a situation arises that requires urgent discussion by the Review Committee.

Chiquita, the IUF, and COLSIBA will each identify a contact person responsible to facilitate communication and the timely resolution of any emergency issues that may be identified between meetings of the review committee.

Commitment to Fair Dealing and Continuous Improvement. . . . During the term of this Agreement, CHIQUITA and the IUF/COLSIBA agree to:

Negotiate in good faith with the best interest of all parties in mind; Communicate in an open, honest and straightforward manner; Avoid actions which could undermine the process spelled out in this Agreement, such as public international campaigns or anti-union retaliatory tactics, until such time as one or the other party declares there has been a failure to agree. A time frame for discussion and mutually satisfactory resolution of the issue will be agreed case-by case by the Review Committee. No failure to agree can be declared before the expiry of that time frame. . . .